THE ENCYCLOPEDIA OF
WATERCOLOR TECHNIQUES

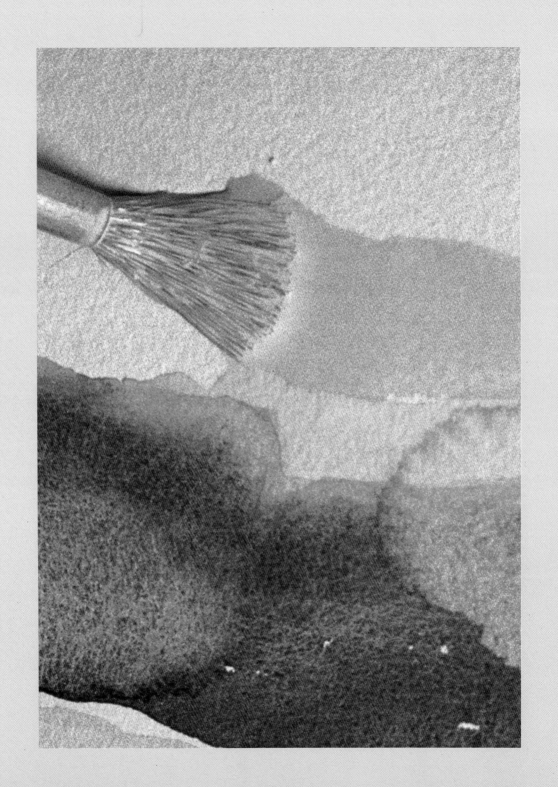

THE ENCYCLOPEDIA OF
WATERCOLOR TECHNIQUES

HAZEL HARRISON

RUNNING PRESS
PHILADELPHIA, PENNSYLVANIA

A QUARTO BOOK

Copyright © 1990 Quarto Publishing plc

First published in the USA in 1990 by
Running Press Book Publishers
125 South Twenty-second Street
Philadelphia, Pennsylvania 19103

Canadian representatives: General Publishing Co. Ltd.
39 Lesmill Road, Don Mills, Ontario M3B 2T6

ISBN: 0-89471-893-2

9 8 7 6 5 4 3

Digit on the right indicates the number of this printing.

This book was designed and produced by
Quarto Publishing plc
The Old Brewery
6 Blundell Street
London N7 9BH

Senior Editor Susanna Clarke

Editor Michelle Clark

Picture Researcher Angela Gair
Designer Hugh Schermuly

Art Director Moira Clinch
Assistant Art Director Chloë Alexander
Picture Manager Joanna Wiese

Typeset by Ampersand Typesetting
(Bournemouth) Ltd
Manufactured in Hong Kong by Regent Publishing
Services Ltd
Printed by Leefung Asco Printers Ltd, Hong Kong

This book may be ordered directly from the publisher.
Please add $2.50 for postage and handling for each copy. *But
try your bookstore first!* Running Press Book Publishers,
125 South Twenty-second Street, Philadelphia,
Pennsylvania 19103.

CONTENTS

PART ONE

TECHNIQUES 8

BACKRUNS · BLENDING · BLOTS · BODY COLOR · BROKEN COLOR ·
BRUSH DRAWING · BRUSHMARKS · BUILDING UP · COLOR CHANGES ·
CORRECTIONS · DRAWING · DRY BRUSH · GLAZING · GUM ARABIC · HARD
AND SOFT EDGES · HIGHLIGHTS · LIFTING OUT · LINE AND WASH ·
MASKING · MIXED MEDIA · SCRAPING BACK · SCUMBLING · SPATTERING ·
SPONGE PAINTING · SQUARING UP · STIPPLING · STRETCHING PAPER ·
TEXTURES · TONED GROUND · UNDERPAINTING · WASH · WASH-OFF · WAX
RESIST · WET-IN-WET · WET-ON-DRY

PART TWO

THEMES 72

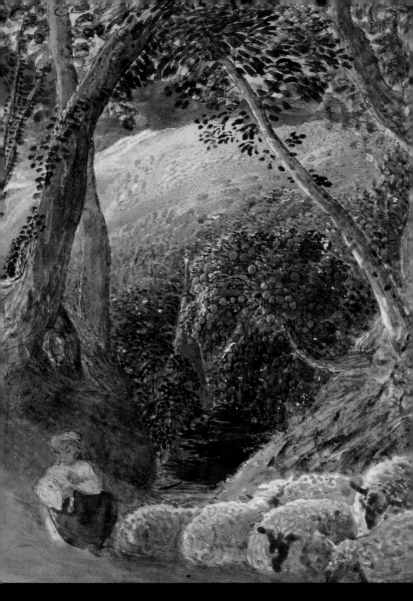

Samuel Palmer, *The Magic Apple Tree,*
$13\frac{3}{4} \times 10\frac{3}{4}$ IN (34.9×27.3 CM),
WATERCOLOR AND PEN AND INK

The main body of Palmer's work was in oil and was efficient, but uninspired. His early watercolors, however, are works of true poetic imagination, owing much to the example of William Blake, whom he met in 1824. Works such as this one, painted in 1830, are highly personal visions, and his desire to express his ideas led him to an inventive and original use of watercolor techniques.

INTRODUCTION

Watercolor is an enormously popular painting medium and has been since the nineteenth century. Ironically, however, its very popularity gave it something of a bad name at one time. Because so many amateur painters used it in Victorian times, the phrase "painting in watercolor" conjured up a mental picture of neatly dressed ladies sitting at easels in the countryside producing small, rather timid landscapes in pale, delicate colors. This image has not been entirely dispelled even today – among the non-painting public, there is still a tendency to regard watercolor painting as a pleasant pastime on a level with flower arranging. Artists, however, do not see it in this way, and an increasing number are now choosing it in preference to other mediums, exploiting it in inventive and creative ways for every possible subject.

Another old myth that is fast losing credence is that there is a "correct" way of working in watercolor, that is, brushing on washes of transparent pigment and allowing the white paper alone to stand as the highlights. This "classic" technique produces very beautiful results, but there are many other methods. And besides, not all watercolor paints are transparent – gouache and acrylic are also watercolors and, more surprisingly, so are the tempera paints that Michelangelo used to paint the Sistine Chapel ceiling. Nowadays no shame attaches to mixing watercolor with opaque white, combining transparent and opaque paints and even mixing several media in one painting. All paints and pastels are made from pigment, and the only real distinction is between the oil-based and the water-based ones.

This book covers the subject of watercolor painting in the broad sense of the term, suggesting ways of working with gouache and acrylic as well as explaining the time-honored techniques associated with transparent watercolor. I hope that it will help banish some preconceptions, provide some new ideas and demonstrate the inspiringly broad range of the water-based paints.

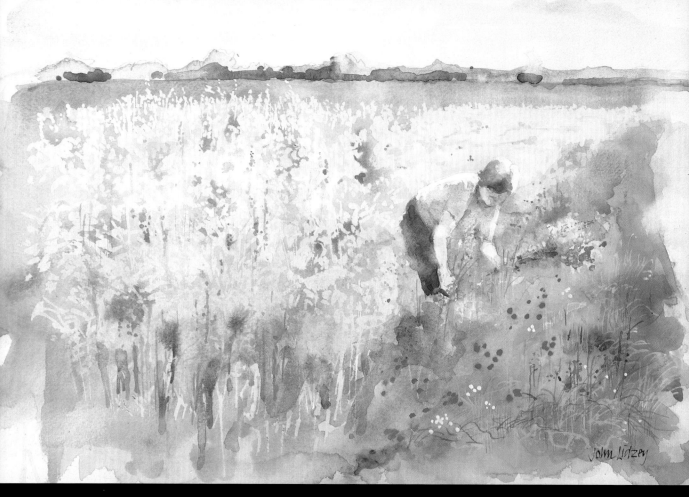

John Lidzey, *Figure in a Cornfield,*
APPROX. 13½ × 20 IN (34.3 × 50.8 CM),
WATERCOLOR

Lidzey is an artist who enjoys
experimenting with different

the shapes with liquid mask (see
MASKING) and laying washes on
top. The mask is then removed to
leave white "negative" shapes,
parts of which have been left

PART ONE

TECHNIQUES

The nineteenth-century academic obsession with correct technique bred a revolt in the early part of this century, to the extent that teaching students how to apply paint began to be regarded as almost immoral – stifling self-expression and creativity. However, while it is true that no amount of technical knowledge and expertise can be a substitute for vision, there is nothing more frustrating than knowing you have something to say, but not having the means to say it. No art exists in a vacuum – we can always learn from other artists and should never be ashamed to study their methods as well as their subject matter – this is and always has been part of the quest for a personal artistic language.

The aim of this first alphabetical section of the book is to show you not what you should do but what you can do. Even in the relatively narrow field of water-based media, there are almost endless different ways of applying paint to paper, and I have tried to show a comprehensive selection of them here. Some of the techniques described may strike a chord, while others may not, but I hope you will try them out. Learning to understand the capabilities of a medium has a wonderfully liberating effect – it enables you to "find your own voice" and express your ideas with confidence and vigor. Always remember, though, that technique is only a tool – the way you paint should never

BACKRUNS

These are both a nuisance and a delight to watercolor painters. If you lay a WASH and apply more color into it before it is completely dry, the chances are that the new paint will seep into the old, creating strangely shaped blotches with hard, jagged edges – sometimes alternatively described as "cauliflowers." It does not always happen: the more absorbent or rough-textured papers are less conducive to backruns than smoother, highly sized ones, and with practice it is possible to avoid them completely.

There is no remedy for a backrun except to wash off the entire area and start again. However, many watercolor painters use them quite deliberately, both in large areas such as skies or water and small ones such as the petals of flowers, as the effects they create are quite unlike those achieved by conventional brushwork. For example, a realistic approximation of reflections in gently moving water can be achieved by lightly working wet color or clear water into a still-damp wash. The paint or water will flow outward, giving an area of soft color with the irregular, jagged outlines so typical of reflections. It takes a little practice to be able to judge exactly how wet or dry the first wash should be, but as a guide, if there is still a sheen on it, it is too wet and the colors will merge together without a backrun, as they do in the WET-IN-WET technique.

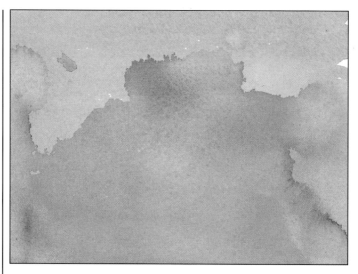

◀ The results of working into a wash before it is thoroughly dry vary widely according to the paper used and the degree of wetness or dryness, but it can look something like this example. Experienced watercolorists learn to make use of such effects, which can often be used descriptively in a painting.

▼ Here backruns have been deliberately induced and then blown with a hairdryer so that they form definite patterns. Techniques such as this are particularly useful for amorphous shapes such as clouds, reflections or distant hills.

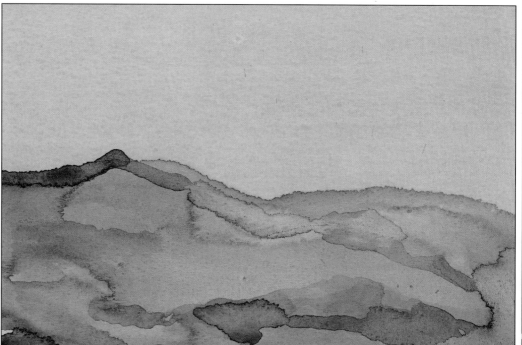

▲ The artist has worked into a wash which has "gone wrong" and flooded and created a sky effect not previously planned.

▶ William Tillyer, *Swiss Lakes series*, $22\frac{1}{2} \times 30$ IN (57.3×76.2 CM) WATERCOLOR
A deliberate backrun enhances this painting, creating a soft curve that echoes those of the hills below.

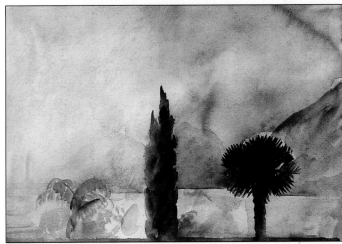

BLENDING

This means achieving a soft, gradual transition from one color or tone to another. It is a slightly trickier process with water-based paints than with oil or pastel, because they dry quickly, but there are various methods that can be used.

One of these is to work WET-IN-WET, keeping the whole area damp so that the colors flow into one another. This is a lovely method for amorphous shapes such as clouds, but is less suited to precise effects, such as those you might need in portraits, as you cannot control it enough. You can easily find that a shadow intended to define a nose or cheekbone spreads haphazardly.

To avoid the hard edges formed where a WASH ends or meets another wash, brush or sponge the edge lightly with water before it is dry. To convey the roundness of a piece of fruit or the soft contours of a face, use the paint fairly dry, applying it in small strokes rather than broad washes. If unwanted hard edges do form, they can be softened by "painting" along them using a small sponge or cotton swab dipped in a little water.

The best method for blending acrylics is to keep them fluid by adding retarding medium. This allows very subtle effects, as the paint can be moved around on the paper. Opaque gouache colors can be laid over one another to create soft effects, though the danger is that too much overlaying of wet color stirs up and muddies the earlier layers. One way to avoid this is to use the DRY BRUSH technique, applying the paint thickly, with the minimum of water.

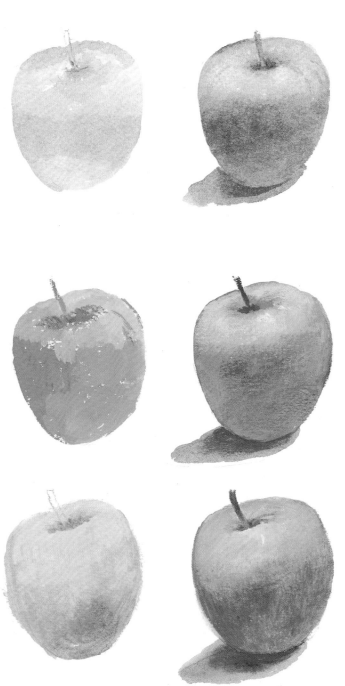

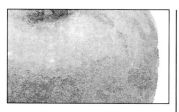

Watercolor. A pale green wash is laid and some darker greens and browns flooded into it while still wet. This is allowed to dry and the tones are built up with small brushstrokes of paint carefully blended together with a moistened brush.

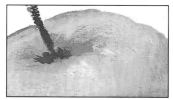

Gouache. The same technique can be used for thin gouache, but here the paint is used thickly, with the blending done by working very dry paint over the underlayer with a bristle brush. On the top of the apple, light paint has been applied over dark.

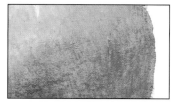

Acrylic. Because acrylic dries so fast, it cannot be moved around on the paper as watercolor can, so retarding medium has been used to slow the drying time. This also increases the transparency of the paint, so that the brushstrokes used to build up the shadows are clearly visible.

BLOTS

Blot painting is a technique most often associated with monochrome ink drawing, but since watercolors are available in liquid (ink) form I have included this technique here. The other reason for its inclusion is that it is an excellent way of loosening up technique and providing new visual ideas. Like BACKRUNS, blots are never entirely predictable, and the shapes they make will sometimes suggest a painting or a particular treatment of a subject quite unlike the one that was planned. Allowing the painting to evolve in this way can have a liberating effect and may suggest a new way of working in the future.

The shapes the blots make depend on the height from which they are dropped, the consistency of the paint or ink and the angle of the paper. Tilting the board will make the blot run downhill; flicking the paint or ink will give small spatters; wetting the paper will give a diffused, soft-edged blot. A further variation can be provided by dropping a blot onto the paper and then blowing it, which sends tendrils of paint shooting out into various directions. Blots can also be used in a controlled, selective way to suggest the texture of trees, flowers or pebbles in a particular part of a painting.

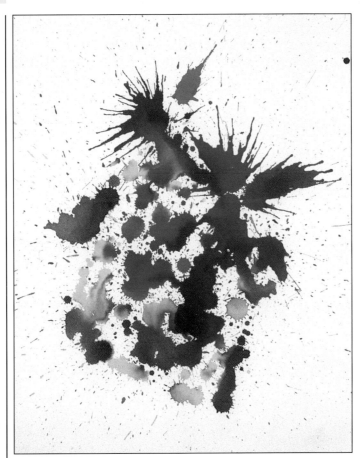

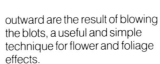

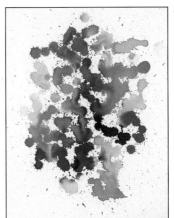

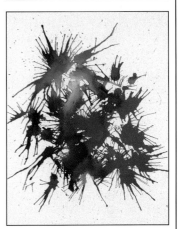

Blot painting is a form of constructive doodling. Because you are freed from the constraints imposed by the need to "make a painting," you can loosen up and enjoy yourself. Sometimes a random effect of colored blots will suggest a subject which can be developed into a roughly representational treatment, but often, as here, they are simply pleasing as abstract patterns. These examples have been produced by dropping colored inks onto the paper from different heights. Some of the colors have been used undiluted and some mixed with a little water. The lines and tendrils of ink spreading outward are the result of blowing the blots, a useful and simple technique for flower and foliage effects.

BODY COLOR

This slightly confusing term simply means opaque water-based paint. In the past it was usually applied to the mixture of either Chinese white with transparent watercolor in parts of a painting or used straight out of the tube for highlights. Nowadays, however, it is often used as an alternative term for opaque gouache paint.

Some watercolor painters avoid the use of body color completely, priding themselves on achieving all the highlights in a painting by reserving areas of white paper. There are good reasons for this, as the lovely translucency of watercolor can be destroyed by the addition of body color, but opaque watercolor is an attractive medium when used sensitively.

Transparent watercolor mixed with either Chinese white or gouache zinc (not flake) white is particularly well suited to creating subtle weather effects in landscapes, such as mist-shrouded hills. It gives a lovely, milky, translucent effect slightly different from that of gouache itself, which has a more chalky, pastel-like quality.

A watercolor that has gone wrong – perhaps become overworked or too bright in one particular area – can often be saved by overlaying a semi-opaque wash, and untidy highlights can be cleaned up and strengthened in the same way.

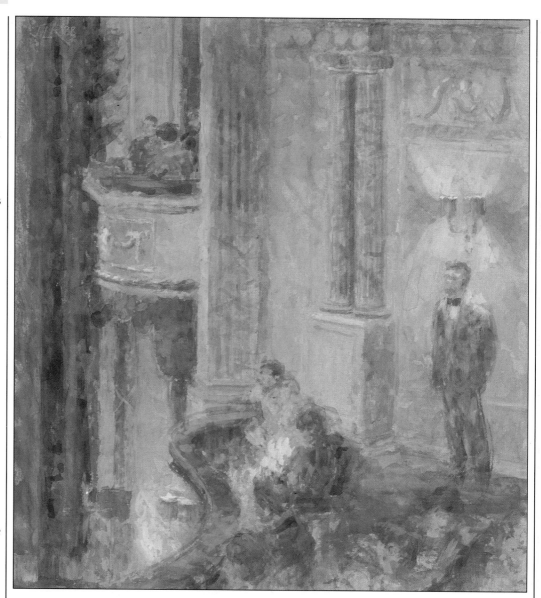

Jacqueline Rizvi, *Interval at the Globe Theatre*, 12 × 11 IN (30.5 × 27.9 CM), WATERCOLOR AND BODY COLOR

This artist uses watercolor mixed with opaque white and builds up very gradually, using the paint rather dry and usually working on a toned paper (the ground for this painting is a light beige-gray). The red of the velvet was brought out in places by laying transparent red watercolor over a slightly opaque crimson and white mixture.

Moira Huntly RI, RSMA, *Still Life with Teapot and Decanter,* 18⅞ × 15⅛ IN (48 × 38.5 CM), WATERCOLOR AND GOUACHE

Huntly likes to exploit the physical contrast between thin and thick paint and in some areas has overlaid washes of transparent watercolor with opaque gouache.

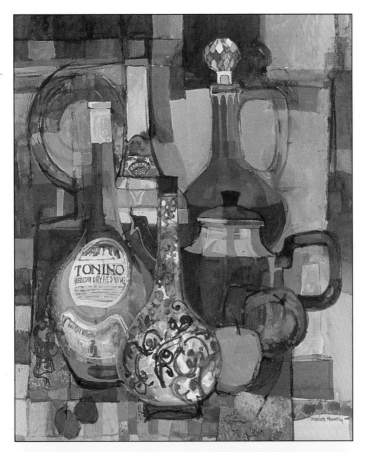

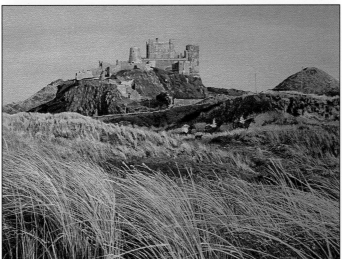

Robert Dodd, *Bamburgh Castle,* 20½ × 28½ IN (52 × 71.1 CM), GOUACHE

This painting is entirely in gouache, used quite thickly, particularly in the foreground. One of the problems with gouache is that the paint becomes dead and muddy-looking if too many layers are built up. Dodd brings up the colors by varnishing them, so that his paint has the appearance of acrylic.

BROKEN COLOR

It is one of the paradoxes of painting that a large area of flat color seldom appears as colorful, or, indeed, as realistic, as one that is textured or broken up in some way. The Impressionists, working mainly in oils, discovered that they could best describe the fleeting, shimmering effects of light on foliage or grass by placing small dabs of various greens, blues and yellows side by side instead of using just one green for each area. This technique can be adapted very successfully to watercolor, but there are many other ways to break up color.

If you "drag" a WASH over a heavily textured paper, the paint will sink into the troughs, but will not completely cover the raised tooth of the paper – a broken color effect much exploited by watercolorists. If you then apply drier paint over the original wash – in a different color or a darker version of the same one – the effect will be even more varied and the painting will have a lively and interesting surface texture.

In gouache and acrylic, broken color effects are best achieved by applying the paint rather dry with a stiff brush (see also DRY BRUSH and SCUMBLING). Acrylic is perfect for this kind of treatment as, not only does it dry fast, it is immovable once dry, which means that more or less endless layers can be laid one over the other. This is not true of gouache: although it is opaque, it is also absorbent and so too many new layers will simply disappear into those below.

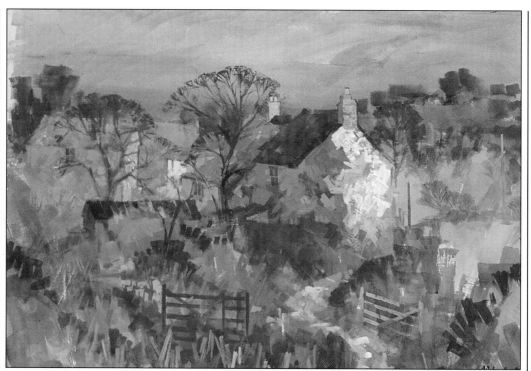

▲ Michael Cadman, *Cornish Farm I*, 18 × 25 IN (45.7 × 63.5 CM), ACRYLIC AND WATERCOLOR

Cadman has used no vivid colors, but the way each area is broken up into a multitude of separate "pieces" by the brick-like brushstrokes gives the painting a bright and sparkling quality. He likes acrylic because it holds the marks of the brush well.

▶ John McPake RE, *Frame Tent*, 14 × 19½ IN (35.6 × 49.5 CM), WATERCOLOR AND GOUACHE

The rather somber color scheme is enlivened by the loose application of paint, with clearly visible brushmarks. McPake has thickened his paint by adding acrylic medium to the water as well as to some of the paint mixtures.

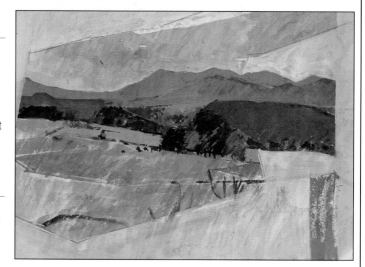

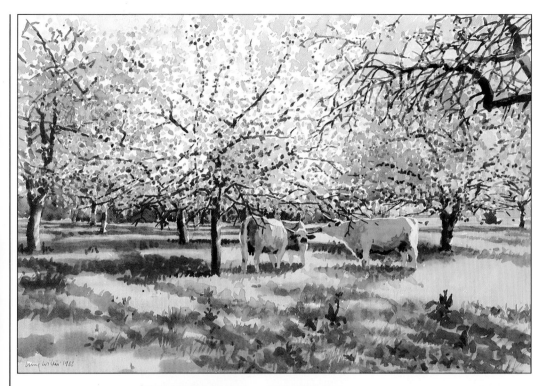

Lucy Willis, *Cattle in the Orchard,*
15 × 22 IN (38.1 × 55.9 CM), WATERCOLOR

Willis works on dry paper, with no preliminary drawing, beginning by making little dots and dashes of color and then working in turn on different parts of the composition. She keeps her effects fresh and clear by leaving each brushstroke or tiny wash to settle undisturbed except where she wants a soft gradation, in which case she regulates the amount of water carefully to avoid unwanted pools.

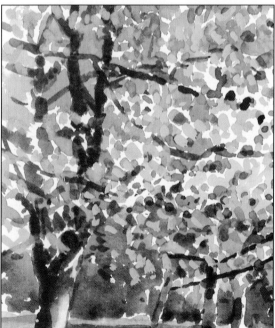

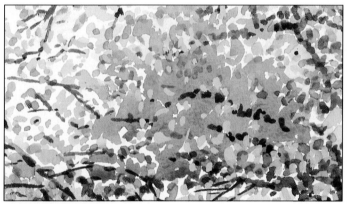

These two details show the lovely impression of dappled light created by means of small, separate brushmarks with areas of white paper left uncovered.

BRUSH DRAWING

Drawing freely and directly with a brush is enormously satisfying and, like BLOTS, is an excellent way to loosen up your technique. Artists down the centuries have made brush sketches, sometimes using pen marks as well, sometimes not, and the Chinese and Japanese made the technique into a fine art.

Opaque paints are not suitable for brush drawing, as the marks and lines must be fluid – flowing easily from brush to paper. You can use ordinary watercolors, watercolor inks or acrylics thinned with water; good, springy brushes are also essential.

Light pressure with the tip of a medium-sized pointed brush will give precise, delicate lines. A little more pressure and the line will become thicker, so that it is possible to draw a line that is dark and thick in places and very fine in others. More pressure still, bringing the thick part of the brush into contact with the paper, will give a shaped brush mark rather than a line. Thus, by using only one brush, you can create a variety of effects; and, if you use several brushes, including broad, flat-ended ones, the repertoire is almost endless.

The technique can be combined with others in a painting and is particularly useful for conveying a feeling of movement, in figures, animals or even landscape.

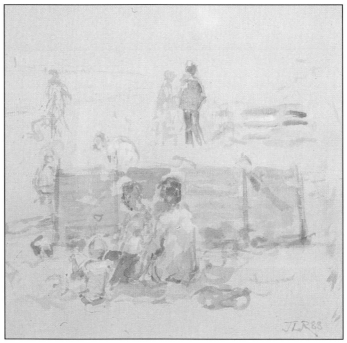

◀ Jacqueline Rizvi, *Family on the Beach*, WATERCOLOR AND BODY COLOR ON PALE GRAY PAPER
Working rapidly on the spot, the artist has used the brush very much as a drawing medium.

▼ Christopher Baker, *Rydal Water*, 10 × 18 IN (25.4 × 45.7 CM), WATERCOLOR
This sketchbook study (on cartridge paper) was initially drawn with a brush and then toughened with a dip-pen where necessary. In the background, the paper was damped to allow the paint to spread, thus maintaining the softness of the forms.

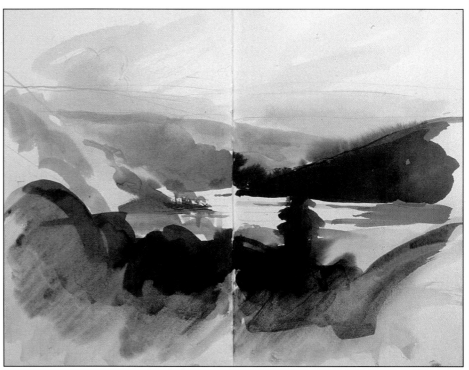

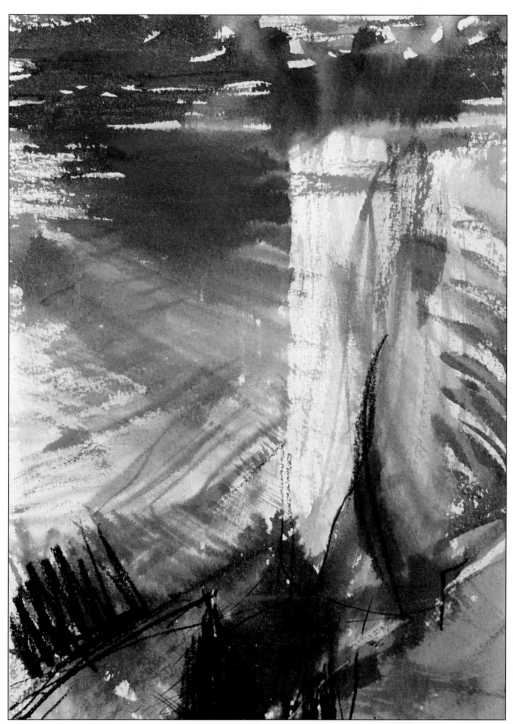

Christopher Baker, *Beachy Head,*
12 × 8 IN (30.5 × 20.3 CM), WATERCOLOR,
CHARCOAL, PENCIL AND PEN

In this study for a large oil
painting, Baker has combined
expressive brush drawing with
the more overtly linear marks of
pen and charcoal.

BRUSHMARKS

The marks made by the brush as a contributing factor to a finished painting are exploited most fully in the thick, buttery medium of oil paint. This has often led people to ignore the importance of brush marks in watercolor, but they can play a vital and expressive part in a painting, making all the difference between a lively, dynamic picture and a dull, routine one.

The most obvious example of visible brush marks in watercolor occurs in the technique of STIPPLING. Then the painting is built up entirely with tiny strokes of a pointed brush. However, it is possible to discern the strokes of the brush in most watercolors to a greater or lesser degree. Some artists use a broad, flat brush, allowing it to follow the direction of a form, while others use a pointed one to create a network of lines in different colors and tones. A popular technique for creating the impression of squalls of rain or swirling mist is to work into a wet WASH with a dry bristle brush to "stroke" paint in a particular direction, while an exciting impression of foliage can be conveyed by dabbing or flicking paint onto paper using short strokes of a small square-ended brush. Another useful technique for foliage – a notoriously tricky subject – is DRY BRUSH, which creates a pleasing feathery texture because the dry paint only partially covers the paper.

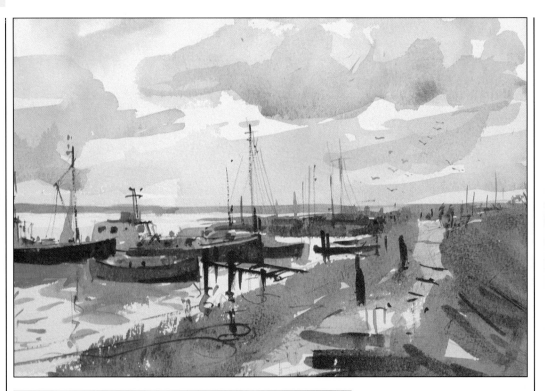

▲ John Tookey, *Blackwater at Heybridge*, 10 × 14 IN (25.4 × 35.5 CM), WATERCOLOR

Sweeping strokes of a large, soft brush define the sky and much of the foreground, contrasting with the finer, linear marks for the boats and their reflections.

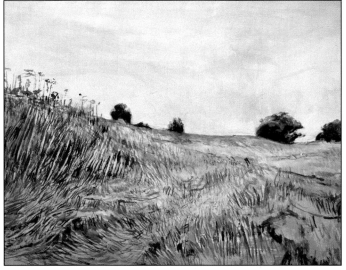

◄ Donald Pass, *Top of the Hill*, 18 × 26 IN (45.7 × 66 CM), WATERCOLOR

The excitement and feeling of movement in this painting derives from the distinctive and highly individual use of directional brushstrokes.

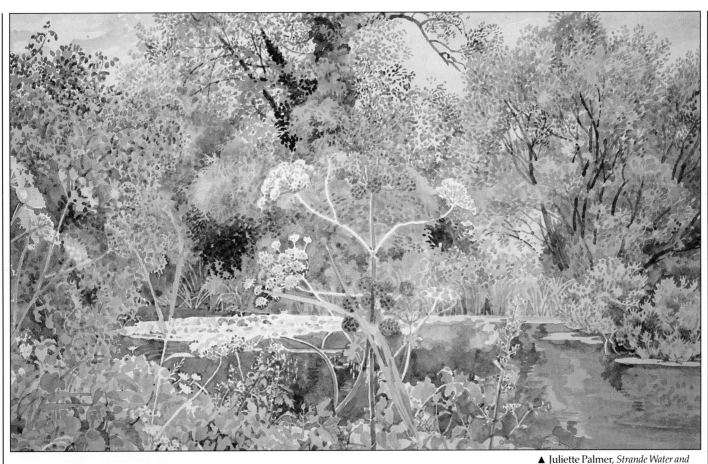

◄ Ronald Jesty, *Durdle Door*, APPROX.
16 × 11 IN (40.6 × 27.9 CM), WATERCOLOR

This artist always paints WET-ON-DRY so that his brushmarks remain crisp and clear with no blurring of edges. Here he has "drawn" with the brush, making marks of different shapes and sizes to describe the clouds, rock textures and patterns of the water.

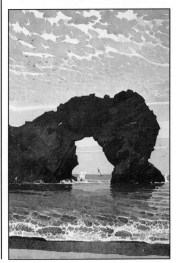

▲ Juliette Palmer, *Strande Water and Hogweed*, APPROX. 11 × 16 IN
(27.9 × 40.6 CM), WATERCOLOR

Palmer uses her small brushmarks descriptively to build up pattern and texture. Notice the variety of different marks – little leaf-shaped blobs and dots at the top; long strokes for the clumps of rushes, and broader squiggles for the reflections.

BUILDING UP

WATERCOLOUR

Because watercolors are semi-transparent, light colors cannot be laid over dark. Thus, traditional practice is to begin a painting with the lightest shades and build up gradually toward the darker ones by means of successive washes or brushstrokes.

Many, but by no means all, artists start by laying a flat WASH all over the paper, leaving uncovered any areas that are to become pure white highlights (known as reserving). This procedure obviously needs some planning, so it is wise to star with a pencil drawing to establish the exact place and shape of the highlights to be reserved. The shade and color of the preliminary wash also needs to be planned as it must relate to the overall color key of the finished painting. A deep blue wash laid all over the paper might be the correct color and intensity for the sky in a landscape, but would not be suitable for a foreground containing pale yellows and ochers. Another variation of the overall wash is to lay one for the sky, allow this to dry, and then put down another one for the land. Both these procedures have the advantage of covering the paper quickly so that you can begin to assess colors and tones without the distraction of pure white paper.

Overpainting

When the first wash or washes are dry, the process of intensifying certain areas begins, done by laying darker washes or individual brushstrokes over the original ones. A watercolor will lose its freshness if there is too much overpainting, so always assess the strength of color needed for each layer carefully and apply it quickly, with one sweep of the brush, so that it does not disturb the paint below. As each wash is allowed to dry, it will form hard edges, which usually form a positive feature of watercolor, adding clarity and crispness.

Other methods

Some artists find it easier to judge the tone and color key of the painting if they begin with the darkest area of color, then go back to the lightest, adding the middle tones last when the two extremes have been established.

Building up a painting in washes is not the only method. Some artists avoid washes altogether, beginning by putting down small brushstrokes of strong color all over the paper, sometimes modifying them with washes on top to soften or strengthen certain areas.

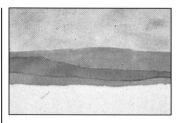

1, 2 Having laid a gray-blue wash over the sky and a slightly darker one for the distant hills, the artist blocks in the details of the middle distance (below). He leaves these washes to dry and then paints the dark trees in the foreground.

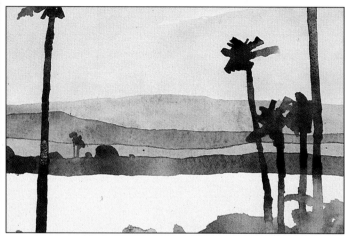

3 The final touch is to lay a green-ocher wash over the area behind the trees. The warm color creates a sense of recession, as it advances toward the front of the picture, while the cool blues are pushed back.

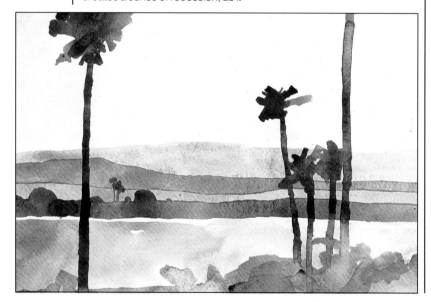

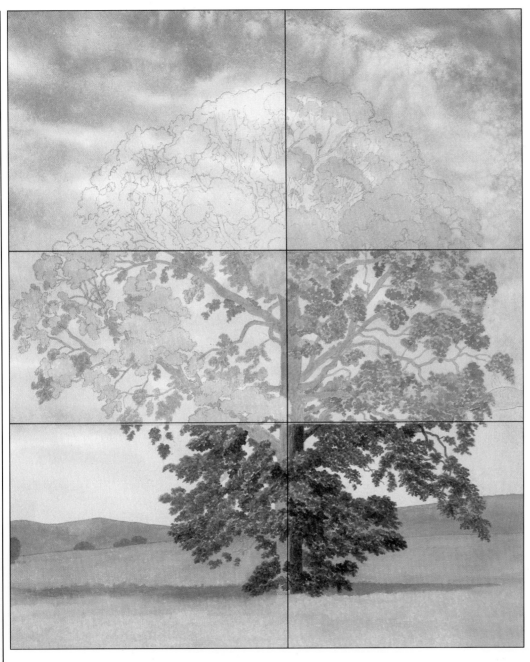

Reading from left to right, this demonstrates the traditional way of building up a watercolor. The sky is the lightest part of the picture, so this is painted first. While it is still damp, a light green wash is taken over the whole of the tree and the foreground. Blue-green paint is then applied to the more distant areas of the tree, and a light brown to the branches. The paper is allowed to dry completely before the darkest tones are added, as these need to have crisp, clear edges. The foliage is given depth by the use of cooler, bluer greens at the back of the tree.

BUILDING UP

GOUACHE AND ACRYLIC

If either of these paints is used thinly, without the addition of white, the procedures are much the same as those for watercolor described on the previous pages. The beauty of acrylic, however, is that no amount of overpainting will stir up earlier paint, because, once dry, it is immovable (a disadvantage of this being that LIFTING OUT is impossible). If used opaquely, acrylic can be built up in more or less infinite layers, dark over light or light over dark. Paintings in opaque gouache can, to a certain extent, be built up from dark to light. If the paint is used thick and dry, a light layer will cover a dark one completely, but there is a limit to the number of layers you can apply, as this paint continues to be soluble in water even when dry, so that a new application of moist paint will churn up and muddy that underneath. The most satisfactory method is to begin by using the paint thin, increasing its opacity gradually as you work. The building up process is aided by working on a TONED GROUND, which serves the same function as a preliminary wash in watercolor and helps to avoid too many layers of paint.

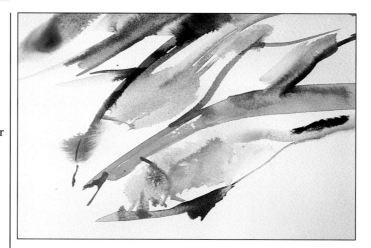

1 Working in gouache, the artist begins with the paint well thinned, laying broad washes and allowing runs to occur in places.

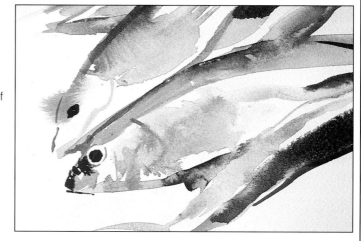

2 When the first washes have dried, she begins to define the detail. The paint is still used as watercolor in most areas, but she intends to build up the textures of the fish more thickly and has applied a broad stroke of opaque yellow.

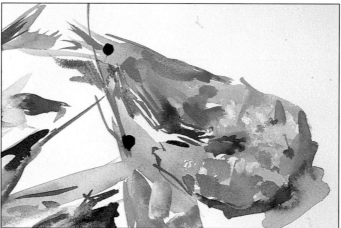

3 The shrimp are painted less solidly than the fish, as befits their delicate, slender forms, and the opaque paint is restricted to small areas of highlight.

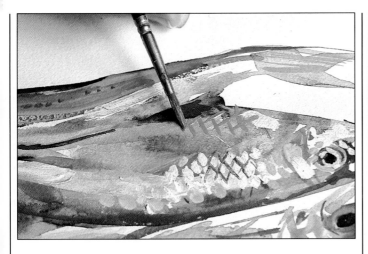

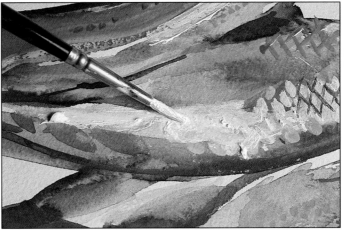

4 Using a strong mixture of gouache, the artist "draws" with the point of the brush on the belly of the fish.

5 Now using really opaque white, she accentuates the silvery highlights. Raised blobs and swirls of paint can be seen where the pigment has been used straight from the tube.

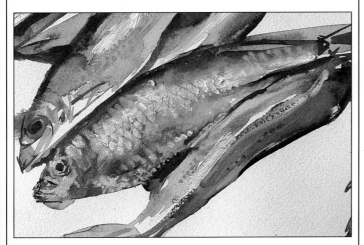

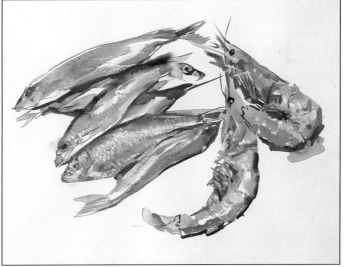

6 The scales of the fish are suggested by a combination of scraping into the paint and working small brushstrokes both WET-IN-WET and WET-ON-DRY.

7 One of the exciting properties of gouache is that it allows a contrast of thick and thin paint, thus providing additional surface interest.

COLOR CHANGES

Newcomers to watercolor often find it difficult to judge the strength and quality of the first color to be applied. There are two reasons for this: one is that the paint becomes a great deal lighter when dry, the other is that it is hard to judge a color against pure white paper – the first wash inevitably looks too dark or too bright.

If you find the first colors are wrong, do not despair. Because watercolors are built up in a series of overlaid washes or brushstrokes, the first color and tone you put down is by no means final: many further changes can be made on the paper itself. If a pale yellow wash is covered – partially or completely – with a blue one, the color changes to become green, and the tone darkens because there are now two layers of paint. By the same token, a wash that is too pale is very easily darkened by applying a second wash of the same color or a slightly darker version of it. Although it is often stated in books about watercolor that light colors cannot be laid over dark ones, this only means that they will not become lighter, but colors can be modified in this way, particularly greens. A green that is too "cool," that is, with too high a proportion of blue, can be changed into a warmer, richer green by laying a strong wash of yellow on top.

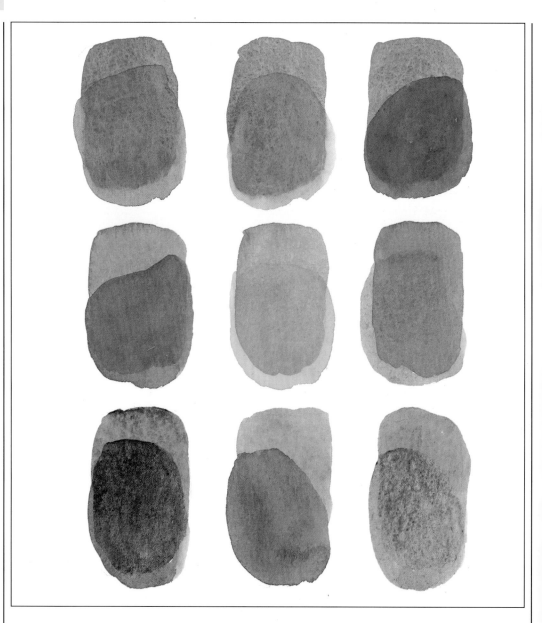

It is surprising how radically even quite a strong color can be altered by overlaying another one. Second and subsequent colors should be applied quickly and surely to avoid stirring up those below. The colors shown here are as follows (left to right).

Top row: first color ultramarine, with Payne's gray, Winsor blue, Winsor violet. Second row: first color cadmium red, with alizarin crimson, cadmium yellow, raw sienna. Third row: first color raw umber, with ultramarine, alizarin crimson, viridian green. Notice

how in some cases the second color has broken up (precipitated) to give a granular effect. This can be used to give additional texture and interest to a painting (see WASH: TEXTURES).

CORRECTIONS

It is a common belief that watercolors cannot be corrected, but, in fact, there are several ways of making changes, correcting or modifying parts of a painting.

If it becomes clear early on that something is badly wrong, simply put the whole thing under cold running water and gently sponge off the paint. For smaller areas, wet a small sponge in clean water and wipe away the offending color, or, for a very tiny area, use a wet brush.

It must be said, though, that some colors are more permanent than others – sap green, for example, is hard to remove totally – and that some papers hold onto the pigment with grim determination. Arches is one of the latter, but other papers will wash clean very well.

As a painting nears completion, you may find that there are too many hard edges or not enough HIGHLIGHTS. Edges can be softened by the water treatment described above, but here the best implement to use is a dampened cotton swab. Both these and sponges are near-essentials in watercolor painting, as they are ideal for LIFTING OUT areas of paint to create soft highlights. Any small specks of dark paint that may have inadvertently flicked onto a white or light-colored area can be removed with an art knife blade, but use the side in a gentle scraping motion, as pressure with the point could easily make holes in the paper.

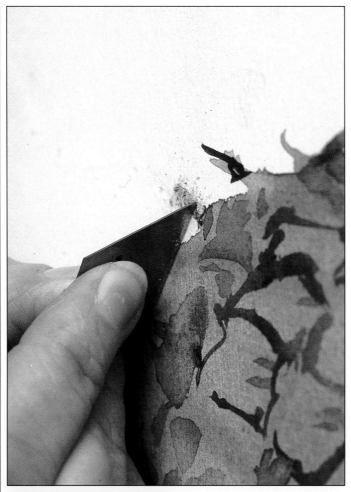

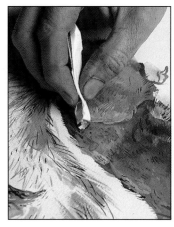

▲ If one color floods into another to create an unwanted effect, the excess can be mopped up with a small sponge or piece of blotting paper.

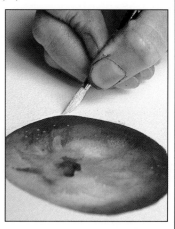

▲ Small blots and blemishes are easily removed by scraping with a knife or razor blade. Be careful not to apply too much pressure, or you could make holes in the paper.

▲ Ragged edges can either be cleaned up with a knife, as in the first example, or with opaque white gouache paint, as here.

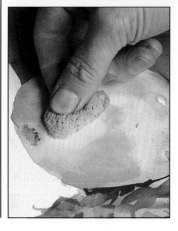

◄ Here the artist finds he needs to lighten the color in this area, so he lifts out some of the paint with a damp sponge.

DRAWING

Because watercolors cannot be changed radically (except by washing off and beginning again), they need to be planned in advance, so it is usual to begin a painting by drawing the subject directly onto the paper. Some artists dispense with this stage, but this is usually because they are familiar with the subject, have painted it before and have a clear idea of how they want the finished painting to look.

There are certain inherent problems with underdrawings for watercolor. One is that the drawn lines are likely to show through the paint in the paler areas. The lines should, therefore, be kept as light as possible and any shading avoided so that the drawing is nothing more than a guideline to remind you which areas should be reserved as highlights and where the first washes should be laid.

Another problem is that on certain papers, erasing can scuff the surface, removing parts of the top layer, so that any paint applied to these areas will form unsightly blotches. If you find that you need to erase, use kneadable putty, applying light pressure.

For a simple landscape or seascape, your underdrawing will probably consist of no more than a few lines, but a complex subject, such as buildings or a portrait, will need a more elaborate drawing. Then you may find that the SQUARING UP method is helpful, using either a sketch or photograph of the subject.

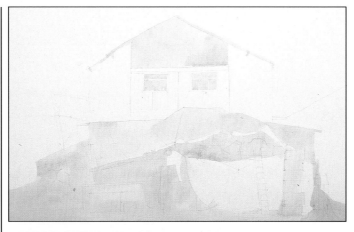

Having made a preliminary drawing with a very sharp B pencil, the artist lays the first washes. The pencil lines can be erased at this stage, but it is not always necessary as they are unlikely to show in any but the palest areas of the painting.

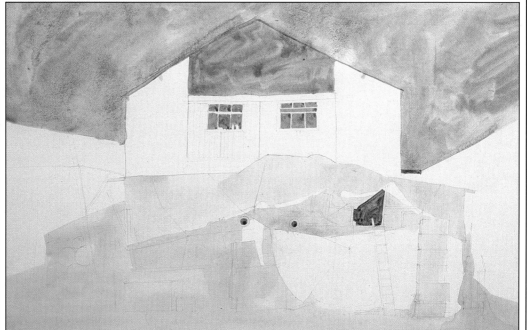

DRY BRUSH

This technique is just what its name implies – painting with the bare minimum of paint on the brush so that the color only partially covers the paper. It is one of the most often used ways of creating TEXTURE and BROKEN COLOR in a watercolor, particularly for foliage and grass in a landscape or hair and fur textures in a portrait or animal painting. It needs a little practice: if there is too little paint, it will not cover the paper at all, but if there is too much, it will simply create a rather blotchy wash.

As a general principle, the technique should not be used all over a painting, as this can look dull and monotonous. Texture-making methods work best in combination with others, such as flat or broken washes.

Opaque gouache and acrylic are also well suited to the dry brush technique. In both cases the paint should be used with only just enough water to make it malleable – or even none at all – and the best effects are obtained with bristle, not soft sable or synthetic-hair brushes (these are, in any case, quickly spoiled by such treatment).

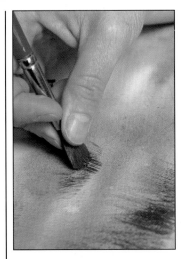

1 The artist uses a square-ended brush, fanning out the hairs slightly with his thumb and forefinger and then dragging it over the paper to create a series of fine, roughly parallel lines. The paint must be fairly dry, so before you begin, flick off the excess or dab the brush lightly on blotting paper.

2 As can be seen from this detail, dry brush is the perfect technique for grass textures, and effects of considerable depth and variety can be created by building up layers of different colors and tones.

3 It is usually more effective to restrict techniques like this to one area of a painting, as the artist has done here. The dry paint and spiky, linear marks in the foreground stand out well in contrast with the broad, free treatment of the buildings and sky.

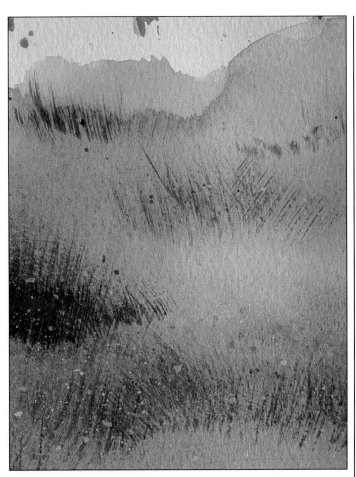

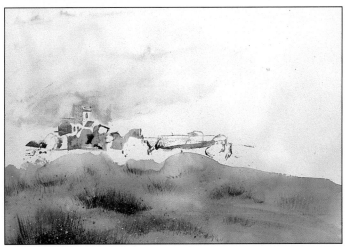

GLAZING

This is a technique that was perfected by the early painters using oils. They would lay thin skins of transparent pigment one over the other to create colors of incredible richness and luminosity. In watercolor painting, overlaying washes is sometimes described as glazing, but this is misleading as it implies a special technique, whereas in fact it is the normal way of working.

Acrylic paint is perfectly suited to the glazing technique because it dries so fast: each layer must be thoroughly dry before the next one is applied. The effects the technique creates are quite different from those of color applied opaquely, as light seems to reflect through each layer, almost giving the appearance of being lit from within. The use of a brilliant white ground (acrylic gesso is ideal) on a smooth surface such as masonite or plain illustration board further enhances the luminosity.

Special mediums are sold for acrylic glazing – available in both gloss and matte – and these can be used either alone or in conjunction with water.

A whole painting can be built up layer by layer in this way – as can be seen in some of David Hockney's acrylic paintings – but this is not the only way of using the technique. Thin glazes can also be laid over an area of thick paint (impasto) to great effect. The glaze will tend to slide off the raised areas and sink into the lower ones – a useful technique for suggesting textures, such as that of weathered stone or tree bark.

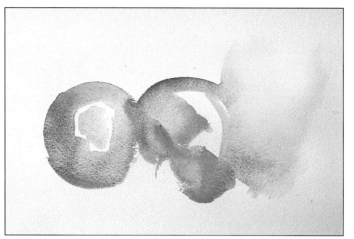

1 Working in acrylic on watercolor paper, the artist starts with the paint heavily diluted with water. Acrylic used in this way is virtually indistinguishable from watercolor, but it cannot be removed once dry, a considerable advantage in the glazing technique.

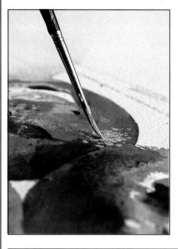

2 A layer of darker color mixed with special glazing medium has been laid over the orange, and the artist now builds up the highlights with opaque paint.

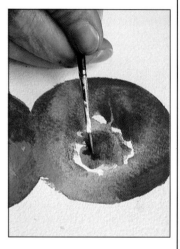

3 Deep-toned glazes are now laid on the apple. The way earlier layers of color reflect back through subsequent glazes gives a rich, glowing effect.

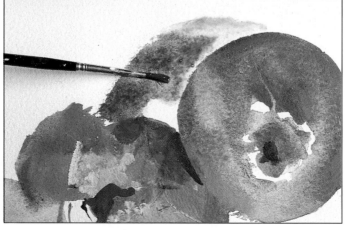

4 Here the transparent, slightly gluey quality of the paint can be seen. Either water or the special medium can be used for acrylic glazes, but it takes a little practice to achieve the right consistency.

GUM ARABIC

This is the medium that, together with gelatine, acts as the binder for watercolor pigment (watercolors also contain glycerine to keep them moist).

Gum arabic can be bought in bottled form and is often used as a painting medium. If you add a little gum to your water when mixing paint, it gives it extra body, making it less runny and easier to blend. It is particularly suitable for the kind of painting that is built up in small, separate brushstrokes, as it prevents them from flowing into one another.

Its other important property is as a varnish. If a dark area of a painting, such as a very deep shadow, has gone dead through too much overlaying of washes, a light application of gum arabic will revive the color and give additional richness. It should never be used alone, however, as this could cause cracking.

Experience will teach you how much to dilute it when using it as a painting medium, but a general rule of thumb is that there should be considerably more water than gum (it is sometimes referred to as gum water for this reason).

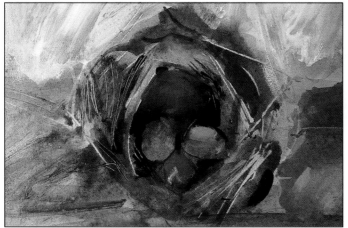

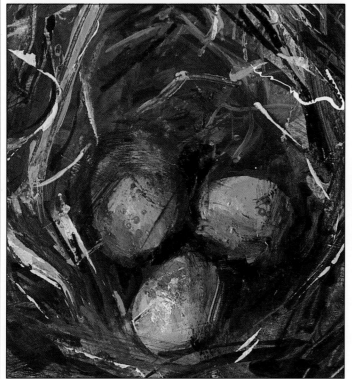

1 Gum arabic can be used with either watercolor or gouache, and here the artist has used a combination of both. Because the gum is soluble in water, it is much easier to lift out areas of paint (see LIFTING OUT), and here sharp, clear lines have been "drawn" with the point of a brush dipped in water and scratched with the brush handle.

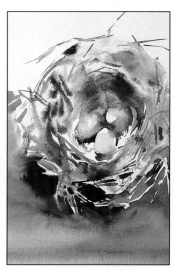

3 This photograph shows the same subject, in this case painted in pure watercolor. Here the colors have merged together softly, but where the gum has been used, distinct brushmarks can be seen, particularly noticeable in the detail on the left, and the paint has stayed where it was put.

2 Gouache mixed with gum arabic behaves more like opaque acrylic than like watercolor, allowing clear, decisive brushmarks and avoiding the matte, dead look the paint sometimes has when too many layers are built up. Here there is considerable overpainting, but the colors have maintained their freshness and sparkle.

HARD AND SOFT EDGES

A wet watercolor WASH laid on dry paper forms a shallow pool of color which, if left undisturbed, will form hard edges as it dries, rather like a tidemark. This can be alarming to the novice, particularly in the early stages of a painting, but it is one of the many characteristics of the medium that can be used to great advantage. By laying smaller, loose washes over previous dry ones, you can build up a fascinating network of fluid, broken lines that not only help to define form and suggest shapes but give a lovely sparkling quality to the work. This is an excellent method for building up rather irregular shapes such as clouds, rocks or ripples on water.

You will not necessarily want to use the same technique in every part of the painting, however. A combination of hard and soft edges describes the subject more successfully and also gives the picture more variety.

There are several ways of avoiding hard edges. One is to work WET-IN-WET by dampening the paper before laying the first wash and then working subsequent colors into it before it dries so that they blend into one another with subtle transitions. A wash on dry paper can be softened and drawn out at the edges by using a sponge, paintbrush or cotton swab dipped in clean water to remove the excess paint. A wash "dragged" or "pulled" over dry paper with either a brush or sponge will also dry without hard edges, since the paint is prevented from forming a pool.

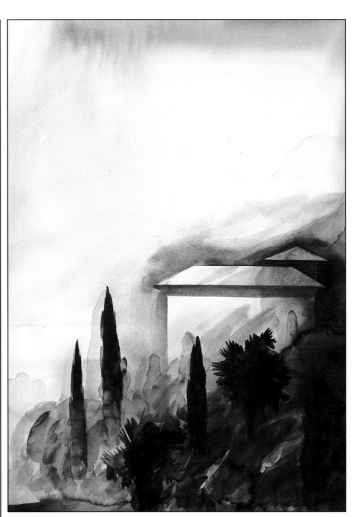

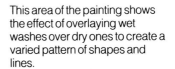

This area of the painting shows the effect of overlaying wet washes over dry ones to create a varied pattern of shapes and lines.

William Tillyer, *Swiss Lakes series*, 30 × 22½ IN (76.2 × 57.2 CM) WATERCOLOR

This artist's work shows an obvious delight in the fluid, aqueous quality of pure watercolor, which he uses in a way that makes full use of its potential. The soft suggestion of rain or mist at the top of the sky has been achieved by working WET-IN-WET, with the board at an angle so that the paint runs down the paper, while further down, a pale wash has been laid over dry paint to hint at the outline of mountains. These gentle gradations set up an exciting opposition to the hard, clear edges of the building and the dark, spiky shapes of the trees.

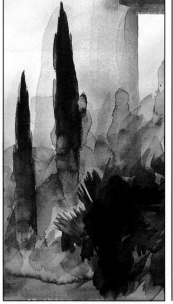

Paul Riley, *Roses and Damsons*,
14½ × 21½ IN (36.8 × 54.6 CM),
WATERCOLOR

Riley also exploits the effects of watercolor to the full, using the pale, delicate colors that we tend to associate with the medium, but with strong, decisive brushwork that gives a taut, linear quality to the painting.

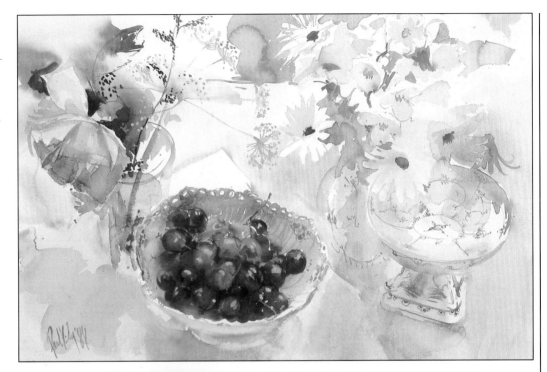

This detail shows a carefully controlled use of hard/soft contrast, with the paint blended WET-IN-WET in places (notably the bowl of fruit) and allowed to form edges in others. An extra touch of crispness is provided by the little dots and lines made with the point of the brush.

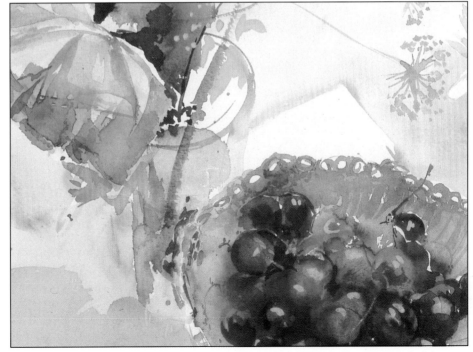

HIGHLIGHTS

The light reflecting off white paper is an integral part of a watercolor painting, giving good watercolors their lovely translucent quality. For this reason, the most effective way of creating pure, sparkling highlights is to "reserve" any areas that are to be white by painting around them. This means that when you begin a painting, you must have a clear idea of where the highlights are to be, so some advance planning is necessary.

Not all highlights, of course, are pure white: in a painting where all the tones are dark, too many whites could be over-emphatic. Thus, before the painting has advanced very far, you will have to decide whether to reserve areas of an initial pale wash or to build up really dark tones around a later, mid-toned one.

When you lay a wash around an area to be reserved for a highlight, it will dry with a hard edge. This can be very effective, but it is not necessarily what you want. You might, for example, need a softer, more diffused highlight on a rounded object such as a piece of fruit. In such cases, you can achieve a gentler transition by softening the edge with a brush, small sponge or cotton swab dipped in water, so that it blends into the white area.

Small highlights, such as the points of light in eyes or the tiny sparkles seen on sunlit, rippling water, which are virtually impossible to reserve, can either be achieved by MASKING or added with thick Chinese white or zinc white gouache paint as a final stage. Highlights can also be made by removing paint (see LIFTING OUT and SCRAPING BACK).

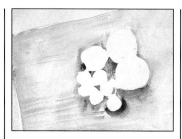

1 The shapes of the fruit are initially left white, their outlines defined by the pale brown wash.

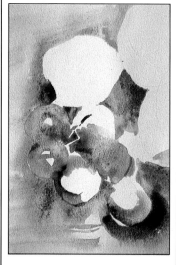

2 Paint is carefully taken around the highlights, and darker color is flooded in WET-IN-WET. The paint is kept loose and fluid: hesitant niggling in the early stages can quickly destroy the freshness of the color.

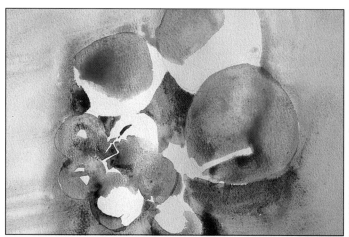

3 Instead of applying a flat wash all over the fruit and then adding darker tones, each area of color is treated separately, though some washes will overlap at a later stage.

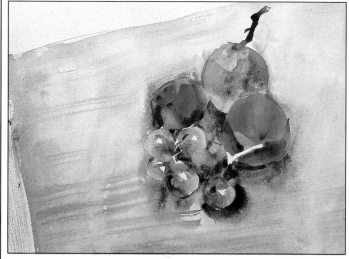

4 With all the paper covered and the main washes in place, the artist decides where further light and dark emphasis is needed.

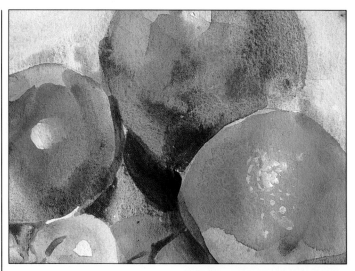

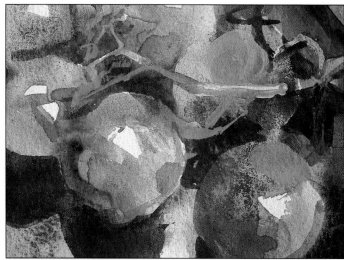

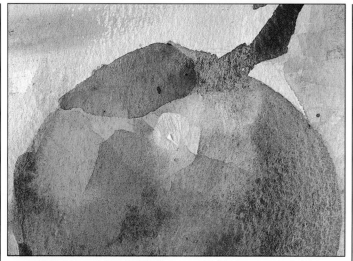

5 She darkens the cast shadows on and below the green apple and uses opaque white to add additional highlights on the fruit at left and right. Those on the orange have been applied lightly with the point of the brush, giving a realistic impression of the slightly pitted texture of the peel. The artist has been conscious of texture throughout, using the granulated quality of the wetly applied paint to add surface interest (see WASH: TEXTURES).

6 The grapes are given further modeling, with the dark paint again kept very wet. The original reserved highlights are not touched again, but the stalks are defined with a combination of opaque paint and reserving.

7 The treatment is impressionistic rather than literal, and the patch of dark green at the top of the apple, which could be either a shadow or a leaf, has been added primarily to separate it from the background and emphasize the highlighted areas.

LIFTING OUT

Removing paint from the paper is not only a correction method, it is a watercolor technique in its own right and can be used to great effect to soften edges, diffuse and modify color and create those HIGHLIGHTS that cannot be reserved. For instance, the effect of streaked wind clouds in a blue sky is quickly and easily created by laying a blue wash and wiping a dry sponge, paintbrush or paper tissue across it while it is still wet. The white tops of cumulus clouds can be suggested by dabbing the wet paint with a sponge or blotting paper.

Paint can also be lifted out when dry by using a dampened sponge or other such tool, but the success of the method depends both on the color to be lifted and the type of paper used. Certain colors, such as sap green and phthalocyanine blue, act rather like dyes, staining the paper, and can never be removed completely, while some papers absorb the paint, making it hard to move it around. Bockingford, Saunders and Cotman papers are all excellent for lifting out in this way, so if you become addicted to the technique, choose your paper accordingly. Another useful aid to lifting out is GUM ARABIC. Add it in small quantities to the color you intend to remove partially.

Large areas of dry paint can be lifted with a dampened sponge, but for smaller ones, the most useful tool is a cotton swab. Never apply too much pressure when using a cotton swab, as the stick may poke through the cotton tip and scratch the surface of the paper.

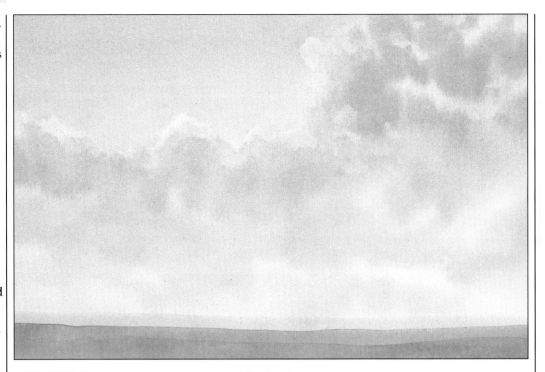

▲ Surprisingly complex sky effects can be obtained by lifting out from wet paint. Here a light ocher wash was laid and allowed to dry, a blue wash was taken over the whole area and the clouds blotted immediately with a crumpled tissue. The paper was then damped and pale gray added in small strokes that were allowed to spread, leaving areas of the original yellow untouched.

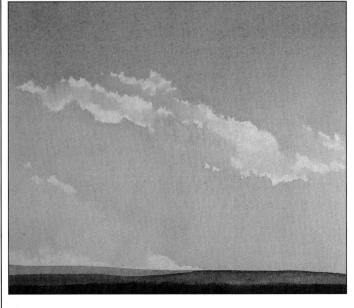

◄ This dramatic sky has been created very simply, by laying a warm gray gradated wash (see WASH: GRADATED AND VARIEGATED) over a dry merged wash of yellow and red. While the gray was still wet, the clouds were lifted out with a piece of tissue formed into a blunt point.

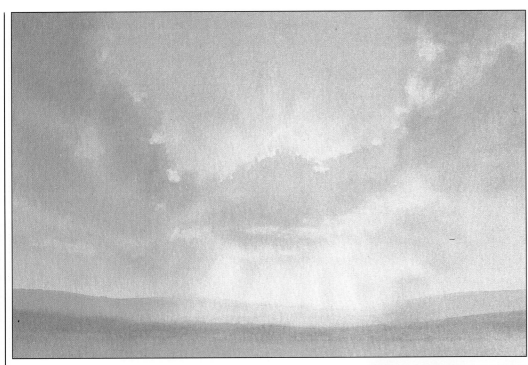

◄ Here a gradated wash of blue was laid over the whole sky and gray added when still wet. The lighter areas of the clouds and the sun's rays were lifted out with tissue rolled into a point.

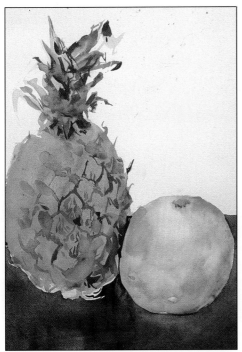

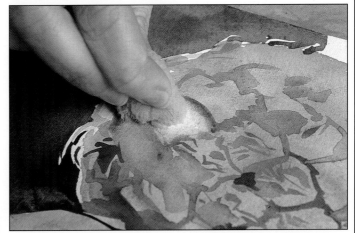

◄ ▲ With this fruit group (left) nearly complete, the artist has decided to lighten certain areas, using a dampened sponge (above) to coax the paint off the paper. The success of lifting out dry paint depends very much on the paper used (this is Bockingford), but highlights created in this way can be very effective, as they are softer and less obtrusive than reserved areas of white paper.

LINE AND WASH

This technique has a long history and is still much used today, particularly for illustrative work. Before the British watercolorists of the eighteenth century began to exploit the full possibilities of watercolor as a painting medium, it had been used mainly to put pale, flat tints over pen drawings, a practice that itself continued the tradition of the pen and ink-wash drawings often made by artists as preliminary studies for paintings.

The line and wash technique is particularly well suited to small, delicate subjects such as plant drawings or to quick figure studies intended to convey a sense of movement. Rembrandt's sketchbooks are full of monochrome pen and wash drawings, conveying everything he needed to record in a few lines and one or two surely placed tones.

The traditional method is to begin with a pen drawing, leave it to dry and then lay in fluid, light color with a brush. One of the difficulties of the technique is to integrate the drawing and the color in such a way that the washes do not look like a "coloring in" exercise, so it is often more satisfactory to develop both line and wash at the same time, beginning with some lines and color and then adding to and strengthening both as necessary. You can also start back to front, as it were, laying down the washes first to establish the main tones and then drawing on top, in which case you will need to begin with a light pencil sketch as a guideline.

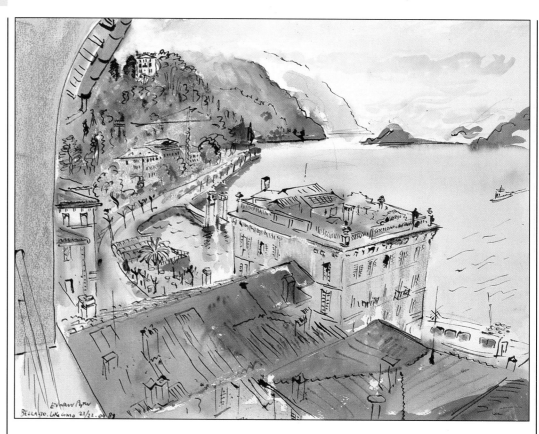

Edward Piper, *Bellagio, Lake Como*, 22 × 30 IN (55.9 × 76.2 CM), WATERCOLOR AND PEN

Piper achieves a perfect harmony between line and color by using both with a light and delicate touch. He never attempts to outline areas of color with line; instead, the washes are allowed to escape their "boundaries" to merge together in places, and the quality of the lines is lively and varied.

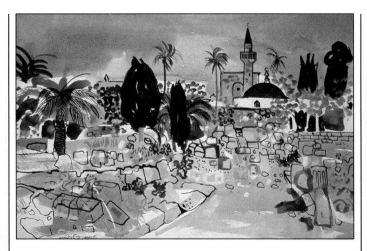

Doreen Osborne, *Ancient Agora, Kos*,
13 × 20½ IN (33 × 52 CM), GOUACHE
AND PEN

Osborne has created a strong
sense of pattern in her painting,
with the bold line drawing in the
foreground providing a nice
balance to the dark shapes of the
trees and mosque roof.

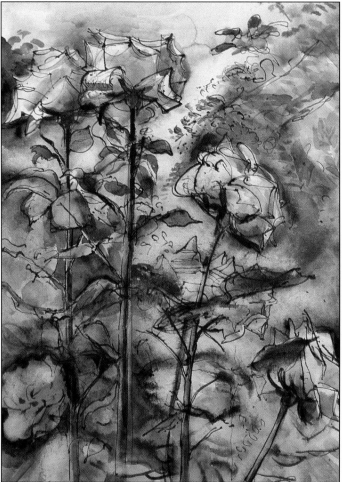

Audrey Macleod, *Roses Against a
Blue Sky*, 15 × 11 IN (38.1 × 27.9 CM),
WATERCOLOR AND PEN

This lovely study was done out of
doors directly from the subject.
The artist has expressed the
delicacy of the subject by
restricting the definition to the line
drawing, using the paint very
fluidly so that it does not so much
describe the forms as create a
soft, diffused halo around them.

MASKING

Some watercolorists feel a certain disdain for masking methods, regarding them as "cheating" or as being too mechanical. It is true that if they are over-used, they can detract from the spontaneity that we associate with watercolors, but masking is a method that can be used creatively, giving exciting effects that cannot be obtained by using the more classic watercolor techniques.

The two main purposes of masking are to create highlights by reserving certain areas of a painting and to protect one part of a picture while you work on another. If you have planned a painting that relies for its effect on a series of small, intricate highlights, such as a woodland scene with a pattern of leaves and twigs catching the sunlight, or a seascape where the light creates tiny bright points on choppy water, liquid mask can be the answer.

The liquid is available in two types. One has a slight yellow tint, the other is colorless. Both are applied with a brush and, once dry (completely), washes are painted over it. When the painting or the particular area of it is complete, the mask is removed by gently rubbing with a finger or an eraser. Be warned, however: if the paper is too rough or too smooth, it will either be impossible to remove or will spoil the paper – the best surface is a medium one (known as Not).

The beauty of liquid mask is that it is a form of painting in negative – the brushstrokes you use can be as varied in shape as you like, and you can create lovely effects by using thick and thin lines, splodges and little dots. The advantage of the yellow-tinted fluid is that

you can see how the brushstrokes look as you apply them, whereas with the white version, it is rather a matter of guesswork. The disadvantage is that the yellow patches are always visible as you paint and tend to give a false idea of the color values.

Sometimes a painting needs to be approached rather carefully and methodically, be dealt with in separate parts, and this is where the second main function of masking comes in. Liquid mask or masking tape (ideal for straight lines) can be used as a temporary stop for certain areas of the painting. Suppose your subject is a light-colored, intricately shaped building set against a stormy sky or dark foliage, and you want to build up the background with several layers of color. Covering the whole area of the building with liquid mask or putting strips of masking tape along the edges will allow you to paint freely without the constant worry of paint spilling over to spoil the sharp, clean lines. Once the background is finished, the mask can be removed, and the rest of the painting carried out as a separate stage. It may be mechanical, but it is a liberating method for anyone who wishes to have complete control over paint.

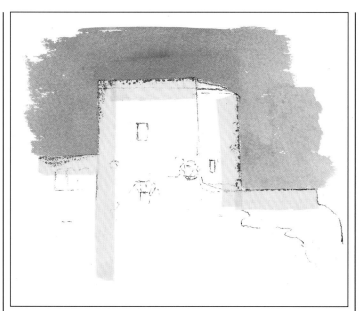

Masking tape can be very helpful for buildings. It takes the tension out of painting, allowing you to work freely without the danger of spoiling an edge that needs to be straight and crisp.

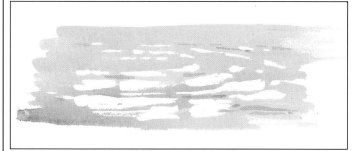

Liquid mask is ideal for hard-edged highlights such as the ripples on water. Such effects are difficult to achieve by the classic technique of reserving (see HIGHLIGHTS), as the paint in the darker areas can easily become overworked and the edges lose their crispness and clarity. This is a very direct and satisfying way of working, as the "negative" brushstrokes can be as varied and expressive as the "positive" ones.

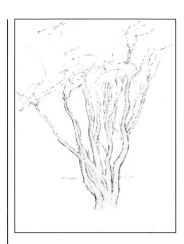

1 The tree trunks are carefully drawn, liquid mask is applied, and then left to dry before any further work is done. The artist is working on Bockingford paper with a Not surface, from which the rubbery liquid is easily removed; it is not suitable for use on Rough papers as it sinks into the "troughs" and cannot be peeled off.

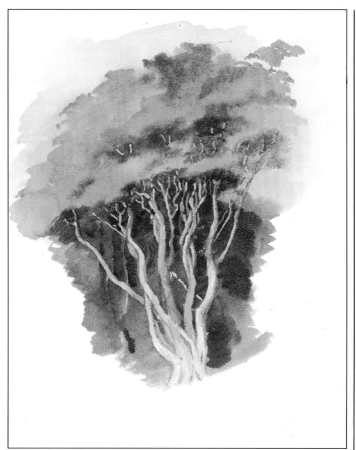

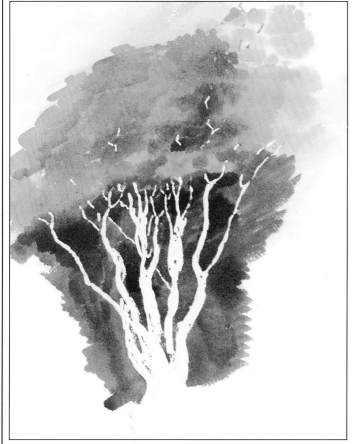

2 With the mask protecting the intricate shapes of the trunks and branches, dark washes are built up behind and above without fear of paint splashing onto the pale areas. When the washes are dry, the mask is removed by rubbing it with a finger.

3 The trunks and branches are modeled with darker paint in places and touches of white gouache define the highlights.

MIXED MEDIA

Although many artists know that they can create their best effects with pure watercolor, more and more are breaking away from convention, finding that they can create livelier and more expressive paintings by combining several different media.

To some extent, mixing media is a matter of trial and error, and there is now such a diversity of artist's materials that there is no way of prescribing techniques for each one or for each possible combination. However, it can be said that some mixtures are easier to manage than others. Acrylic and watercolor, for example, can be made to blend into one another almost imperceptibly because they have very much the same characteristics, but two or more physically dissimilar media, such as LINE AND WASH, will automatically set up a contrast. There is nothing wrong with this – it may even be the point of the exercise – but it can make it difficult to preserve an overall unity.

The only way to explore the natures of the different materials and find out the most effective means of using them is to try out various combinations. You could use a failed watercolor as a basis – many successful mixed-media paintings are less the result of advance planning than of exploratory re-working.

Watercolor and acrylic
Acrylic used thinly, diluted with water but no medium or white, behaves in more or less the same way as watercolor. There are two important differences between them, however. One is that acrylic has greater depth of color so that a first wash can, if desired, be extremely vivid, and the other is that, once dry, the paint cannot be removed. This can be an advantage, as further washes, either in watercolor or acrylic, can be laid over an initial one without disturbing the pigment. The paint need not be applied in thin washes throughout: the combination of shimmering, translucent watercolor and thickly painted areas of acrylic can be very effective, particularly in landscapes with strong foreground interest, where you want to pick out small details like individual flowers or grass heads (very hard to do in watercolor). It is often possible to save an unsuccessful watercolor by turning to acrylic in the later stages.

Watercolor and gouache
These are often used together, and many artists scarcely differentiate between them. However, unless both are used thinly, it can be a more difficult combination to manage, as gouache paint, once mixed with white to make it opaque, has a matte surface, which can make it look dead and dull beside a watercolor wash.

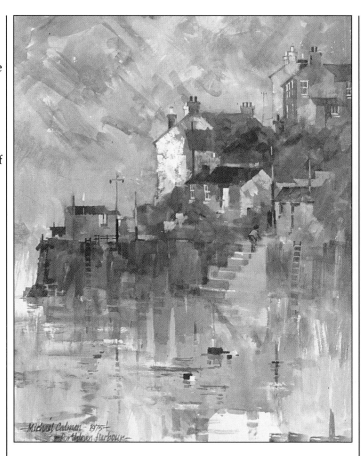

Michael Cadman RA, ARCA, *Low Tide, Cornish Harbour,* APPROX. 20 × 14 IN (50.8 × 35.6 CM), WATERCOLOR, ACRYLIC AND GOUACHE

Cadman regularly mixes the three water-based paints, using them thickly or thinly as the painting demands. Here brushstrokes of transparent color have been laid over one another, with touches of thick, opaque white on the buildings and water.

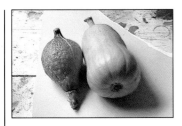

1 One of the most attractive qualities of these gourds (above) is the contrast in textures. As the first stage in building up the pitted surface of the orange gourd, the artist mixes her paint with GUM ARABIC, which makes it settle unevenly, with a slight bubbling.

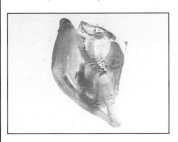

2 Still using transparent watercolor, she paints the yellow gourd WET-IN-WET, allowing the colors to blend softly together.

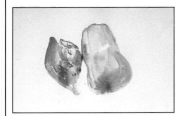

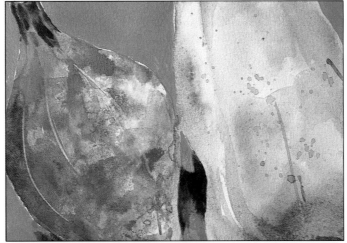

3 Opaque gouache is now used for the flat background and some areas of the fruit. The texture of the orange gourd is achieved by further applications of paint mixed with gum arabic. This is blotted with a damp sponge (see LIFTING OUT).

4 The finished result shows the pleasing variety of paint quality typical of mixed-media paintings.

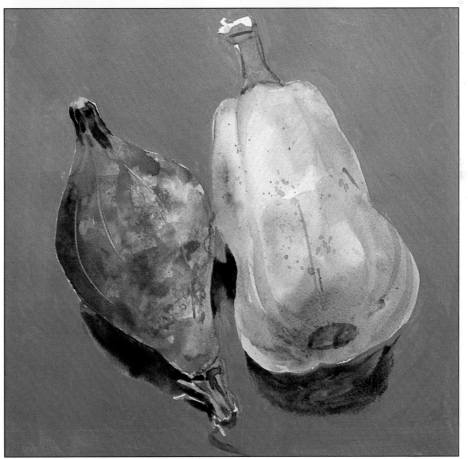

MIXED MEDIA

PAINT AND PASTEL

Soft pastels can be used very successfully with watercolor and provide an excellent means of adding texture and surface interest to a painting.

Sparkling broken colors can be created by overlaying a watercolor wash with light strokes of pastel, particularly if you work on a fairly rough paper.

Oil pastels have a slightly different, but equally interesting, effect. A light layer of oil pastel laid down under a watercolor wash will repel the water to a greater or lesser degree (some oil pastels are oilier than others) so that it sinks only into the troughs of the paper, resulting in a slightly mottled, granular area of color.

Gouache and pastel

These have been used together since the eighteenth century when pastel was at the height of its popularity as an artist's medium. Some mixed-media techniques are based on the dissimilarity of the elements used, which creates its own kind of tension and dynamism, but these two are natural partners, having a similar matte, chalky quality.

Watercolor crayons

These are, in effect, mixed media in themselves. When dry, they are a drawing medium, but as soon as water is applied to them, they become paint and can be spread with a brush. Very varied effects can be created by using them in a linear manner in some areas of a painting and as paints in others. They can also be combined with traditional watercolors, felt-tipped pens or pen and ink.

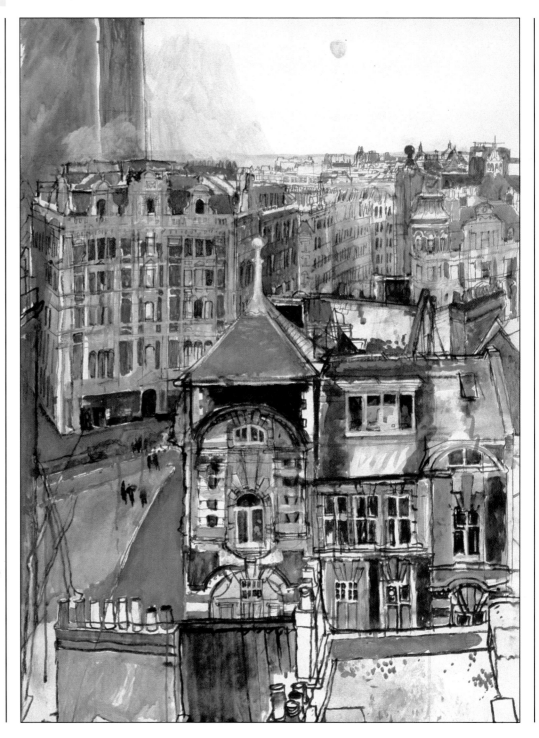

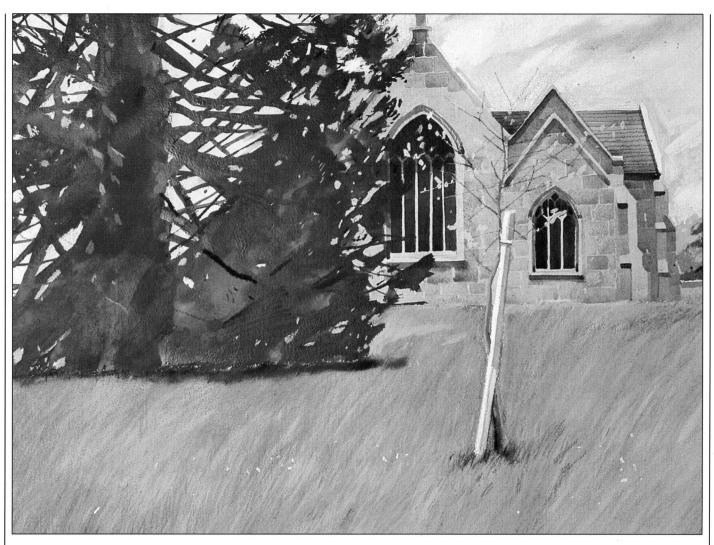

◄ Ian Simpson, *From St. Martin's, London*, 33 × 23 IN (84 × 58.5 CM), ACRYLIC, PENCIL AND CHARCOAL

This was painted on the spot (from a window). It began as a charcoal drawing, which was then fixed, and the painting built up with acrylic, pencil, and more charcoal. The paint is transparent in places and opaque in others, and large areas of paper have been deliberately left uncovered.

▲ Ian Sidaway, *Churchyard*, 11¼ × 16 IN (28.6 × 40.6 CM), WATERCOLOR, PASTEL AND CONTÉ PENCIL

This combination of media has produced a lively contrast of textures. The building and tree are pure watercolor, while the sky and grass are pastel worked over an initial watercolor wash. Details have been picked out lightly with conté pencil.

SCRAPING BACK

Sometimes called *sgraffito*, this simply means removing dry paint so that the white paper is revealed. The method is most often used to create the kind of small, fine highlights that cannot be reserved, such as the light catching blades of grass in the foreground of a landscape. It is a more satisfactory method than opaque white applied with a brush, as this tends to look clumsy and, if laid over a dark color, does not cover it very well.

Scraping is done with a sharp knife, such as an art knife, or with a razor blade. For the finest lines, use the point of the knife, but avoid digging it into the paper. A more diffused highlight over a wider area can be made by scraping gently with the side of the knife or with a razor blade, which will remove some of the paint but not all of it.

This technique is not successful unless you use a good-quality, reasonably heavy paper – it should be no lighter than 140lbs. On a flimsier paper you could easily make holes or spoil the surface.

The same method can be used for gouache and acrylic, but only if the surface is one that can withstand this treatment.

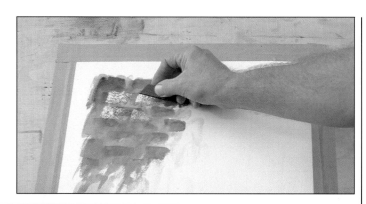

▶ Large areas of paint can be scraped back with the flat of a knife blade or razor blade. This only removes the raised tooth of the paper, leaving color still in the "troughs" and creating a mottled, broken-color effect rather similar to WAX RESIST.

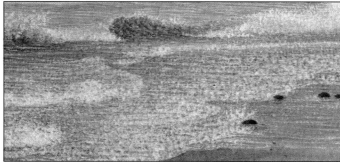

◀ ▼ The delicate, complex pattern of the frothy water in the painting below was created by scraping with a sharp point. The effect, which can be seen clearly in the detail (left), would be impossible to achieve by any other means. Opaque white gouache or acrylic could be used, but the texture would be less interesting and the lines less fine and crisp.

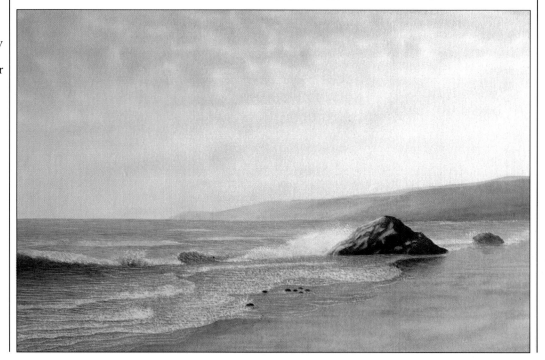

SCUMBLING

This is one of the best-known of all techniques for creating texture and BROKEN COLOR effects, particularly in the opaque media. It involves scrubbing very dry paint unevenly over another layer of dry color so that the first one shows through, but only partially. It is most frequently used in oil painting, but is in many ways even better suited to acrylic and gouache because they dry so much faster – the oil painter has to wait some time for the first layer to dry.

Scumbling can give amazing richness to colors, creating a lovely glowing effect rather akin to that of a semi-transparent fabric with another, solidly colored one beneath.

There is no standard set of rules for the technique, as it is fundamentally an improvisational one. You can scumble light over dark, dark over light or a vivid color over a contrasting one, depending on the circumstances, but do not try to use a soft, sable-type brush or the paint will go on too evenly (and you will quickly ruin the brush). A bristle brush is ideal, but other possibilities are stenciling brushes, sponges, crumpled tissue paper or your fingers.

The particular value of the method for gouache is that it allows colors to be overlaid without becoming muddy and dead looking – always a danger with this medium.

Scumbling is less well suited to watercolor, but it is possible to adapt the DRY BRUSH method to scumbling, using the paint as thick as possible – even straight out of the tube – and working on rough paper.

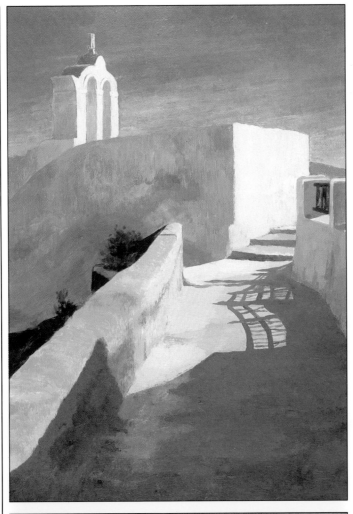

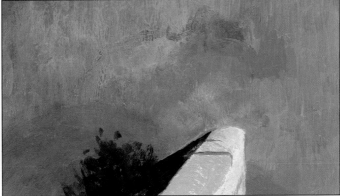

Hazel Harrison, *Sun and Shadow, Santorini*, 20½ × 14½ IN (52 × 36.8 CM), ACRYLIC ON SMOOTH ART BOARD

Here successive layers have been built up over a pre-tinted yellow ocher ground. In places thick paint has been scumbled over thinner applications, and in others, notably the shadow, transparent color thinned with acrylic medium has been glazed over opaque paint. The detail (below) shows thin over thick scumbling with a bristle brush.

SPATTERING

Spraying or flicking paint onto the paper, once regarded as unorthodox and "tricksy," is now accepted by most artists as an excellent means of either enlivening an area of flat color or of suggesting texture.

Spattering is a somewhat unpredictable method and it takes some practice before you can be sure of the effect it will create, so it is wise to try it out on some spare paper before running the risk of spoiling a painting. Any medium can be used, but the paint must not be too thick or it will simply cling to the brush. To make a fine spatter, load a toothbrush with fairly thick paint, hold it horizontally above the paper, bristle side down, and run your index finger over the bristles. For a coarser effect, use a bristle brush, loaded with paint of the same consistency, and tap it sharply with the handle of another brush.

The main problem with the method is judging the tone and depth of color of the spattered paint against that of the color beneath. If you apply dark paint – and thick watercolor will of necessity be quite dark – over a very pale tint, it may be too obtrusive. The best effects are created when the tonal values are close together. If you are using the technique to suggest the texture of a pebbled or sandy beach, for which it is ideal, you may need to spatter one pale color over another. In this case the best implement is a mouth diffuser of the kind sold for spraying fixative. The bristle brush method can also be used for watery paint, but will give much larger drops.

1 The forms and textures of the trees are to be built up by spattering, so the first washes are deliberately uneven, with the paint almost thrown from the brush in the sky area. A white patch is left in the foreground for the path.

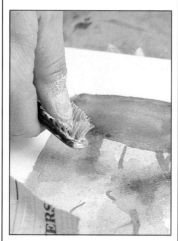

2 A loose newspaper mask protects the top of the picture while paint is spattered onto the trees and foreground. The yellow, being a lighter tone than the dark green, needs to be thickened if it is not to disappear into the darker color, so a mixture of watercolor and acrylic is used.

3 At this stage, the artist takes stock of the painting to see where further definition is needed. The trees are still rather pale and formless, but the sky area above them, where the paint has formed a BACKRUN, enhances the composition by echoing the curves below.

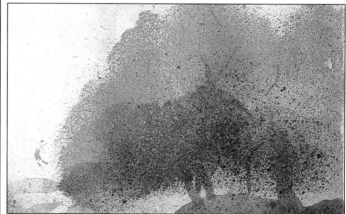

4 Another layer of spattered paint has given texture and depth of color to the trees. This detail clearly shows the thickened paint, which has formed little raised blobs on the surface.

5 In the final stages, opaque paint is used to sketch in the trunks and branches, and the area of path in the foreground, which was too uncompromisingly white, is darkened. The accidental blot in the sky directly above the path will be removed with a knife blade (see CORRECTIONS).

▶ In this example, slightly diluted gouache white was used for spattering. The soft, misty effect of the wave top was produced by taking the wash for the sky and sea right across the paper and LIFTING OUT with a tissue. The lower part was dampened when painting the sea, after which the whole wave was again dampened and shadows run in while still wet.

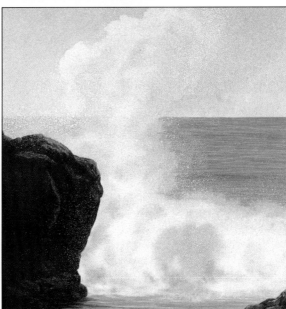

SPONGE PAINTING

Sponges are an essential part of the artist's toolkit. They are useful for mopping up unwanted paint, cleaning up edges and making corrections, and they can be used for applying paint – either alone or in conjunction with brushes as well.

Laying a flat WASH is just as easy (some claim it is easier) with a sponge as it is with a brush. The only thing it cannot do satisfactorily is take a wash around an intricate edge – for which a brush is best – but if you intend to begin a painting with an overall wash of one color, a sponge is ideal. For a completely even wash, with no variations, keep the sponge well saturated and squeeze it out gently as you work down the paper. If you want a less regular wash, squeeze some of the paint out so that the sponge is only moistened. This will give a slightly striated effect, which can be effective for skies, seas, the distance in a landscape or hair in a portrait.

Dabbing paint onto paper with a sponge gives an attractive mottled effect quite unlike anything that can be achieved with a brush, particularly if you use the paint reasonably thick. This method is an excellent way in which to describe texture, and you can suggest form at the same time by applying the paint lightly in some areas and densely in others.

There is no reason why whole paintings should not be worked using this method, but the one thing the sponge cannot do is create fine lines or intricate details, so brushes are usually brought into play for the later stages of a picture when extra definition is needed.

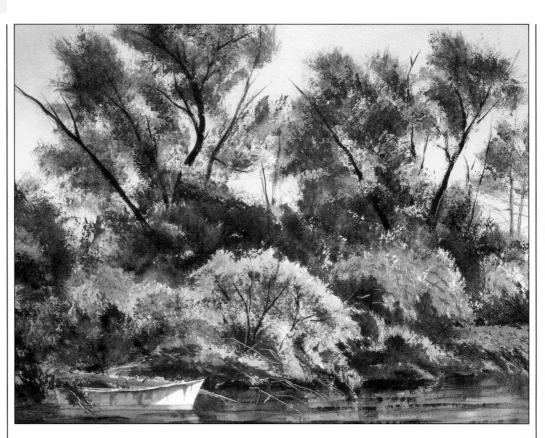

Arthur J. Barbour, *Lone Boat*,
WATERCOLOR

A small natural sponge is ideal for suggesting the texture of summer foliage. The artist has built up a rich, glowing range of colors by applying one over another, varying the pressure of the sponge so that some areas are dark and solid while others have a lightly stippled appearance. The decisive brushwork used for the branches, water and boat provide an exciting contrast to the soft textures and BROKEN COLOR.

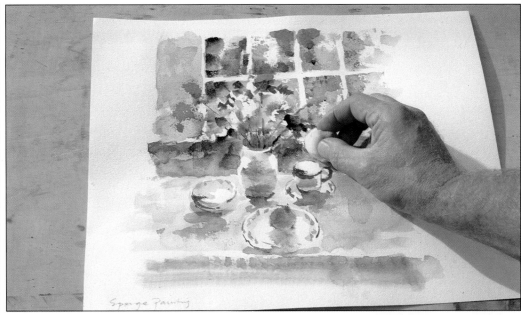

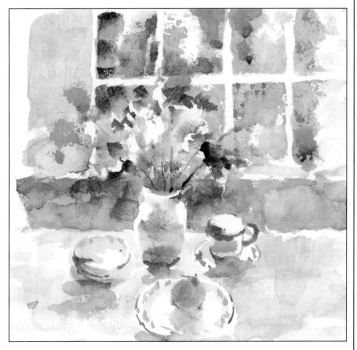

1, 2 It is often necessary to employ some system of MASKING when painting with a sponge, as you cannot take paint around edges as precisely as you can with a brush. The artist has masked the window bars, which are to remain white, by the simple method of holding a ruler against each edge as he works. He does not worry unduly if paint splashes over in places, as he is aiming at a soft, impressionistic overall effect.

3 Working carefully, the artist continues to build up the painting, using the paint fairly wet so that each new application merges with the surrounding colors.

4 One of the problems with combining sponge painting and brushwork is that the contrast of techniques, if over-emphasized, can destroy the unity of the composition. Although the artist has used conventional brush washes in places, he has kept the paint loose and fluid throughout, blurring the edges of the brush marks on the crockery so that they blend in with the sponge work.

SQUARING UP

It is not always necessary to begin a painting with a detailed drawing, but some subjects, such as portraits, call for a careful, methodical approach in the early stages.

One way of avoiding too much drawing and erasing on the paper, which can spoil the surface, is to make a smaller study of the subject first and then to transfer it to the watercolor paper by squaring it up to the size desired. A photograph can be used instead of a drawing, providing you have taken it yourself for this purpose. However, photographs do tend to flatten and distort perspective, and sometimes present an insufficiently clear image, so try to use them only in conjunction with sketches, observation and imagination.

Squaring up is a slightly laborious process, but it is not difficult and really does pay off when the effect of the painting depends on the accuracy of the drawing.

Using a ruler, draw a measured grid over the study or photograph, then draw another grid on the watercolor paper, using light pencil marks. This must have the same number of squares, but if you want to enlarge the drawing, they must obviously be larger. If you use a 1 in. (2.5 cm) grid for your original drawing and a 1½ in. (3.8 cm) one for the painting, it will be one-and-a-half times the size, and so on. When the grid is complete, look carefully at the drawing, note where each line intersects a grid line and transfer the information from one to the other.

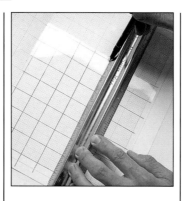

1 The method demonstrated here avoids damaging the original drawing or photograph. A grid is drawn with a felt-tipped pen on a sheet of acetate. The grid is traced from a sheet of graph paper below, which saves time and is very accurate.

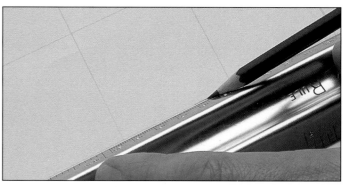

2 The next stage is drawing an enlarged version of the grid on the working paper. Pencil, T-square and ruler are needed for this, and the pencil lines should be as faint as possible.

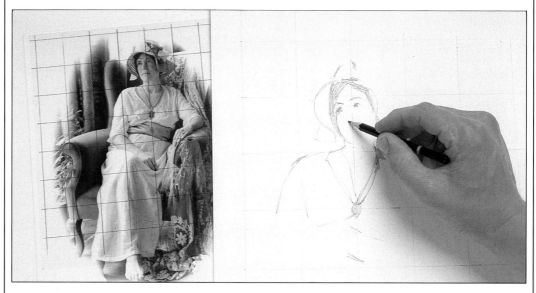

3 The acetate sheet is then placed over the photograph or working drawing, and the image is transferred to the working paper square by square. Do not rush this process, and check carefully as you work, as you could place one part of the composition in the wrong square.

STIPPLING

This is a method of applying paint in a series of separate, small marks made with the point of the brush, so that the whole image consists of tiny dots of different colors. It was and still is a technique favored by painters of miniatures, and is seldom used for large paintings for obvious reasons. However, for anyone who enjoys small-scale work and the challenge of a slow and deliberate approach, it is an attractive method and can produce lovely results quite unlike those of any other watercolor technique.

The success of stippled paintings relies on the separateness of each dot: the colors and tones should blend together in the viewer's eye rather than physically on the paper. Like all watercolors they are built up from light to dark, with highlights left white or only lightly covered so that the white ground shows through, while dark areas are built up gradually with increasingly dense brush marks. However, it is quite permissable to use BODY COLOR to emphasize the smaller highlights and to establish a larger, darker area of color by laying a preliminary wash.

The beauty of the technique is that it allows you to use a great variety of colors within one small area – a shadow could consist of a whole spectrum of deep blues, violets, greens and browns. As long as they are all close enough in tone, they will still "read" as one color, but a more ambiguous and evocative one than would be produced by a flat wash of dark green.

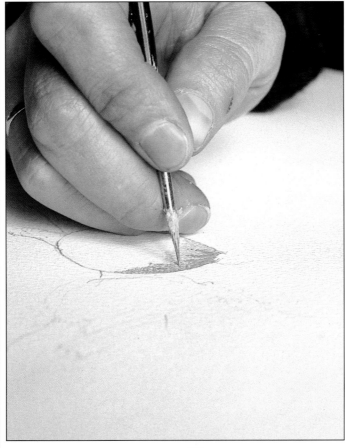

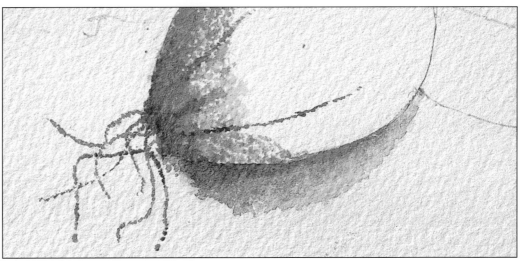

1 The artist has chosen a fairly rough paper to enhance the textural quality of the stippled paint. She begins with an outline drawing and paints carefully and methodically with the point of a sable brush.

2 She continues to build up the tones and colors in the same way. Although she is working on white paper because she likes the sparkling effect of tiny areas of white showing through the dots of color, it is perfectly permissible to establish a large area of color by laying a preliminary wash.

STRETCHING PAPER

This is not strictly speaking a technique, but is included here because so many watercolor techniques depend upon it. Wet paint causes paper to buckle, and lighter papers will remain buckled even when dry. This not only spoils the picture, but is a hindrance to the work in progress, as you cannot place a flat wash on an unevenly corrugated surface. Novice painters tend to be daunted by this task, but it is not difficult, nor is it always necessary – heavier papers do not require stretching. As a general rule of thumb, any paper over 200lbs. can be used without this treatment, though even a 200-lb. paper can buckle slightly if you use a lot of water, as when working WET-IN-WET.

The only real problem with stretching is that it requires pre-planning, as the paper takes a long time to dry, so if you intend to paint in the morning, prepare the paper the night before.

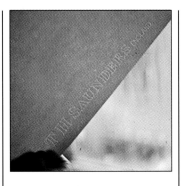

1 Not all papers have a right and wrong side, but those that do have a watermark. Hold the paper up to the light and check that this reads correctly.

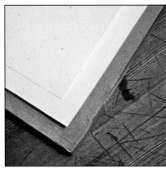

2 Trim the paper to the appropriate size, leaving a good margin at the edges of the board to allow for the gummed tape, which needs to be at least 1 ½ in. (3.8 cm) wide.

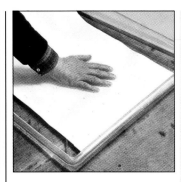

3 Soak the paper thoroughly, making sure it has absorbed water on both sides. Hold it up by one corner and gently shake it to drain the excess water before placing it on the board. Smooth it out from the center to make sure no air is trapped underneath.

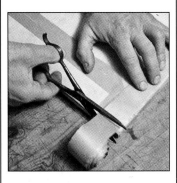

4 Cut the required lengths of gummed strip. It is a good idea to make small pencil marks at each edge of the paper to guide you when putting on the tape, as it is only too easy to paste it on crooked.

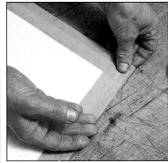

5 Dampen each length of tape immediately before use. With half the width of the tape on the paper and half on the board, place a strip along each edge, beginning with the two long sides, and press down firmly as you go.

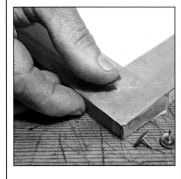

6 To make sure the paper is securely held, place a thumbtack in each corner. Leave the paper to dry flat, and resist the temptation to put it in front of a fire or heater, as this can cause the gummed strip to tear away from the paper.

TEXTURES

There are two main kinds of texture in painting: surface texture, in which the paint itself is built up or manipulated in some way to create what is known as surface interest, and imitative texture, in which a certain technique is employed to provide the pictorial equivalent of a texture seen in nature. These naturally overlap to some extent: surface texture is sometimes seen as an end in itself, but in many cases it is a welcome by-product of the attempt to turn the three-dimensional world into a convincing two-dimensional image.

Surface texture
Since watercolors are applied in thin layers, they cannot be built up to form surface texture, but this can be provided instead by the grain of the paper. There are a great many watercolor papers on the market, some of which – particularly the handmade varieties – are so rough that they appear almost to be embossed. Rough papers can give wonderfully exciting effects, as the paint will settle unevenly (and not always predictably), breaking up each area of color and leaving flecks of white showing through. Reserved highlights on rough paper stand out with great brilliance – because the edges are slightly ragged, the white areas appear to be standing proud of the surrounding colors.

Acrylic paints are ideal for creating surface interest because they can be used both thickly and thinly in the same painting, providing a lively contrast. You can vary the brushmarks, using fine, delicate strokes in some places and large, sweeping ones in others. You can put on slabs of paint with a knife and you can even mix the paint with sand or sawdust to give it an intriguing grainy look.

Imitative texture
Several of the best-known techniques for making paint resemble rocks, tree bark, fabrics and so on are described in other entries (see DRY BRUSH, SCUMBLING, SPATTERING, SPONGE PAINTING, WAX RESIST), but there are some other tricks of the trade you might like to experiment with. One of these – unconventional but effective – is to mix watercolor paint with soap. The soap thickens the paint without destroying its translucency. Soapy paint stays where you put it instead of flowing outward, and allows you to use inventive brushwork to describe both textures and forms.

Intriguingly unpredictable effects can be obtained by a variation of the resist technique. If you lay down some turpentine or paint thinner on the paper and then paint over it, the paint and the oil will separate to give a marbled appearance. A slightly similar effect can be gained by dropping crystals of sea salt into wet paint. Leave it to dry, brush off the salt, and you will see pale, snowflake shapes where the salt has absorbed the surrounding paint. If the crystals are close together, these shapes will run into one another to form a large mottled blob resembling weathered rock.

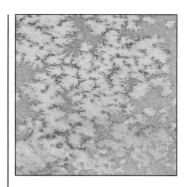
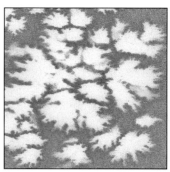

Fascinating effects can be made by scattering salt crystals in wet paint. Elaborate textures can be built up by laying further washes over one salt-scattered area and then repeating the process.

The results obtained by the salt technique vary according to how close the crystals are to one another and how wet the paint is. Here crystals have been sprinkled into a very wet wash, while in the first example the paint was left to dry a little first.

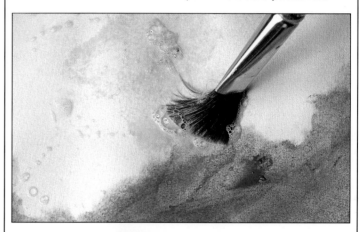

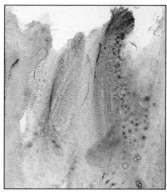

◄ ▲ Mixing paint with soap has a similar effect to mixing it with GUM ARABIC. It loses much of its fluidity, holding the marks of the brush very well, and thus providing considerable scope for textural painting. The bubbles leave pronounced rings and blobs on the paper when dry. This is a less predictable method than salt scattering, but it is an enjoyable one to experiment with.

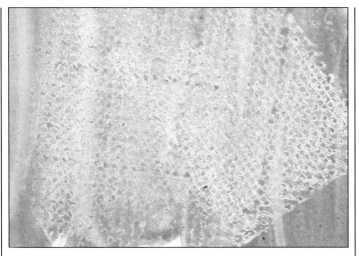

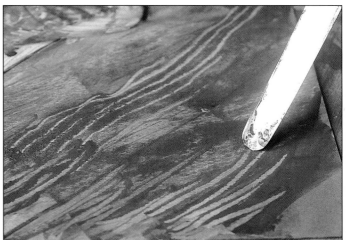

This method, known as a "blot-off," is a very direct way of creating texture. It is basically a simple printing technique, involving pressing a textured paper or piece of fabric on wet paint and then removing it, so that its imprint is left behind. Almost anything can be used for this technique, and quite intricate textures can be built up by using several different printing surfaces in one area of a painting.

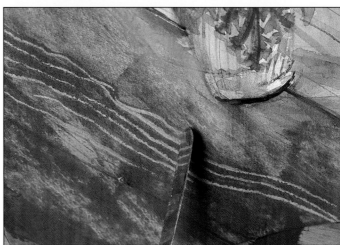

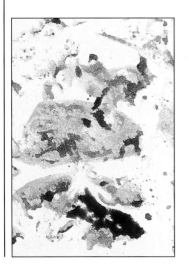

This is another version of the method shown above, but here the paint is not lifted off, but dabbed on. In this example, the color was applied with a crumpled piece of paper, but again, more or less anything can be used, and the variety of effect that can be created is almost unlimited.

Sgraffito, which means scratching into paint, is another well-known texturing method, here used to give the effect of wood grain. It is not suitable for transparent watercolor, but is excellent for thick gouache or acrylic. Broad areas can be scraped with the side of a knife and fine lines made with a pointed implement.

TONED GROUND

For a picture that is planned as an exercise in dark, rich tones and colors, it can be an advantage to begin with a pre-tinted ground. It is possible to buy heavy colored papers for watercolor work, but these have to be sought out; few of the smaller, less specialist art supply shops stock them.

A quick and simple way to pre-tint watercolor paper is to lay an overall wash of thinned acrylic (after stretching the paper if you are doing this). The color, when dry, will be permanent, so there is no danger of stirring it up with the next layer of paint.

The advantages of toned grounds are two-fold. First, they help you to achieve unity of color because the ground shows through the applied colors to some extent, particularly if you leave small patches uncovered. Second, they allow you to build up deep colors with fewer washes, thus avoiding the risk of muddying. They are especially well suited to opaque gouache work where muddying occurs very easily.

The main problem with pre-tinting is deciding what color to use. Some artists like to paint a cool picture, such as a snow scene, on a warm, yellow ocher ground so that the blues, blue-whites and grays are heightened by small amounts of yellow showing through. Others prefer cool grounds for cool paintings and warm grounds for warm ones. You need to think carefully about the overall color key of the painting, and you will probably have to try out one or two ground colors before you find out which ones suit you best.

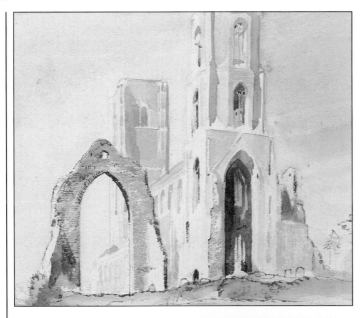

◄ Charles Knight RWS, ROI, *Church Ruins*, 11¼ × 13¾ IN (28.6 × 34.9 CM), WATERCOLOR WITH PEN ON TINTED PAPER

This artist likes to achieve his effects by means of a very free and direct application of paint, with as little overlaying of washes as possible. The cream-colored paper chosen for this painting has been left uncovered on large parts of the building, so that it stands as a color in its own right.

► John Martin, *Interior with Sunlight*, 14 × 12 IN (35.6 × 30.5 CM), GOUACHE ON TONED PAPER

Martin seldom if ever works on white paper, and he chooses a ground color that sets the key for the painting. Here the paper is a warm medium brown, and the paint, fairly dry and thick, is lightly applied so that the base color shows through in places.

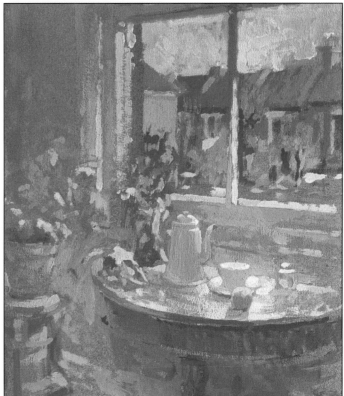

UNDERPAINTING

This involves building up a painting over a monochrome tonal foundation. It is usually associated with oil painting, but the early watercolorists used a modified version of the same technique, particularly for detailed topographical or architectural subjects. You can see the effects of underpainting if you have ever had to wash down a watercolor by dunking it in a sink. Faint shadows of the original will remain, which can often provide a good basis for the next attempt. This kind of "accidental" underpainting highlights the value of a deliberately planned one: establishing the tonal balance of a painting is not always easy, and doing this at the outset means you do not have to alter, correct (and possibly overwork) the painting later on.

It is essential to use a pale color and one that will not interfere with the colors to be placed on top. In a predominantly green landscape, for instance, blue would be a good choice and, since blues tend to stain the paper, a blue wash is less likely to be disturbed by subsequent washes. The paper should be a fairly absorbent one, such as Arches, which allows the undercolor to sink into it. Any areas to be reserved as bright highlights should, of course, be left uncovered.

An underpainting for acrylic is much less restricted as it will be permanent when dry and the tonal range can be greater because the later colors can be used opaquely to cover the first one. Underpainting provides a good basis for the technique of GLAZING, in which colors are built up in successive thin skins.

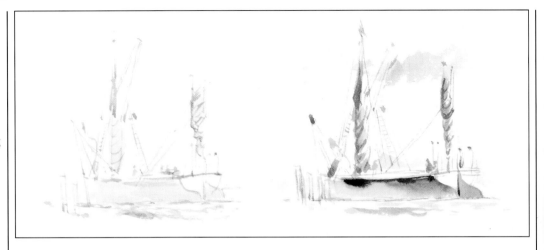

1, 2 A tonal underpainting can provide a better basis than an outline drawing, as pencil lines quickly become obscured. The artist begins with a very light gray, building up to deeper tones in areas that are to remain as dark shadows.

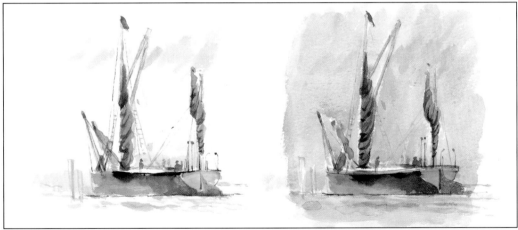

3, 4 The gray chosen for the underpainting is slightly modified by the colors laid over it, but in the shadows it remains virtually unchanged, which highlights the importance of choosing the right color. Notice that the brightest parts, the stern of the boat and areas of the water, have been left white in the underpainting.

WASH

FLAT

The term "wash" is a rather confusing one, as it implies a relatively broad area of paint applied flatly, but it is also sometimes used by watercolor painters to describe each brushstroke of fluid paint, however small it may be. Here it refers only to paint laid over an area too large to be covered by one brushstroke.

A flat wash in watercolor, thinned gouache or acrylic can be laid either with a large brush or a sponge (see SPONGE PAINTING), and the paper is usually dampened to allow the paint to spread more easily, though this is not essential. Washes must be applied fast with no dithering, so mix plenty of paint before beginning – you always need more than you think. Tilt the board slightly so that the brushstrokes flow into each other but do not dribble down the paper. Load the brush with paint, sweep it horizontally across the paper, starting at the top of the area, and immediately lay another line below it, working in the opposite direction. Keep the brush loaded for each stroke and continue working in alternate directions until the area is covered.

Sometimes it is necessary to lay a wash around an intricate shape, such as a skyline of roofs or chimneys. In this case the wash must start at the bottom, not at the top, to allow you to paint carefully around the shapes, so you will have to turn the board upside down. If you are dampening the paper first, dampen only up to the edge, as the paint will flow into any wet part of the paper.

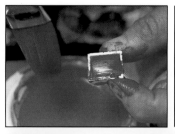

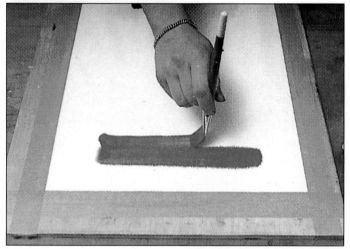

1 A wash uses up a surprising amount of paint, so always mix more than you think you will need or you will have to stop halfway and the paint will dry with a hard edge.

2 Opinions are divided as to whether the paper should be dampened or not before applying a flat wash, and results also vary according to the type of paper used. On some papers, a wash will go on very well either wet or dry, but on the whole it is probably wiser to dampen first. Here a wash is laid with a large, square-ended brush on wet, stretched paper. Some artists prefer soft, round brushes, while others like housepainter's brushes, which can cover large areas rapidly.

3 Begin by laying a single strip of color across the top, and then continue backwards and forwards down the paper. The board must be tilted slightly so that each strip of color runs down and mingles with the next.

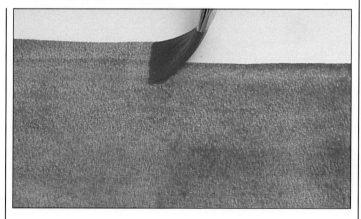

WASH

GRADATED AND VARIEGATED

Colors in nature are seldom perfectly flat and uniform, and it is often necessary to lay a wash that shifts in tone from dark to light or one that contains two or more different colors.

A gradated wash shades from dark to light, and is laid in the same way as a flat wash, the only difference being that more water is added to the pigment for each successive line of paint. It is a little tricky to achieve a really even gradation, as too much water in one line or not enough in another will result in a striped effect. Keep the paint as fluid as possible so that each brushstroke flows into the one below, and never be tempted to work back into the wash if it does not come out as you wished. You may find a sponge gives better results than a brush, as it is easier to control the amount of water you use.

Variegated washes are those using more than one color and are much less predictable than flat or gradated ones. However, you can achieve very exciting, if unexpected, results by allowing colors to bleed into one another.

If you intend to paint a sky at sunset, blending from blue at the top to yellows, oranges and reds at the bottom, mix three or four suitable colors on your palette and lay them in strips one under the other on dampened paper so that they blend gently into one another.

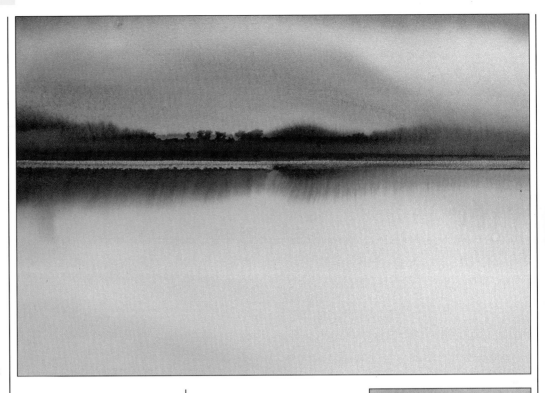

▲ Robert Tilling, *Reservoir Reflections*, WATERCOLOR
This lovely painting relies for its effect on the way each color blends into its neighbor with no hard edges. The artist works with large brushes and very wet paint, tilting his board so that the colors flow down the paper, but controlling them very carefully.

▶ A slight striping occurs if too much or too little water is added for each new brushstroke, but this can be turned to advantage. Here it suggests the almost transparent layer of misty cloud often seen on a clear, still day.

► ▼ Variegated washes need to be applied quickly and with no hesitation, so for both these examples the artist mixed her colors in advance. She worked on well-damped paper with the board at a slight angle. For the sunset (below), she turned the board upside down to allow her to lay the yellow, red and blue from light to dark, turning it back again to add the streaks of gray over the blue. Once the colors had blended together to create the desired effect, the wash was left to dry flat.

WASH

TEXTURES

Watercolor washes can be many things: some simply play the role of a flat backdrop to a visual "drama," while others serve the purpose of providing an underpainting for subsequent work. They can also be an end in themselves, conveying mood and atmosphere by means of a few brushstrokes swept over white paper. One of the best ways to make a wash say more is to use the texture of the paper as an integral part of the painting. Watercolorists who paint mainly in washes choose their supports very carefully, fully aware of the contribution they make to the finished work.

Wet or dry paper

A wash laid on dampened paper has a soft, diffused quality; the paint goes on very evenly because the first application of water draws the paint down into the troughs of the paper. Working on dry paper gives a much sharper, crisper effect, and some painters find it a more controllable method. If you drag a broad brush, not overloaded with paint, over dry, grainy paper, you will create a lovely, sparkling area of color, with the raised parts of the paper standing out clearly. The essence of these dragged washes is unevenness, as any small areas of white paper left uncovered will enhance the effect. Dry washes can be used alone or over previous wet ones – a combination of the two can be wonderfully expressive.

Granulation

Another way to give a touch of something extra to a wash is to use the propensity of certain pigments to precipitate, that is, to separate from the water, when laid on wetly. This causes a slight speckling that is often more suggestive than completely flat color and can be used to great advantage.

Colors that have this property include cerulean and ultramarine blue, burnt umber, raw umber and yellow ocher (though the characteristics of pigments do vary according to the manufacturer).

The degree of granulation that will occur can only be ascertained by trial and error: some colors will granulate only when laid over a previous wash, and if the paint is mixed with a high proportion of water, the process may not occur at all, or be almost imperceptible.

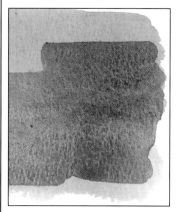

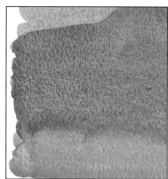

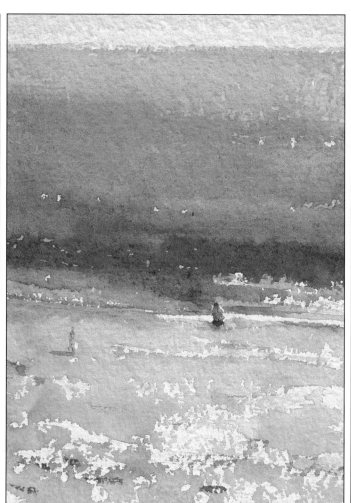

◄ The granulation of the pigment that sometimes occurs when a wet wash is applied over a dry one can add extra interest to a painting. It is particularly useful in shadow areas, which can become flat and dull.

▲ Christopher Baker, *Tor Cross, Devon* 18 × 10 IN (45.7 × 25.4 CM), WATERCOLOR
The artist has built up his painting mainly in flat washes, but because he has worked on a very heavily textured rag paper they have a lively, BROKEN COLOR appearance. The sandy beach and the wavelets on the water are created simply by leaving areas of paper unpainted.

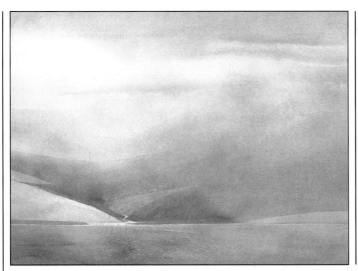

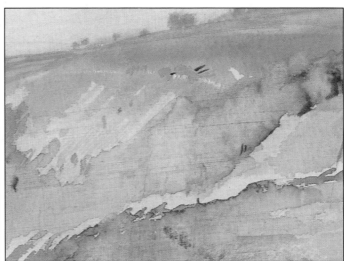

▲ Colin Paynton, *Welsh Elements VII*,
20¾ × 29 IN (52.7 × 73.6 CM),
WATERCOLOR

Paintings with little color or tonal contrast can all too easily become monotonous, but the slightly granular paint quality has given this atmospheric composition a lovely touch of sparkle. Paynton has achieved this by working on an absorbent, low-sized paper, normally used for etching.

▶ Charles Knight, *Evening Light, Cotswolds*, 10¾ × 14¾ IN (27.3 × 37.5 CM), WATERCOLOR AND WAX CRAYON

This artist frequently combines watercolor with wax and pencil, or sometimes both. Here areas of the foreground and middle distance have been subtly textured by a light underlay of wax crayon. This can be clearly seen in the detail (top right), where an interesting variety of texture has been achieved by allowing wet washes to form BACKRUNS on top of the slight striations made by the wax.

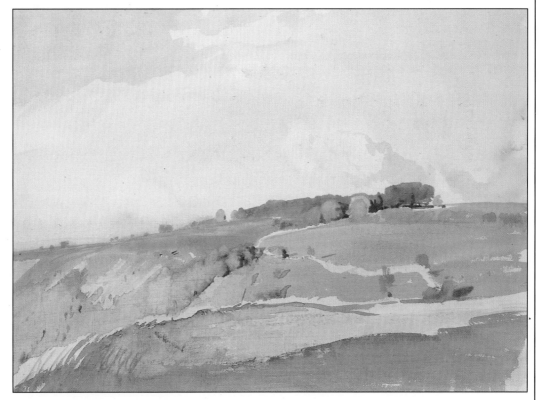

WASH-OFF

This is an unusual and fascinating technique that exploits the properties of India ink and gouache. It is not difficult, but it is slow, involving careful planning and a methodical approach.

Basically, the method involves painting a design with thick gouache paint, covering the whole picture surface with waterproof ink and then holding it under running water. This washes off the soluble paint and the ink that covers it, leaving only the ink in the unpainted areas to form a negative image.

First, the paper must be stretched – essential, as it has to bear a considerable volume of water. A light wash is then laid over it and left to dry, after which the design is painted on with thick, white gouache paint. White paint must be used, as a color could stain the paper and destroy the clear, sharp effect. For the same reason, the wash should be as pale as possible: its only purpose is to allow the white paint to show up as you apply it.

Once the paint is thoroughly dry, cover the whole picture surface with waterproof ink (make sure it really is waterproof and is clearly marked as such on the bottle). Allow the ink to dry completely before washing it off.

The "negative" can either be left as a black-and-white image or it can be worked into with new colors, using gouache, watercolor or acrylic.

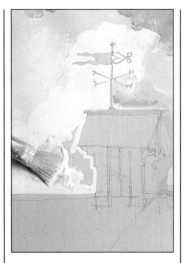

1 Working with a large brush, the artist applies thick gouache paint, having first stained the paper so that she can see what she is doing.

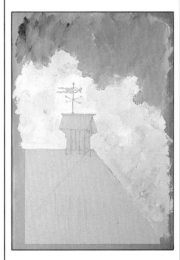

2 She continues to build up the sky which, although to be partially removed in the washing process, will remain as an element of the finished painting.

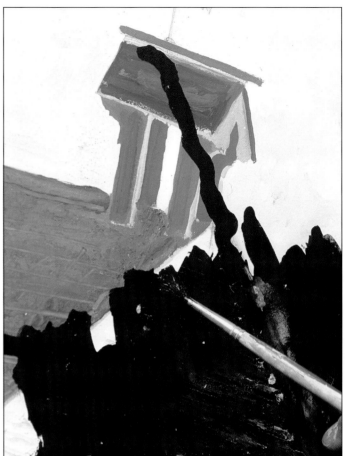

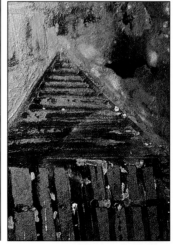

3 With the gouache painting stage completed, the whole surface is covered with ink. For a complete wash-off, the ink should be applied flat, as in a WASH, but in this case the artist intends to leave the paint and the ink to mingle in places, so she applies it deliberately unevenly, in a scrubbing motion.

4 The thicker areas of paint are not completely covered by the ink.

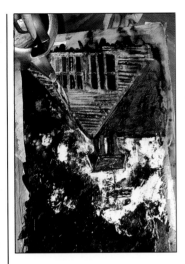

5 Hot water is poured onto the surface, washing off some of the soluble pigment and the ink on top of it. There is a danger that too much water will break up the ink and remove more than is wanted, so any stubborn areas are coaxed off gently with a sponge.

6 In a complete wash-off, the whole sky would have been removed, necessitating repainting, but in this version of the technique, large areas of the original gouache have remained, with the small patches of black adding both definition and drama

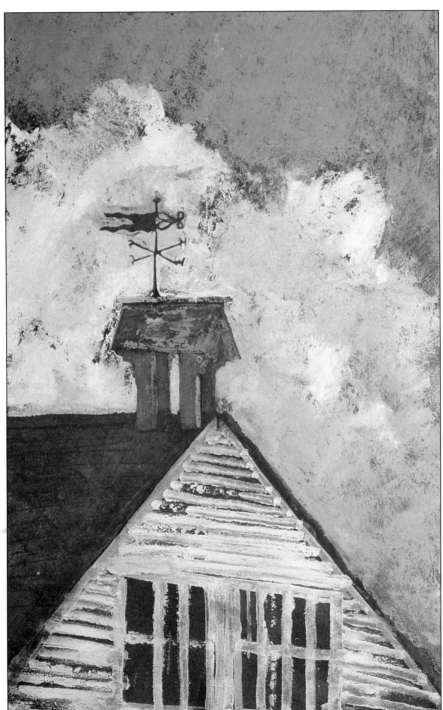

WAX RESIST

This, a valuable addition to the watercolorist's repertoire, is a technique based on the antipathy of oil and water, and involves deliberately repelling paint from certain areas of the paper while allowing it to settle in others.

The idea is simple, but can yield quite magical results. If you draw or lightly scribble over paper with wax and then overlay this with watercolor, the paint will slide off the waxed areas. You can use either an ordinary household candle or the type of inexpensive wax crayons produced for children. The British sculptor Henry Moore (1898-1986), also a draftsman of great imagination and brilliance, used crayons and watercolor for his series of drawings of sleeping figures in the London Underground during World War II.

The wax underdrawing can be as simple or as complex as you like. You can suggest a hint of pattern on wallpaper or fabric in a still-life group or portrait by means of a few lines, dots or blobs made with a candle or do something more complex by making quite an intricate drawing using crayons, which are smaller and have good points.

Wax beneath watercolor gives a delightfully unpredictable speckled effect, which varies according to the pressure you apply and the type of paper you use. It is one of the best methods for imitating natural textures, such as those of rocks, cliffs or tree trunks, but like all tricks of the trade, should be reserved for certain areas of the painting only, as textured areas make more of an impact if they are juxtaposed with smooth

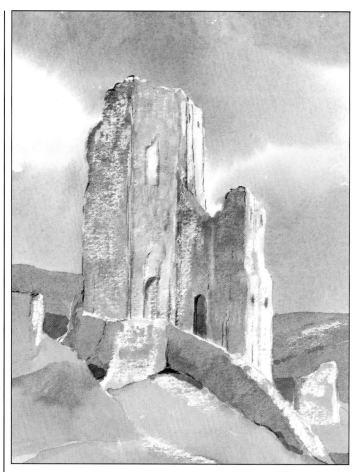

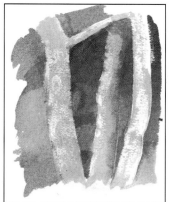

In both these examples (above and left), a stick of white wax oil pastel was scribbled over paper with a Not surface and watercolor washes were then laid on top. In some areas, the paint was left to dry and the process repeated. A more pronounced texture can be gained by working on Rough paper.

One of the best ways of learning how combinations of media can be used is by making rough doodles like those shown below, in which colored wax crayons were overlaid with watercolor.

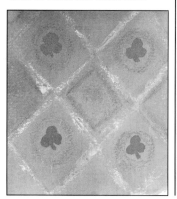

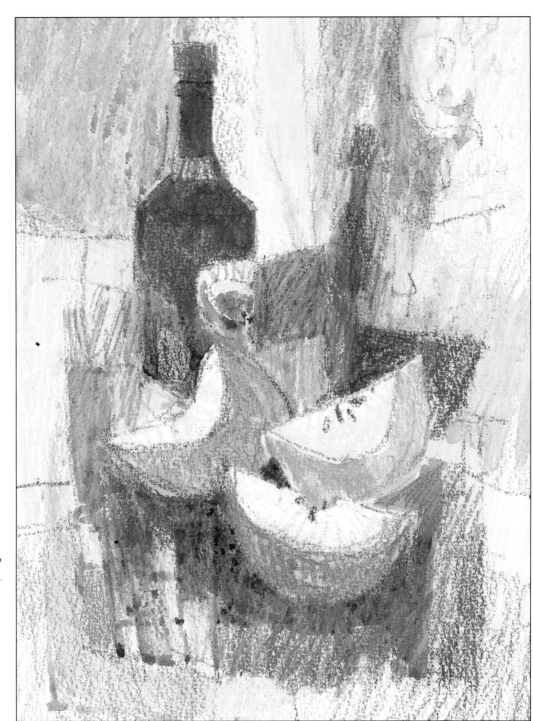

Moira Huntly RI, RSMA, *Still Life with Melon Pieces*, 10 × 7 IN (25.5 × 17.9 CM), WATERCOLOR, WAX AND WAX CRAYON

The artist has created vibrant colors and lively textures by using candle wax under the paint and wax crayons both under and over it. Rich surfaces can be built up in this way, and further variety can be achieved by scraping into an overlay of wax crayon with a razor blade.

WET-IN-WET

This means exactly what its name implies – applying each new color without waiting for earlier ones to dry, so that they run together with no hard edges or sharp transitions. This is a technique that is only partially controllable, but is a very enjoyable and challenging one for precisely this reason. Any of the water-based media can be used, providing no opaque pigment is added, but in the case of acrylic, it is helpful to add retarding medium to the paint to prolong the drying time.

The paper must first be well dampened and must not be allowed to dry completely at any time. This means, first, that you must stretch the paper (unless it is a really heavy one of at least 200lbs.) and second, that you must work fast. Paradoxically, when you keep all the colors wet, they will not actually mix, although they will bleed into one another. Placing a loaded brush of wet paint on top of a wet wash of a different color is a little like dropping a pebble into water; the weight of the water in the new brushstroke causes the first color to pull away.

The danger with painting a whole picture wet-in-wet is that it may look altogether too formless and undefined. The technique is most effective when it is offset by edges and linear definition, so when you feel you have gone as far as you can, let the painting dry, take a long, hard look at it, and decide where you might need to sharpen it up.

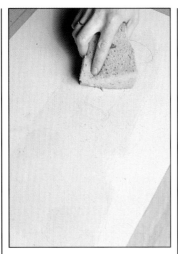

1 Having made a preliminary outline drawing on dry paper, the artist damps it thoroughly with a sponge. She is using slightly colored water to provide a background tint.

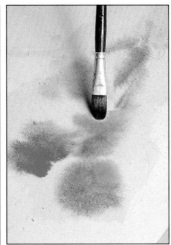

2 Using the point of a large brush, she begins to drop in areas of color, allowing them to spread and merge.

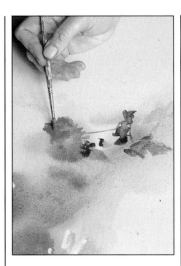

3 She lets the paper dry slightly before touching in darker colors, as she wants crisper edges in these areas.

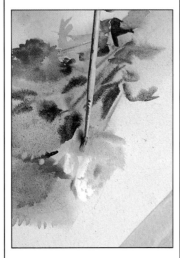

4 As highlights cannot be reserved when working in this way, she has used opaque white in places.

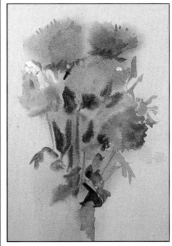

5 She continues to build up, using slightly thickened paint.

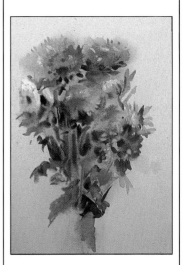

6 Touches of soft definition give depth and form to the leaves and flower heads.

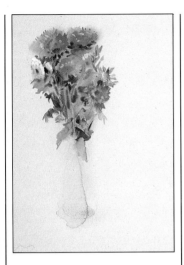

7 The flowers are now complete, but the vase is still no more than a suggestion, with the outline drawing still visible under the pale wash.

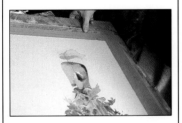

8 Having applied a loose, wet wash of darker paint, the artist tilts the board so that the color flows in the right direction. This is the best way of controlling wet paint and is surprisingly accurate. She is now working wet-in-wet only in the area of the vase, having allowed the surrounding paper to dry so that the wash will not spread beyond the edges.

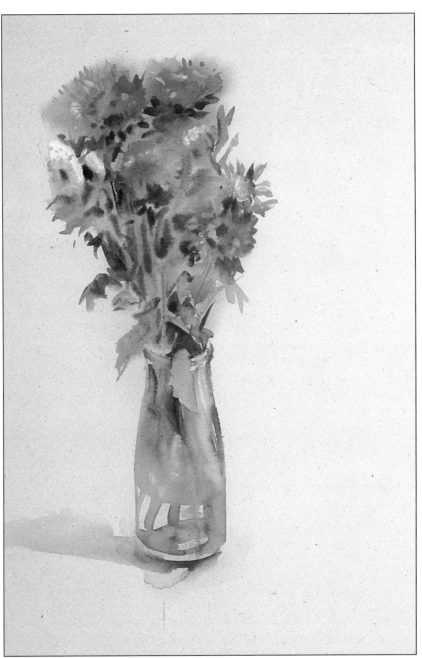

9 Wet-in-wet is such an enjoyable and seductive technique that it is difficult to know when to stop, and if it is taken too far, the whole painting can become wooly and formless. Here, although the general effect is pleasingly soft, there is enough definition and tonal contrast to pull the composition together.

WET-ON-DRY

Laying new (hence wet) washes over earlier ones that have been allowed to dry is the classic method of building up a watercolor. Because it is difficult to achieve great depth of color with a preliminary wash, the darker and richer areas of a painting are achieved by overlaying colors in successive layers.

One of the more irritating aspects of watercolor work is that of having to wait, sometimes for long periods, for paint to dry before the next color is added. It is perfectly permissible to use a hairdryer to hasten the process, but avoid using it on really wet paint, as you can find you are blowing a carefully placed wash all over the paper. It is equally permissible, of course, to paint some parts of a picture wet-on-dry and others WET-IN-WET, indeed the most exciting effects are achieved by combining the two methods. The danger with wet-on-dry is that you can overwork the painting and muddy the colors if you allow too many layers to accumulate, so if you are working mainly in flat washes, always try to make the first one really positive.

In acrylic, wet-on-dry is the most natural way to work, as the paint dries almost as soon as you put it on, but gouache, although also fast drying, presents more of a problem. If you do use this method, begin by using the paint as watercolor (with water but no white) and gradually build up to thicker paint for the final stages. If you lay one thick layer over another, the colors will quickly become dull and muddy because they will mix together on the paper.

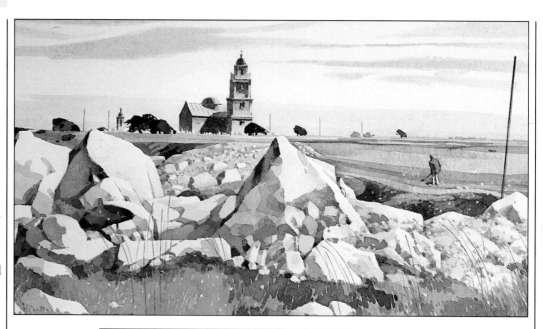

▲ Ronald Jesty, *St. George's, Portland*, 10 × 17 IN (25.4 × 43.2 CM), WATERCOLOR
Working wet-on-dry in the way that this artist does, with clearly delineated areas of light and dark, produces a lovely crispness and clarity, but it calls for a careful and methodical approach.

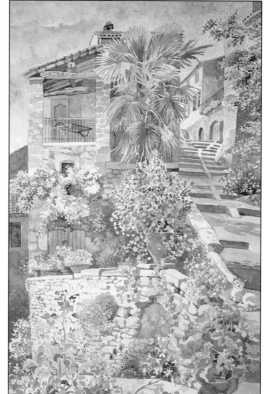

◄ Juliette Palmer, *St. Privat Cats*, 41.9 × 30.5CM (16½ × 12 IN), WATERCOLOR
While the painting above contrasts bold shapes of light and dark, Palmer uses a more limited tonal range to achieve a gentler effect. She has built up her painting in a series of small brushstrokes, waiting for each layer of paint to dry before applying another, but keeping overpainting to a minimum.

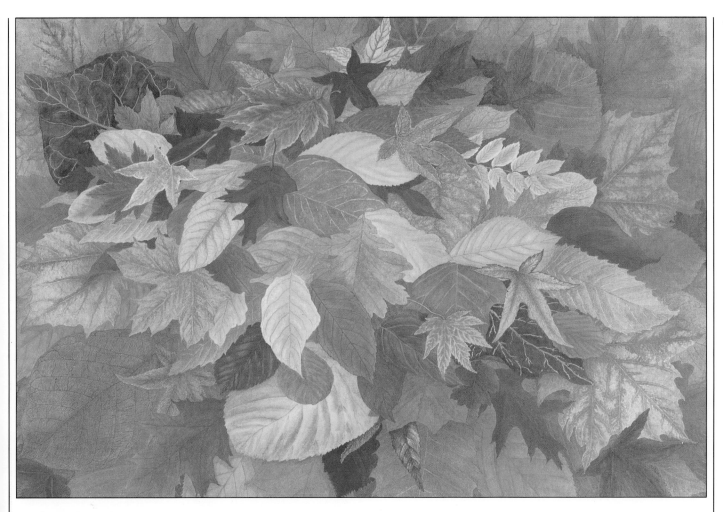

Jean Canter, *Autumn Leaves,*
16 × 23½ IN (40.6 × 59.7 CM),
WATERCOLOR

For this painting, unlike the two on the opposite page, the artist has combined the wet-on-dry and WET-IN-WET methods, beginning by painting each leaf individually on slightly damp paper and allowing the color to spread. A variety of texturing methods was used on the leaves, including DRY BRUSH, STIPPLING and scattering salt into wet paint (see TEXTURES). The effect of the delicate white veins was achieved by MASKING, while the darker ones were drawn into wet paint with a toothpick.

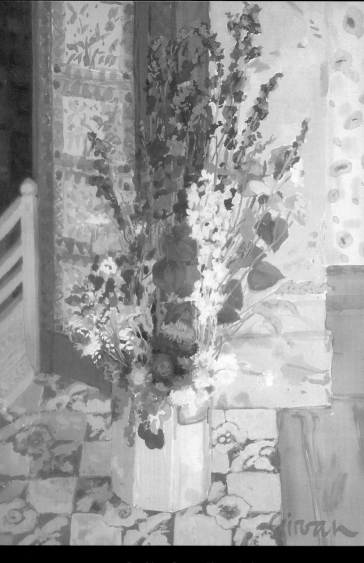

Geraldine Girvan, *Flowers in the Hearth*, 27⅛ × 19¼ IN (68.9 × 48.9 CM), GOUACHE

This artist loves color and pattern, and finds that gouache is the medium best suited to her particular preoccupations.

THEMES

In the first part of the book I outlined the techniques most frequently used by watercolor painters as well as introducing some of the more unusual and unconventional ones. I hope that these will provide some food for thought and experiment, but it is important to remember also that painting techniques are no more than vehicles for the expression of ideas. My aim in this second part of the book is to show you, by means of step-by-step demonstrations and finished paintings, how other artists have harnessed their technical skills and experience of the medium to their own personal vision.

I have chosen eight main themes – animals, the human figure, buildings, flowers, landscape, skies, still life and water. A wide variety of techniques and different approaches is shown in each of these subject areas, together with some explanations of the particular difficulties associated with certain subjects. I hope that everyone will find something to inspire them in the selection of paintings – looking at the work of other artists is never time wasted, and analyzing their methods can often suggest a new direction. Someone who has never dared to paint animals or has consistently failed with skies may see the perfect method for the first time and say, "So that's how it's done. I could do that, too." You probably can.

The animal kingdom presents the most common of all problems to the would-be recorder of its glories: none of its members stay still long enough to be painted. One can usually bribe a friend to sit reasonably still for a portrait, but you cannot expect the same cooperation from a dog, cat or horse. If movement is the essence of a subject, however, why not learn to make a virtue of it?

Observing movement

Watch an animal carefully and you will notice that the movements it makes, although they may be rapid, are not random – they have certain patterns. If you train yourself to make quick sketches whenever possible and take photographs as an aid to understanding, you will find that painting a moving animal is far from impossible – and it is also deeply rewarding.

We in the twentieth century are lucky, because we benefit from the studies and observations of past generations. We know, for instance, that a horse moves its legs in a certain way in each of its four paces – walking, trotting, cantering and galloping – but when Edgar Degas (1834-1917) began to paint his marvelous racing scenes, he did not fully understand these movements. He painted horses galloping with all four legs outstretched, as they had appeared in English sporting prints. It was only when Eadweard Muybridge (1830-1904) published his series of photographs of animals in motion in 1888 that Degas saw his error and was quick to incorporate the newfound knowledge into his paintings. This confirms the value of the camera as a source of reference, but photographs should never be slavishly copied, as this will result in a static, unconvincing image – photographs have a tendency to flatten and distort form and "freeze" movement.

Understanding the basics

Painters and illustrators who specialize in natural history acquire their knowledge in a wide variety of ways. Many take powerful binoculars and cameras into remote parts of the countryside to watch and record birds and animals in their natural habitats, but they also rely on illustrations and photographs in books and magazines or study stuffed creatures in museums. All this research helps them to understand basic structures, such as the way a bird's wing and tail feathers lie or how a horse or cow's legs are jointed. In the past, artists were taught that a detailed study of anatomy was necessary before they could even begin to draw or paint any living creature. Some wildlife painters, whose prime concern is scientific accuracy, still do this, but for most of us this depth of study is unnecessary.

Sketching from life

Although background knowledge is helpful because it will enable you to paint with more confidence, books and magazines are never a substitute for direct observation. When you are working outdoors, whether in a zoo or on a farm, try to keep your sketches simple, concentrating on the main lines and shapes without worrying about details such as texture and coloring. If the animal moves while you are in mid-sketch, leave it and start another one – several small drawings on the same page can provide a surprising amount of information. You may find it difficult at first, but quick sketches are a knack, and you really will get better with practice, partly because you will be unconsciously teaching yourself to look hard at your subject in a really analytical and selective way.

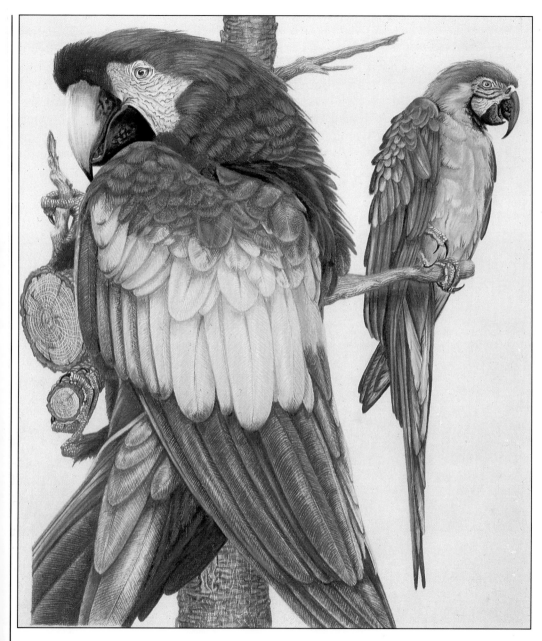

Laura Wade, *Macaws,* WATERCOLOR, GOUACHE AND COLORED PENCILS

The artist has made good use of MIXED MEDIA to build up the birds' vivid colors and delicate textures. Like many professional illustrators, she used photographs as well as drawings from life for her reference; this is the original of a printed illustration in a guide brochure.

BIRDS

Birds are a perennially appealing subject, but they are also a complex one. The fur of a smooth-haired animal does not obscure the structure beneath, but the feathers of a bird do – if you look at a skeleton in a museum you may find it hard to relate it to the living, feathered reality. To portray a bird convincingly, it is important to understand the framework around which it is "built," and the way the small feathers follow the contours of the body while those of the wing and tail extend beyond it. Never be ashamed to draw on the store of knowledge built up by others: look through natural history books and photographs in wildlife magazines as well as sketching birds whenever you can.

If you are painting birds in their natural habitat, for instance geese on a river or seagulls circling around a clifftop, you will need to concentrate on shape and movement rather than detail. Both the LINE AND WASH and the BRUSH DRAWING methods are well suited to this kind of broad impression, but the two most exciting features of birds, particularly exotic ones, are color and texture, and many bird painters employ a more precise and detailed technique to show them in their full glory.

You can practice painting feathers and discover ways of building up texture by working initially from a photograph or another artist's work or even by painting a stuffed bird. If you find that watercolor is hard to control or becomes overworked, you could try gouache, acrylic or one of the many MIXED MEDIA techniques.

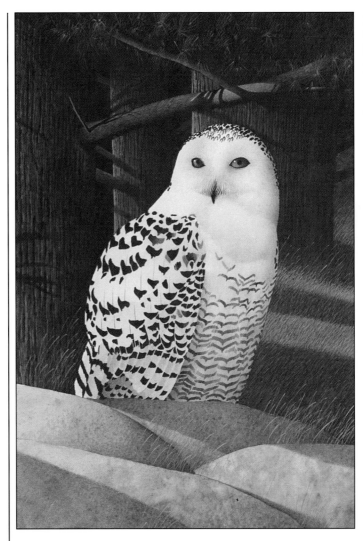

Paul Dawson, *Snowy Owl*, 11 × 8¾ IN (27.9 × 22.2 CM), WATERCOLOR AND GOUACHE

Although the paint has been used thickly in places, this is surprisingly not the case on the bird itself, which was protected with LIQUID MASK throughout the process of building up the background and foreground. The artist wanted the white to be that of the paper (in this case a smooth-surfaced one), which stands out far more brilliantly than opaque white paint.

To achieve the depth of tone in the trees, foliage and grass, Dawson began by laying dark watercolor base washes, over which he worked in gouache. The stones in the foreground are watercolor with a little gouache, stippled on with an old brush with splayed bristles – never throw such brushes away, as they may come in handy later.

The feathers of the bird were then built up carefully with small, delicate brushstrokes; with care taken not to destroy the effect of the white against the deep browns and greens.

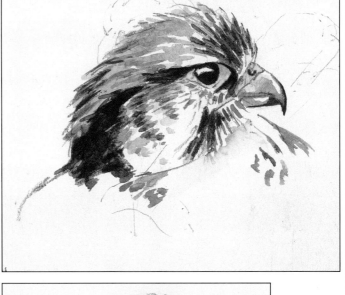

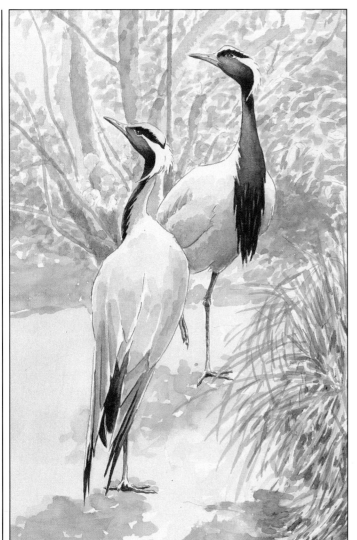

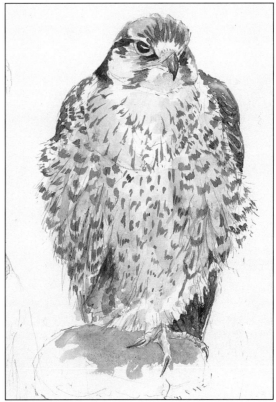

David Boys, *Sketchbook Studies*

Boys is a professional wildlife artist, whose studies, such as those shown here, are used by the London Zoo as part of the information labels outside their aviaries and animal cages. The free and spontaneous appearance of his sketches should not blind us to the fact that they are extremely accurate, and each one is the end-product of several days of careful observation and constant drawing. However, they provide an excellent example of the use of watercolor as a medium for recording rapid impressions.

MOVEMENT

When we watch an animal in movement, such as a horse galloping, our eyes take in an overall impression of shape and color without precise details – these become blurred and generalized in direct ratio to the speed of the animal's movement. The best way of capturing the essence of movement is to choose a technique that in itself suggests it, so try to keep your work free and unfussy, applying the paint fluidly and letting your brush follow the direction of the main lines (see BRUSH DRAWING). Alternatively, you could try watercolor pastels or crayons, which can provide an exciting combination of linear qualities and washes. A sketchy treatment, perhaps with areas of paper left uncovered, will suggest motion much more vividly than a highly finished one – the surest way to "freeze" a moving animal is to include too much detail. This is exactly what the camera does: a photograph taken at a fast shutter speed gives a false impression because it registers much more than the human eye can. Photographs, though, are enormously useful for helping you to gain an understanding of the way an animal moves, and there is no harm in taking snapshots to use as a "sketchbook" in combination with direct observation and on-the-spot studies.

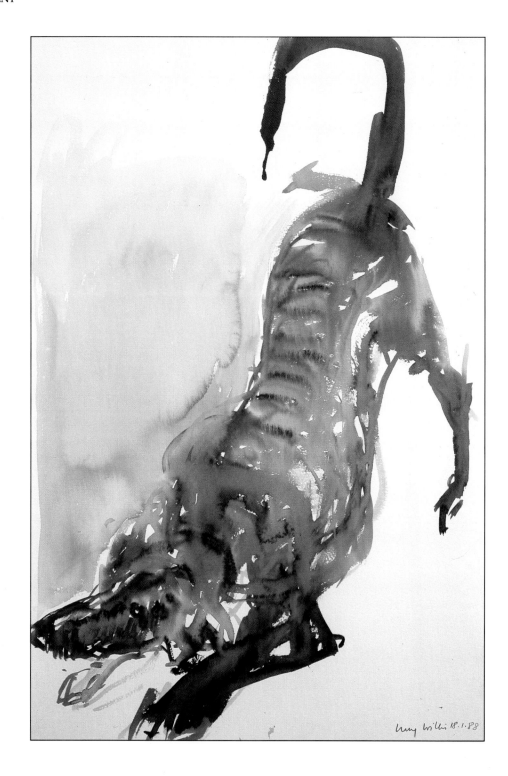

◀ Lucy Willis, *Dog with a Stick III*, 22 × 15 IN (33.9 × 38.1 CM), WATERCOLOR

This is a marvelous example of the fluid and vigorous use of paint to convey movement. Willis has painted very rapidly without waiting for washes to dry, so that some brushstrokes on the dog's body have run together. This is particularly effective on the back and shoulders, where small BACKRUNS have been deliberately used to suggest texture. The soft blurring of the paint in these areas is offset by the crisp, linear brushwork on the muzzle and front paws, and a final lively touch is given by the little exclamation mark of paint that has been allowed to run down from the end of the tail.

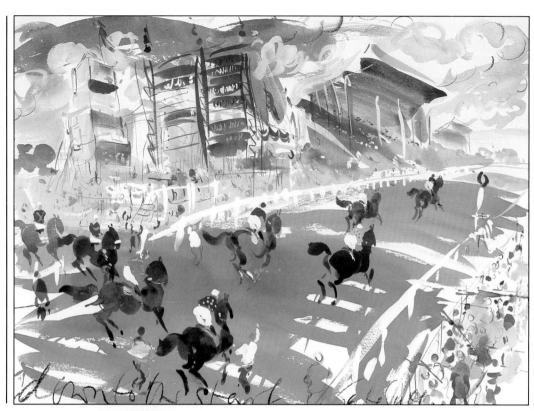

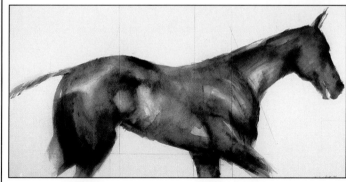

◀ Richard Wills, *Bess*, 30 × 62 IN (76.2 × 157.5 CM), WATERCOLOR AND ACRYLIC

This is a studio study of a horse in movement, made after extensive observation and on-the-spot sketches. It is a large painting, necessitating joining paper by splicing it and glueing it to the board, and the joins have become an integral part of the composition, developed with structural pencil lines. This is a pictorial concept that the artist has taken further in other paintings. The texture on the body has been produced by SPATTERING acrylic paint into wet watercolor.

▲ Jake Sutton, *Down to the Start*, 22½ × 30 IN (57.2 × 76.2 CM), GOUACHE

Movement forms the main theme of this sparkling picture and is expressed in every area, from the scribbled clouds to the blobs and splashes of paint used for awnings and foreground figures. The artist has avoided any overworking of the paint by painting the horses over the rich green of the turf rather than trying to take the green around the shapes.

DOMESTIC AND FARM ANIMALS

All the best paintings in the history of art are of subjects that the artist is deeply familiar with. Rembrandt (1606-69) painted himself, his wife and his children, while much of John Constable's (1776-1837) artistic output was inspired by his native Suffolk. So if you want to paint animals and have a captive subject, such as your own dog, cat or pet rabbit, why not start at home?

One of the great advantages of pets is that they are always around and you can make studies of them sleeping (cats are particularly good for this), running, eating or simply sitting in contemplation. If you live in the country, on or near a farm, sheep, cows and goats are also willing models, as they tend to stand still for long periods when grazing.

One of the most common mistakes in painting an animal is to pay too little attention to its environment, so that it appears to be floating in mid-air. Whether you are painting a cat lying on a windowsill or a cow in a field, always try to integrate the animal with the background and foreground, blurring the edges in places to avoid a cardboard cut-out effect.

The techniques you use are entirely a matter of personal preference and will be dictated by your particular interests, but it is worth saying that if you opt for a very precise method, using small brushstrokes to build up the texture of an animal's fur or wool, you must use the same approach throughout the painting or the picture will look disjointed and unreal.

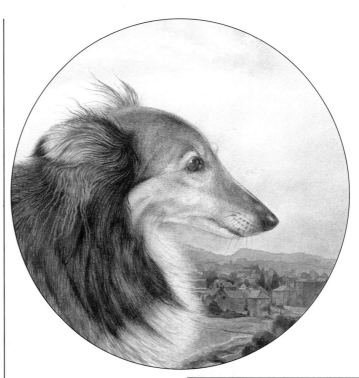

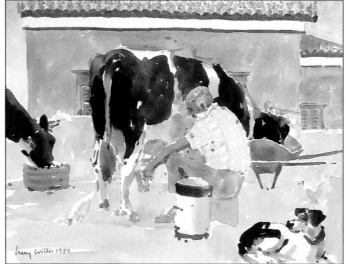

◀ Ronald Jesty, *Shandie*, 11 IN (27.9 CM) DIAMETER, WATERCOLOR

Although this is not a particularly small picture, the artist has chosen a circular format reminiscent of a miniature for his delightful dog portrait and has adapted his technique to suit the idea. His usual style, illustrated elsewhere in this book, is a precise yet bold use of WET-ON-DRY, but here, although still working wet-on-dry, he has used very fine, linear brushstrokes to build up the texture of the fur. The buildings behind are treated in equal detail, but with the tones and colors carefully controlled so that they recede into the background.

▶ Lucy Willis, *Lefteri Milking*, 11¼ × 15⅛ IN (28.6 × 38.5 CM), WATERCOLOR

Willis works directly from life, using a heavy paper that does not need to be stretched, a limited palette and usually only one brush. She says that her aim is simply to translate to paper a selected chunk of what she sees, but she always spends some time looking at her subject before she starts to paint, in order to impress upon herself exactly what it is she is aiming for. Her most frequent preoccupations are with color and light, beautifully conveyed here, as in most of her watercolors. Notice the attractive sparkle given by the little patches of white paper left uncovered between brushstrokes.

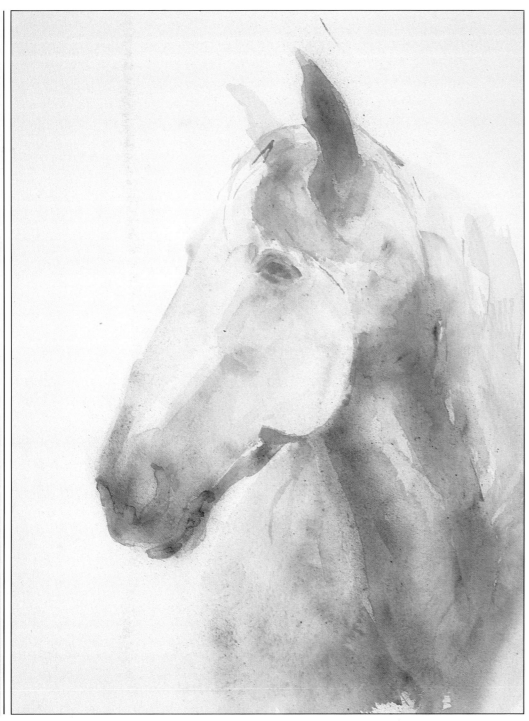

Richard Wills, *White Horse*, 30 × 20 IN (76.2 × 50.8 CM), WATERCOLOR AND ACRYLIC

Wills's control of watercolor is quite breathtaking, and here he has used the most delicate of colors to build up a complex series of forms. Where each pale wash overlaps another, a hard line is formed (see HARD AND SOFT EDGES), and these have been used with absolute precision to define the bony structure of the head and sinewy strength of the neck. This crispness contrasts with the softer areas worked WET-IN-WET, with a light SPATTERING of acrylic into wet watercolor blurring the forms and shadows.

WILD ANIMALS

Painting wild creatures in their natural habitats is becoming an increasingly specialized branch of art, mainly because it involves so much more than simply painting. Professional wildlife artists devote their lives to watching and studying birds and animals in the field, often using sophisticated equipment such as powerful binoculars and cameras with telephoto lenses. However, this does not mean that wild animals are beyond the reach of the ordinary artist. Wildlife is the bread and butter of these specialist painters, and their patrons often require a high standard of accuracy, but not all those who want to paint animals need be so constrained.

There is no need, either, to choose inaccessible subjects. Deer, for example, are eminently paintable and will often come quite close to the viewer in country parks, while shyer, more exotic creatures can be studied and sketched at zoos. A zoo, of course, is not a true habitat for a lion, tiger or monkey, so if you want to use such sketches for a finished painting of a tiger in a forest, you may have to resort to books and magazines for a suitable setting. There is nothing wrong with this – after all, not everyone has the opportunity to paint the forests of Asia and Africa from firsthand experience.

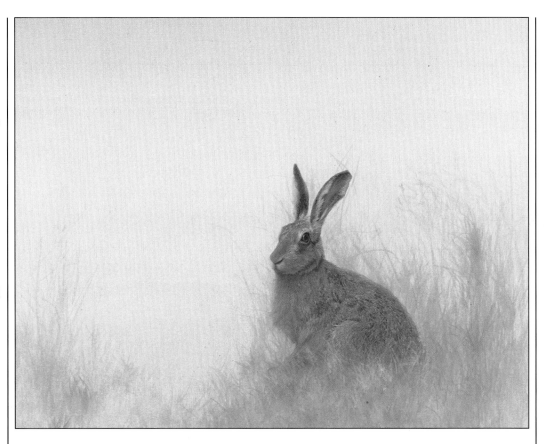

John Wilder, *Brown Hare*, 15 × 20 IN (38.1 × 50.8 CM), GOUACHE

It may seem surprising that this lovely, delicate painting was done in gouache, but it provides an excellent demonstration of the versatility of the medium. Although usually associated with bright, bold work, it can be used as effectively for thin, pastel-colored washes as for vivid, rich impastos. One of its problems is that it dries out very quickly on the palette, but Wilder solves this by using a version of the special palette sold for acrylic, a simple device consisting of wet blotting paper under a layer of parchment paper. The paints are laid out on the parchment and, if covered between working sessions, will stay moist indefinitely.

He started by transferring the main outlines from a working drawing and then laid several very pale overall base washes before beginning to build up the head and body of the hare. Because he likes to leave the outline vague and the brushwork blurred until the final stages, his working process is one of continual painting, blurring, re-defining, overpainting and removing excess paint by sponging or scraping.

The grass was painted when the hare was almost complete, beginning with barely colored water and very gradually increasing the strength. The final touch was to wash over the hare once or twice with the background color, to unify the composition and avoid the cardboard cut-out look seen in many less successful animal paintings.

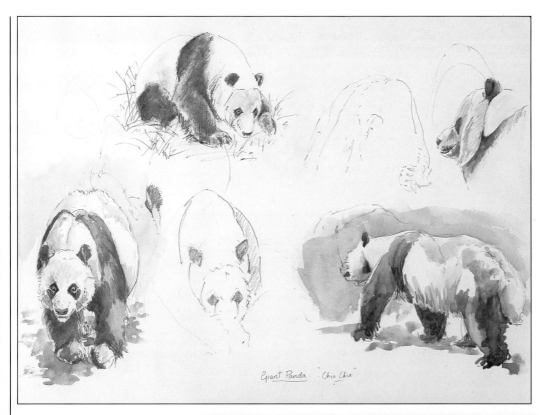

Giant Panda "Chia Chia"

◀ David Boys, *Chia-Chia*, SKETCHBOOK PAGE, WATERCOLOR AND PENCIL

These studies of the giant panda Chia-Chia are the work of the London Zoo artist whose bird sketches are shown on page 77. Although he is a professional wildlife artist, drawing and painting primarily to record precise information, he takes an obvious delight in the watercolor medium, which he uses with great fluency. Notice how the colors have run into one another on the legs of the right-hand panda. This is the result of working on highly sized paper, which can produce interesting results.

▶ Sally Michel, *Ring-tailed Lemur*, WATERCOLOR AND GOUACHE

Michel trained as an illustrator, but began to exhibit paintings when her book illustration work decreased. She became a wildlife artist more or less by accident and is also well known as a painter of cat and dog portraits. She works in both pastel and watercolor and always from life, although she sometimes takes photographs to record a particular pose.

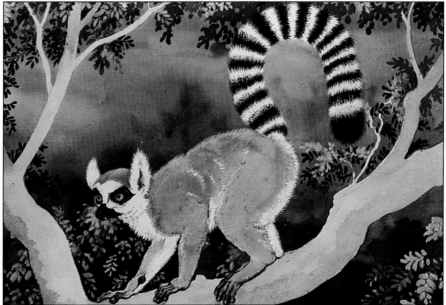

TEXTURES

The fur of an animal or the feathers of a bird are among their most attractive features, but they do present certain problems.

One is that too much attention to texture, the animal's "outer covering," can obscure the underlying form and structure, so you must be careful to paint textures in a way that hints at the body beneath. Perspective makes all objects appear smaller as they recede into the distance, and in the same way, the brushstrokes you make to represent fur must vary in size, becoming smaller as the form recedes away from you.

The other problem is the more technical one of how to represent soft fur or stiff, bristly hair with an aqueous medium. Take heart – this is not a real problem at all, but only in the mind, springing from the widely held belief that watercolor can only be used in a broad and fluid manner. In fact, the medium is an extremely versatile one, as can be seen from the illustrations throughout the book.

Fine, linear brushstrokes are an excellent way of painting fur or feathers and, if necessary, the paint can be thickened with opaque white to give it extra body. Another useful technique is DRY BRUSH, which can be worked over a preliminary wash or straight onto white paper, while the perfect method for highlighting tiny details, such as whiskers catching the light, is SCRAPING BACK with the point of a knife, which gives an infinitely finer line than can be achieved with a brush.

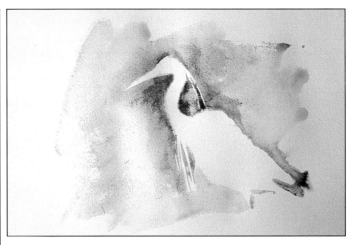

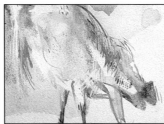

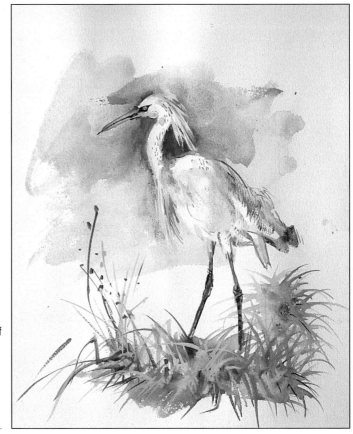

1 The bird is to remain predominantly white, so the background is painted first.

2 The artist now begins to work on the bird's body, defining the shapes and forms. Texture is suggested by means of a light application of wax crayon (see WAX RESIST) under the paint and some equally light pastel smudges over it, but care is taken not to overwork any area.

3 The background is slightly darkened, some additional small marks made on the bird's neck to suggest feathers, and the grass painted with spiky brushstrokes of acrylic.

Kate Gwynn, *Egret*, 20 × 16 IN (50.8 × 40.6 CM), WATERCOLOR AND ACRYLIC

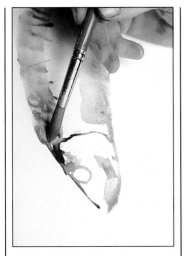

1 The artist begins by working WET-IN-WET, allowing slightly opaque yellow paint to merge into the blue-gray.

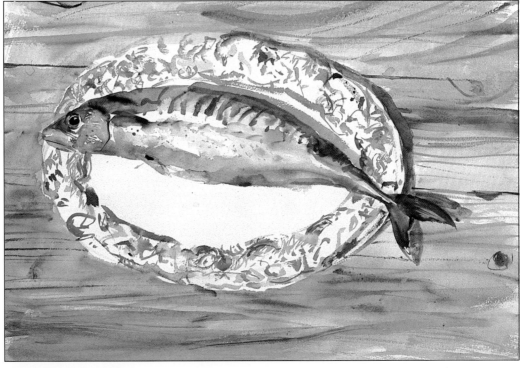

Kate Gwynn, *Mackerel*, 16 × 20 IN (40.6 × 50.8 CM), WATERCOLOR

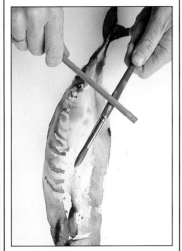

2 Having laid the first washes to establish the main colors and tones, she now spatters paint lightly onto the body (see SPATTERING).

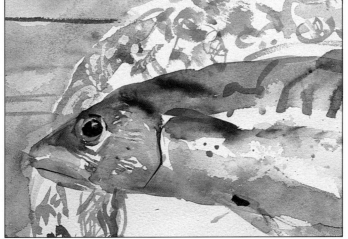

3 This detail of the finished painting shows a skillful use of overlaid wet washes to describe the soft, glowing colors, with the white paper forming the silvery highlights.

A lot of people steer clear of painting buildings because they feel they cannot draw well enough or are unable to come to grips with perspective. This is understandable, but it is a pity, as buildings not only form a major part of the twentieth-century landscape, but are also in many cases beautiful, exciting and highly paintable.

Perspective and proportion

If you want to make detailed, accurate and highly finished paintings of complex architectural subjects, such as the great palaces and cathedrals of Europe, a knowledge of perspective is vital, as are sound drawing skills. This is a specialized kind of painting, but most people have humbler aims, and it is perfectly possible to produce a broad impression of such subjects or a convincing portrayal of a rural church, farmhouse or street scene mainly by means of careful observation. Too much worrying about perspective can actually have a negative effect, causing you to overlook the far more interesting things, such as a building's general character, color and texture. However, there is one important rule that most of us learn at school, but don't pay much attention to: receding parallel lines meet at a vanishing point on the horizon. The horizon is at your own eye-level, and so is determined by the place you have chosen to paint from. If you are on a hill looking down on your subject, the horizon will be high and the parallels will slope up to it, but if you are sitting directly beneath a tall building, they will slope sharply down to a low horizon. It is vital to remember this when painting on the spot, because if you alter your position by, for example, sitting down when you began the painting standing at an easel, the perspective will change, and this can be disconcerting.

If you intend to paint a "portrait" of a particular building, shape and proportion are just as important as they are in a portrait of a person – it is these that give a building its individuality. A common mistake is to misrepresent the size and shape of doors, windows, balconies and so on in relation to the wall area, which not only makes it fail as a portrait, but also creates a disturbing impression, as the building looks structurally impossible.

Before you start to draw or paint, look hard at the building and try to assess its particular qualities. Some houses are tall and thin with windows and doors occupying only a small part of each wall, while others seem to be dominated by their windows. In a street scene, there may be several completely different types of building, built at various periods, and all with distinct characters of their own. You can exaggerate these for extra effect, but you ignore them at your peril.

Shapes and proportions can be checked by a simple measuring system. Hold a pencil or a small pocket ruler up in front of you and slide your thumb up and down it to work out the height or width of a door or window in relation to those of the main wall. Most professional artists do this; the human eye is surprisingly un-trustworthy when it comes to architecture.

The straight line problem

Unless you are a trained draftsman or just one of those lucky people, it can be extraordinarily hard to draw and paint straight lines, and a building that tilts to one side or that has outer walls that are not parallel to each other can ruin the impression of solidity as well as looking bizarre. The ruler is useful here, too – there is nothing wrong with using mechanical aids for your preliminary drawing, as it will quickly be covered by the paint. You can apply colors as freely as you like once you have a good foundation, using the ruled lines as a general guide. Some of the nineteenth-century watercolorists were not above having their drawings done by professional draftsmen – would that we were all so fortunate!

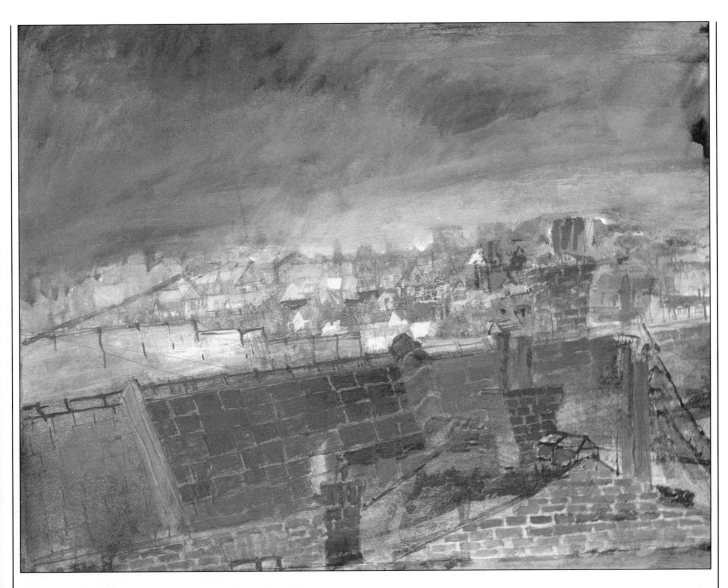

Julia Gurney, *Studio View*, 14 × 18 IN (35.6 × 45.7 CM), WATERCOLOR, ACRYLIC AND INK

Paintings of buildings do not have to be minutely observed and correct in every detail. Here the artist has taken a broader approach, conveying the atmosphere of the city houses under a stormy sky through her bold and decisive use of MIXED MEDIA. Detail is restricted to the foreground, which she has emphasized by picking out the pattern of the bricks and tiles.

TOWN AND CITYSCAPES

In industrialized countries, the rural populations are far outnumbered by those of towns and cities, and yet cityscapes do not rank high in popularity as painting subjects. This is perhaps not very surprising. Although most city dwellers can see a wealth of rich subject matter in their surroundings – colors, textures, shapes and patterns – the prospect of painting them in a convincing manner seems a daunting one. There is the dreaded perspective to contend with, not to mention the straight lines and the complex array of architectural details.

Town houses and streets, however, are marvelous subjects, endlessly varied and open to countless different modes of interpretation. It is mainly a matter of deciding what interests you and making sure that your technique expresses it. An artist whose obsession is architecture may want to paint panoramic townscapes, using fine, precise brushwork to describe every detail of roofs, windows, doors and brickwork, but another might be concerned exclusively with the interplay of geometric shapes or the quality of light, using a broader, more impressionistic technique.

Start in a small way, perhaps with the view from an upstairs window, which provides an interesting viewpoint as well as intriguing details you would not see from street level. Practice drawing whenever possible, and avoid tackling over-ambitious projects until you are sure your skills are up to them, as this could lead to frustration and put you off the whole subject.

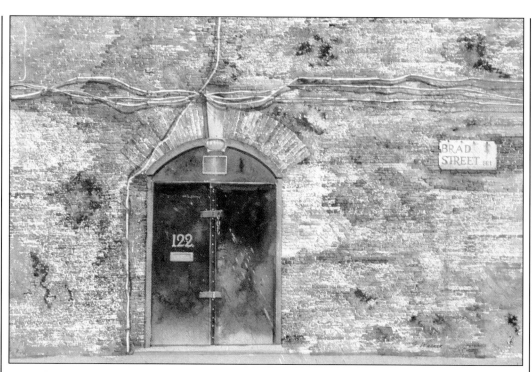

Sandra Walker, *Brad Street II*, 22 × 30 IN (55.9 × 76.2 CM), WATERCOLOR

Walker is fascinated by the atmosphere and textures of buildings and has painted a series of large watercolors of London's crumbling East End, of which this is one. Her draftsmanship is superb, and her paintings are remarkable for their accuracy of detail. She has built up texture by a combination of SPATTERING, DRY BRUSH and scraping with a razor blade.

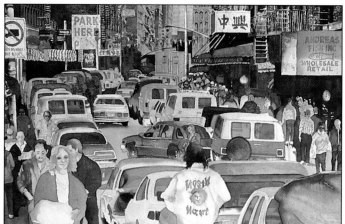

Sandra Walker, *Grand Street*, 30 × 40 IN (76.2 × 101.6 CM), WATERCOLOR

The sheer complexity of this New York cityscape, with its multitude of different shapes, colors and forms, would be enough to daunt most watercolorists. But Walker has been equal to the task, producing a busy and lively composition in which, although every detail has received loving attention, there is no laboring of the paint.

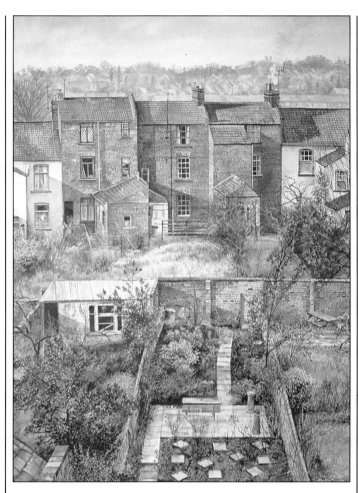

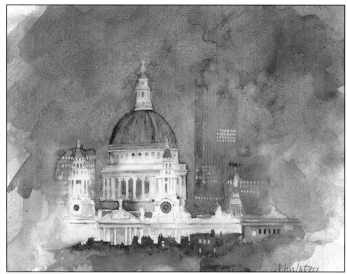

John Lidzey FRSA, *St. Paul's at Night*,
14 × 16 IN (35.6 × 40.6 CM), WATERCOLOR
WITH SOME BODY COLOR

The freedom of this wonderfully
atmospheric painting contrasts
strongly with the tighter
techniques seen elsewhere on
these pages. But it has to be said
that the most spontaneous-
seeming effects in watercolor are
usually the result of a thorough
knowledge of the medium, and so
it is here. The artist began with a
careful drawing, a prerequisite for
complex architectural subjects.
Having given himself a firm
foundation, he was then able to
apply the paint freely, with a large,
soft mop brush, controlling it on
the paper with a piece of damp
absorbent cotton. He proceeded
by allowing clean water to flow on
freshly painted areas, blotting out
as necessary. The details were
added WET-ON-DRY, but softened
with damp cotton in order to keep
the same effect throughout the
painting.

Martin Taylor, *Up the Garden Path*,
20⅞ × 15½ IN (53 × 39.5 CM),
WATERCOLOR AND ACRYLIC

Taylor, like Sandra Walker, loves
detail and includes every brick,
tile, flagstone and blade of grass
in his townscapes. He paints
slowly, working on one area of the
picture at a time, and achieves
depth and variety of color by
considerable overlaying of
brushstrokes and washes.

DETAILS

A building derives much of its character from the details of its architecture, such as doors, windows, balconies and decorative brick- and stonework, all of which make lovely painting subjects in themselves. An open shutter casting a shadow on a whitewashed wall, for instance, could make an exciting composition, providing a contrast of colors and an interplay of vertical and diagonal lines. This kind of subject can all too easily become static and dull, however, so try to keep your brushwork lively and varied, using a combination of fluid washes and crisp lines. You may find the LINE AND WASH technique adds this kind of extra dimension, or you could make texture the main theme of the painting, using the salt spattering (see TEXTURES) or WAX RESIST methods.

Try to relate the chosen detail to the structure of the building and be careful about the viewpoint you choose. If you paint a window from straight on, you will not be able to suggest the depth of the recess and hence the thickness of the wall, giving it the appearance of being stuck on rather than built in. Another common mistake when painting windows is to make them the same dark tone all over, but window glass takes its colors and tones from the prevailing light, often reflecting color from the sky or other buildings or showing glimpses of curtains and walls from the room behind. If you look carefully, you will see considerable variations.

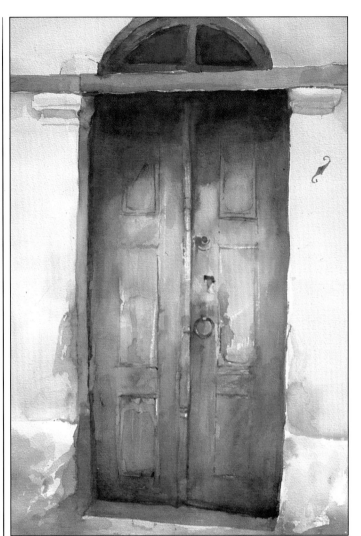

Paul Millichip, *Scorched Door*, 22 × 16 IN (55.9 × 40.6 CM), WATERCOLOR

It takes courage to make an entire composition of one object placed centrally on the paper, but this painting succeeds completely. It is more than just a portrait of a door; it is an essay in color and technique. Working initially WET-IN-WET, Millichip has introduced an astonishing range of colors to the door, echoing the violet-blues in the shadows below and the warm orange-browns in the two small accents of color on right and left of the door. He has been equally cunning in terms of composition. The horizontal bar ties the main shape to the sides of the picture, while the diagonals at the bottom prevent a static look that can result from parallel horizontals.

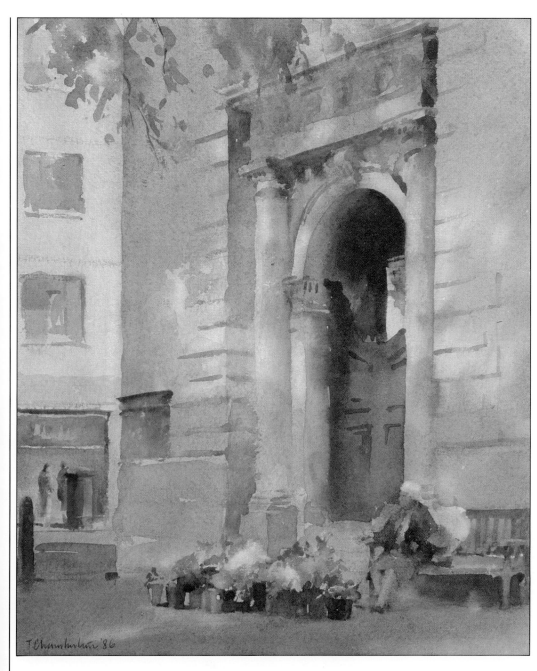

Trevor Chamberlain, *The Flower Seller, Bow Church*, 10½ × 8¾ IN (26.7 × 22.2 CM), WATERCOLOR

This is another example of the skillful use of the WET-IN-WET technique, and it also provides a lesson on the importance of light in architectural subjects. The artist has clearly been excited by the strong, elegant shapes of the church portico, but the painting is really about the quality of the light, he has conveyed this through his choice of colors as well as his technique. The color key is limited, with the same blue-grays and pale yellows repeated throughout the painting to create a gentle and harmonious atmosphere, even the "red" mailbox and the clumps of flowers are muted versions of their true colors.

INTERIORS

Interiors are fascinating painting subjects as they provide so many possibilities for experimenting with the effects of light on composition.

Natural interior light is less intense than outdoor light, but it is more varied because the light source is channeled through the relatively small area of a window, creating warm, bright colors in some places and cool, dark ones in others. This also creates interesting patterns. For instance, the light coming in through a window on a sunny day will be partially blocked by the window bars, setting up an interplay of light and dark geometric shapes that can form a strong or dominant element in a painting.

Artificial light also has great potential for pattern and color. A lamp placed in a dark corner, for example, will throw a strong pool of light below it, and a weaker, more diffused one on the wall behind, breaking up the surfaces into several distinct areas.

Any or all of these effects of light superimposed on the architectural structure of a room with a framework of verticals and horizontals offers more or less endless possibilities. Remember, however, that artificial light has a different quality to daylight – it is much warmer and imparts a yellow or orange tinge to the colors, so, if you intend to paint a lamp-lit interior, you will find it easier to block out the natural light (or wait until after dark). Natural and artificial light can be mixed, but handling the warm and cool contrasts the mixture provides does require some experience.

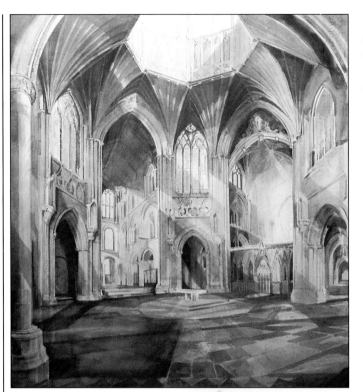

◄ Christopher Baker, *Ely Cathedral*, 26 × 18 IN (66 × 45.7 CM), WATERCOLOR AND PENCIL

Although we tend to think of painting in terms of color, it is perfectly possible to "paint" in monochrome. As can be seen from Baker's sensitive and skillful portrayal, it is an effective way of treating complex subjects like this. It is also a good discipline, as it forces you to think about the balance of lights and darks, an important aspect of painting. Baker built up his painting over a careful drawing, working on Hot Pressed (smooth) paper. After carefully modeling the forms, he lightly tinted some areas to provide an overall warmth to the interior.

▶ John Tookey, *London Café*, 8½ × 11½ IN (21.6 × 29.2 CM), WATERCOLOR WITH SOME GOUACHE

Light coming through a window always creates exciting effects of light and dark, silhouetting some forms and illuminating others, and Tookey has exploited them to the full. Working rapidly on unstretched toned paper, he has boldly blocked in the dark areas, enlivening them with accents of red and yellow. The impressionistic treatment is perfectly suited to the subject.

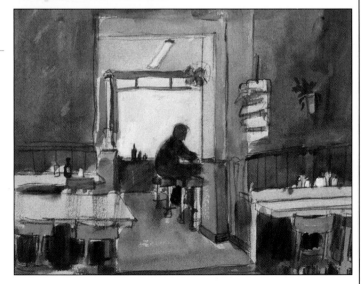

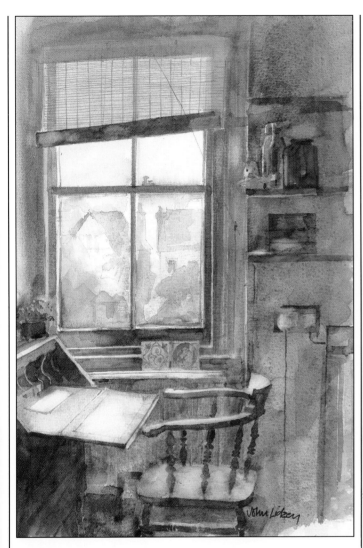

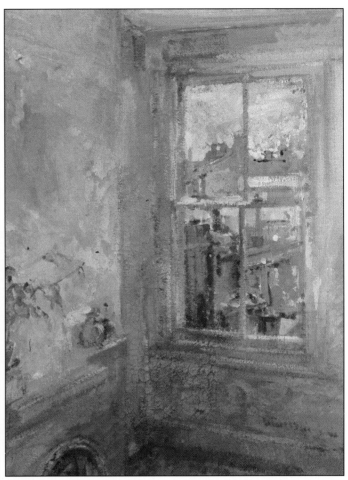

John Lidzey, *Interior with Desk and Chair*, 18 × 24 IN (30.5 × 61 CM), WATERCOLOR

Lidzey has achieved a lovely soft, luminous effect by frequently blotting his freely applied paint with damp cotton, sometimes completely removing and then re-introducing areas of color. This means that there are no obvious brushmarks, which he dislikes, and gives a pleasing, granular texture to the paint. When dry, some areas were wiped with clean water and left again to dry, after which certain details were reinforced with BODY COLOR. The houses outside have been deliberately "held back," with the minimum of tonal contrast and little detail, to enhance the inside/outside quality.

John Martin, *Pinda Cottage*, 18 × 12 IN (45.7 × 30.5 CM), GOUACHE ON TONED PAPER

In two of the paintings on these pages, the window is the main light source, but here light also appears to be coming into the room from another source on the right, giving a more even illumination with less contrast of tone. The focal point, however, is the window, with its framed view of the buildings outside, toward which we are led by the diagonals of the left-hand wall. Martin is particularly fond of interior scenes, as he is of the gouache medium, which allows him to build up rich but subtle color surfaces.

LIGHTING

Light is the single most important factor in all painting: without it, nothing would exist. It is particularly vital when painting buildings, as it is the play of light and shade on their vertical planes that describes their structure and illuminates their color and texture. A building seen at noon will tend to look flat and uninteresting because the shadows cast by an overhead sun are minimal, but a low sun, in the morning or evening, throws long, slanting shadows that not only help to describe the features of the building, but also provide exciting contrasts of color and tone. Light like this makes a building come to life – an ordinary, drab, brick-built row house, for instance, or a view of city rooftops and chimneys, will suddenly present a glowing array of colors, from golden yellows and oranges in the sun-struck areas to purples and blues in the shadows.

It is not always color or detail that you want to emphasize, however. You may be more concerned with the overall shape and want to suppress minor architectural features. In this case, you could use backlighting to give a dramatic or atmospheric impression, silhouetting the massive bulk of a cathedral or a line of rooftops against an evening sky. For this kind of subject, the paint should be used fluidly, applied in broad washes, with any hard edges restricted to the outlines of buildings against sky.

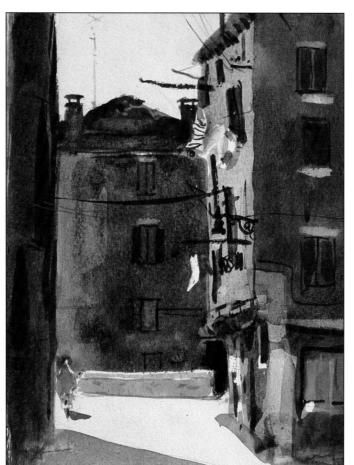

◄ John Tookey, *Venetian Backstreet*, 11½ × 8½ IN (29.2 × 21.6 CM), WATERCOLOR AND FELT-TIP PEN

Imagine what this scene would look like under a flat gray drizzle – the buildings would hold no interest for an artist because there would be almost no color or tonal contrast. Tookey has wisely chosen to paint at a time when the sun has turned the right-hand building into a rich gold and cast a decisive slanting shadow across the street. His color scheme is simple but effective: he has enhanced the yellow by using its complementary, blue-violet, repeated in small patches in several places to unify the composition.

► Michael Cadman, *Gloucester Cathedral III*, 14 × 19 IN (35.6 × 48.3 CM), ACRYLIC AND WATERCOLOR ON TINTED PAPER

A misty, diffused light has allowed the artist to simplify the complex forms of the cathedral. There is a considerable amount of detail on the building, but it is subjugated to shape and color and the lines have been softened by working into an initial wash which is still damp.

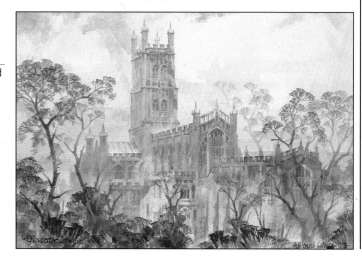

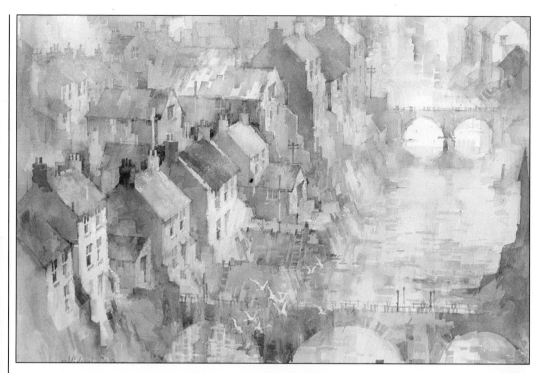

Michael Cadman, *A Memory of Whitby*, 14 × 20 IN (35.6 × 50.8 CM), ACRYLIC AND WATERCOLOR

A shaft of sunlight on a misty day has provided both a focal point and a wealth of glowing but subtle colors, which the artist has exploited beautifully. The painting was built up from initial WET-IN-WET washes laid rapidly to cover the white of the paper, and some of the whites and lighter colors were produced by GLAZING with watercolor over acrylic impasto. The brick-like brushstrokes seen in many of Cadman's paintings are produced by using square-ended brushes (sable and nylon).

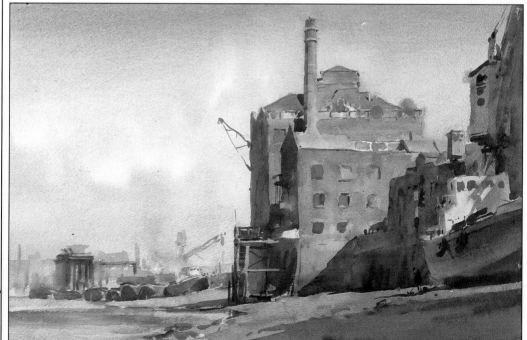

Trevor Chamberlain, *Old Wharf at Rotherhithe*, 14 × 21 IN (35.6 × 53,3 CM), WATERCOLOR

A low evening sun is the perfect time for painting buildings, and Chamberlain, whose major interest is the effects of light, has made the most of it. A subject like this one can be quickly spoiled by overworking, and he suits his technique to the subject by working fluidly yet surely with a minimum of overlaid washes.

VIEWPOINT

The viewpoint you select for an architectural subject needs careful consideration, as it can make all the difference to the composition. This can present you with some problems, however. You might find that sitting on a sidewalk provides an exciting angle for a painting of a city church because the low viewpoint silhouettes it against the sky, but it can be difficult to work in the middle of a busy thoroughfare. It is even more frustrating to find that all the best views are from the middle of a road (they often are because then you are far enough from them to see them in their entirety).

It is a good idea to make one or two preliminary reconnaissances to find the perfect spot. You must be able to see the whole of the building clearly without "panning" up or down, because as soon as you move, your viewpoint changes – in a small way, but enough to distort the perspective.

Windows are often good vantage points, and painting from the inside looking out has two additional benefits. It shields you from both weather and inquisitive eyes, while the window provides a ready-made frame for your subject.

Angle is important, too. It is difficult to make a building look really solid if you paint it from directly in front, whereas an oblique or corner view provides clearly defined diagonals as well as a more interesting composition.

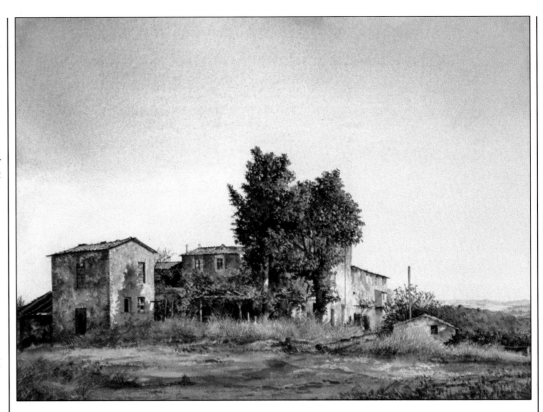

Martin Taylor, *Back of the Castello di Tocchi, Tuscany,* 13¾ × 10¼ IN (26 × 35 CM), WATERCOLOR

Taylor says that he has always been interested in painting the back views of places, partly to avoid the obvious and partly because they are often more interesting. This subject particularly appealed to him because he saw a Corot-like quality in its spaciousness, light and composition. Notice how he has increased the feeling of space by allowing the sky to occupy a large part of the picture area, and has chosen a viewpoint that enables him to convey the solidity of the buildings and make the most of their shapes.

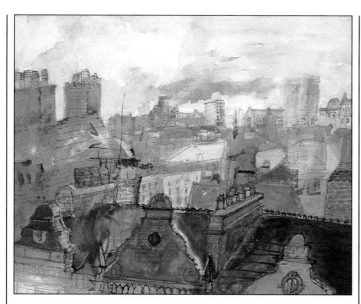

▲ Julia Gurney, *From Peter Jones*,
14 × 17 IN (35.6 × 43.2 CM), WATERCOLOR,
ACRYLIC AND INK

One of the best viewpoints for
buildings is a high one. Not only
do the rooftops and chimneys
form fascinating patterns, but you
also begin to see all sorts of
intriguing details not noticeable
from eye level, such as the
delightfully shaped gable fronts
in this painting. Gurney has
made expressive use of MIXED
MEDIA, drawing with ink on top of
watercolor in a vigorous and
direct style.

▼ Jill Mirza, *Path with Sand Pile,
Cycladic Series*, 18 × 12 IN (45.7 × 30.5
CM), ACRYLIC ON BOARD

Sometimes the viewpoint is not so
much the artist's choice as one
dictated by the lie of the land, as
here, where the buildings are set
on a steeply rising hill. The low
angle from which we see
buildings in hilly towns and
villages shows them to good
advantage, and the converging
parallels sloping downward at a
sharp angle encourage dramatic
compositions. Mirza has made
the most of the intrinsic drama of
the subject by strong contrasts of
tone, suggesting the texture of
the whitewashed walls with a light
SCUMBLING of gray-blues and
yellows.

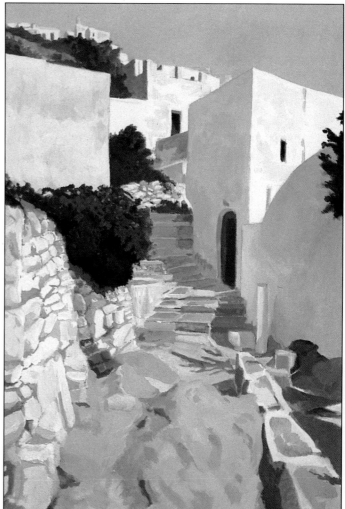

BUILDINGS IN LANDSCAPE

In a town- or cityscape, buildings form the whole subject of the painting – although there may be a "supporting cast" of people, cars and the occasional tree. A farmhouse, church or group of houses, however, can also be part of a landscape, forming just one of its features in the same way that a bush or outcrop of rocks might.

This is a subject with great potential, as it allows you to exploit the contrast between manmade and natural forms in a way that can enhance the qualities of both. There is, however, a danger that the contrast may be too strong. Most people are familiar with the jarring effect of a new building whose architect has not considered its setting. It looks out of place and unrelated, the very quality you want to avoid in a painting.

Many old buildings look as if they have grown naturally out of the landscape they sit in, often because they are built from local materials and reflect the prevailing colors. So try to achieve a similar unity in your painting, in color and above all in technique. Because buildings are less easy to draw and paint than fields and hills, it is always a temptation to treat them in a much tighter and more detailed way than the rest of the painting, which is a recipe for failure. If you would naturally paint the landscape WET-IN-WET, use the same method for the building, or at least parts of it.

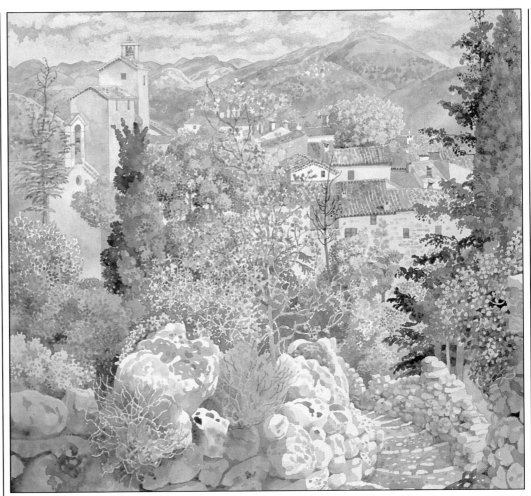

Juliette Palmer, *The Pathway to Molière Cavaillac, Cévennes,* 16 × 16 IN (40.6 × 40.6 CM), WATERCOLOR

In this delightful painting, the buildings are so well integrated into the landscape that they almost appear to be organic forms like the surrounding rocks and trees. This impression is reinforced by the artist's unusual and very individual technique, which stresses pattern by means of small, light brushstrokes of different shapes and sizes. Her skill at reserving highlights is amazing: the intricate tangle of tiny twigs on the left and the little white shapes on the steps were created entirely by painting around them – no scratching out techniques or liquid mask were used.

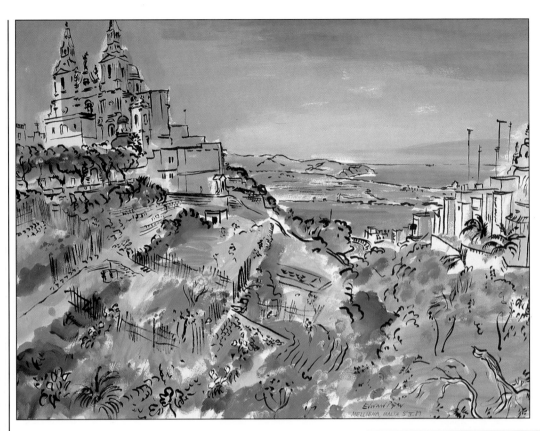

◄ Edward Piper, *Mellieha, Malta,*
22 × 30 IN (55.9 × 76.2 CM), WATERCOLOR
AND PEN

The rose-colored church, rising
up into the deep blue sky, is an
important part of the composition,
but it is not allowed to dominate.
Pattern, color and movement are
the main themes of the painting,
expressed through a lively use of
the LINE AND WASH technique.
Piper does not attempt to outline
areas of color with line, as this
usually works to the detriment of
both. Instead, he places the
colors in an almost random way,
so that they sometimes overlap
the lines and sometimes end well
within them, as on the left side of
the church.

► David Curtis, *Ruined Barracks,
Scotland,* 15 × 22 IN (38.1 × 55.9 CM),
WATERCOLOR

As in Juliette Palmer's painting
opposite, the building looks less
like a manmade structure than
an integral part of the landscape.
Ruins are, of course, a
particularly paintable subject
because they have weathered
and changed shape as parts of
the original structure fall away.
This painting was done directly
from the subject with a fairly
limited palette and has all the
freshness and immediacy of
good on-the-spot paintings.

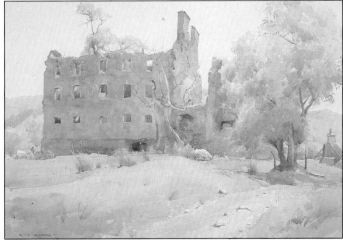

PATTERN AND TEXTURE

Manmade structures provide as much variety of pattern and texture as the natural world, and it is often these that attract us to a particular building rather than its shape or proportion. Building materials vary hugely – there are houses with wooden boarding, great expanses of shimmering glass on modern office buildings, whitewashed houses, mellowed brick mansions and great stone churches. It would be a great pity to ignore the inventiveness of generations of architects and builders and, in any case, if you paint a wall or roof exactly the same color and tone all over, it will look like a cardboard cut-out.

Although in general old buildings provide the most surface interest because the materials have become weathered, new ones also have texture or pattern of some kind, so always look for ways of suggesting these qualities.

There are many techniques ideally suited to painting texture. You could try, for example, the WAX RESIST or SCUMBLING methods or any of those described under the heading TEXTURES in the first part of the book. It is worth experimenting with all these, and you may then evolve your own personal variations.

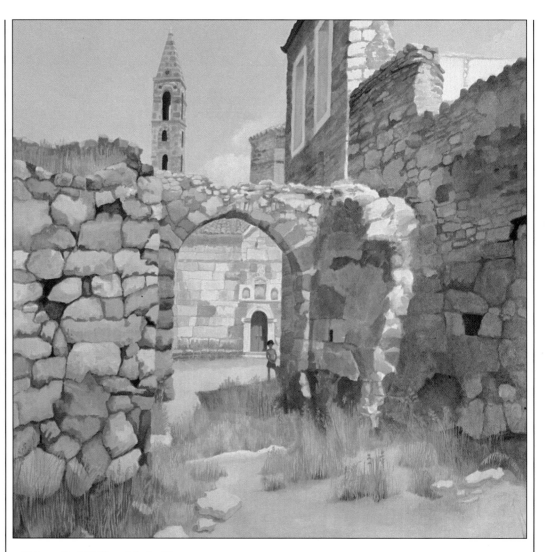

Jill Mirza, *The Old Village of Kardamili, Peloponnese*, 32 × 32 IN (81.3 × 81.3 CM), ACRYLIC ON BOARD

The varied colors and irregular shapes of the building stones and the strong shadows and highlights create a lively pattern throughout the painting. Acrylic can be used in transparent washes just like watercolor, but Mirza uses it very much like opaque gouache, laying light colors over dark and vice versa. The luminous quality of the shadowed walls on the left has been achieved by GLAZING thin paint over underlying colors.

Martin Taylor, *Within the Castle Walls*,
18⅞ × 14⅛ IN (48 × 36 CM), WATERCOLOR
AND ACRYLIC

Taylor has built up the richly textured surface of the old stonework by successive SCUMBLING with a dry watercolor and acrylic mixture over transparent washes. In places he has scuffed the paper with the blade of a knife, applied paint on top and then repeated the process. Good watercolor paper is surprisingly tough and can withstand a good deal of such treatment.

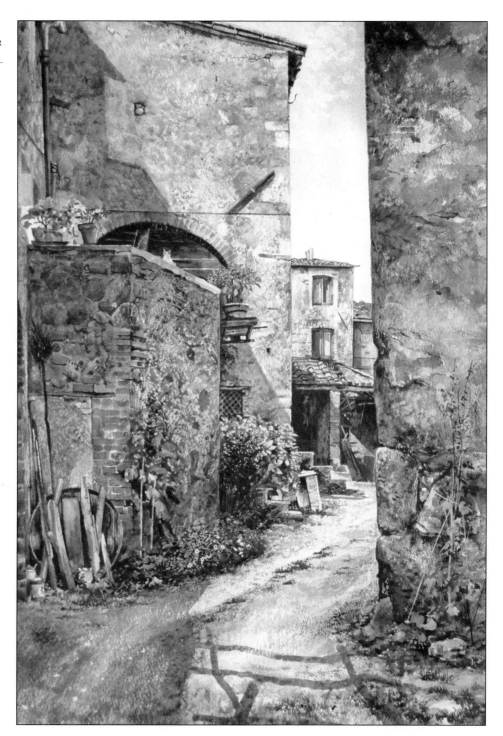

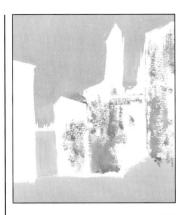

1 Moira Huntly uses a combination of watercolor, gouache and pastel pencils for this painting. Having laid loose washes for sky and water, she applies texture by a simple printing technique of brushing watercolor onto a thick piece of paper and then pressing it firmly onto the working surface. The effect varies according to the texture of the paper and the wetness of the paint.

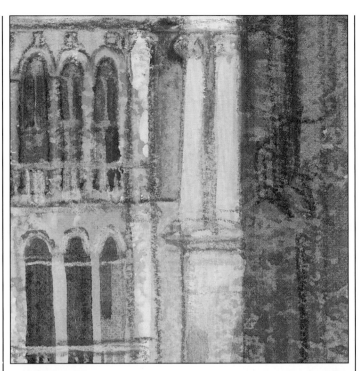

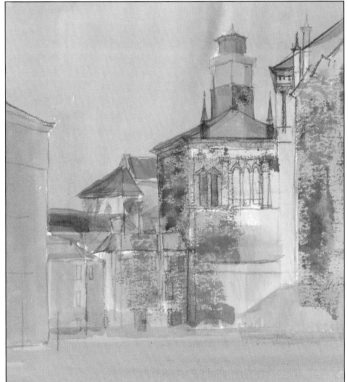

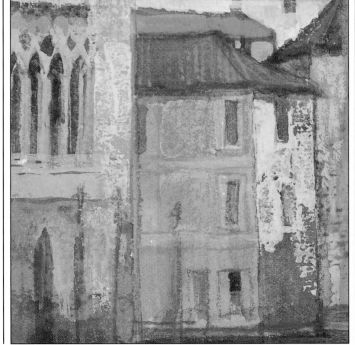

2 Flat washes of orange and raw sienna (the colors used for the printed texture) and the sky color are then brushed over the white shapes, in some areas superimposed over the textures.

Detail is introduced by drawing with dark olive-green and red-brown pastel pencils, with the rough surface of the paper breaking up the line to give a grainy effect.

3 (final stage). Darker shades are painted with watercolor washes of Payne's gray, echoing the sky color, which is the same gray with a small amount of crimson. Gouache is used to introduce further texture in the lighter-toned areas, again using the printing technique and opaque, cream-colored paint. This can be seen clearly on the building at the extreme left (see left, below). A few final details are then added with white pastel pencil to complete the picture.

◄ (detail of finished painting). This shows both the build-up of transparent washes over the printed textures and the textural quality of the pastel line marks.

◄ (detail of finished painting). Texture on the light areas is created by SCUMBLING opaque gouache over transparent washes. The roof tiles are suggested by drawing with a pale-orange pastel pencil over dark washes.

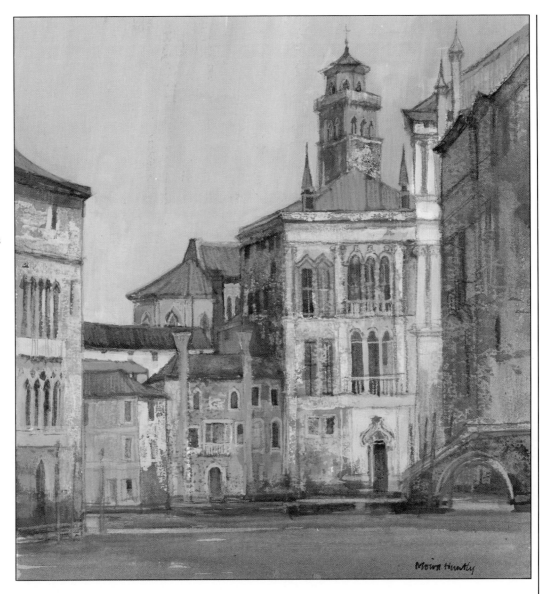

Moira Huntly RI, RSMA, *Venice*,
11¾ × 10¾ IN (30 × 27.5 CM),
WATERCOLOR, GOUACHE AND PASTEL
PENCILS ON STRETCHED PAPER

Watercolor is generally believed to be suited only to certain subjects. It is "perfect" for landscape, of course, and possible for flowers, but surely it is much too uncontrollable to be brought to the service of figure and portrait painting. It is true that there is no strong tradition of figure work in watercolor and that all the most famous paintings of people – those we see in art collections – are in oils, but this has nothing to do with any inherent unsuitability of the medium. The reason for the choice of oils is a much simpler one. In the past, most paintings were done for a fee, and artists had to please their patrons. Those who were wealthy enough to commission a portrait or pay a high price for a nude study wanted a large, imposing painting that would stand the ravages of time, and this meant one in oils.

Nowadays, however, we paint for ourselves and do not have to produce highly finished work with every hair or jewel described in faithful detail. More and more artists are finding that watercolor is a marvelous medium for figure and portrait work, ideal for freer, more impressionistic treatments, and perfectly suited for capturing impressions of light and the delicate, living qualities of skin and hair.

Drawing

No branch of painting is problem-free and, because watercolors cannot be reworked and corrected to any great extent, it is vital to start a painting on a good foundation. This means that, before you can paint figures or faces successfully, you must first be able to draw them.

The best way to approach the complexities of the human figure is to see it as a set of simple forms that fit together – the ovoid of the head joining the cylinder of the neck that, in turn, fits into the broader, flatter planes of the shoulders, and so on. If you intend to tackle the whole figure, avoid the temptation to begin with small details; instead, map out the whole figure first in broad lines.

Proportion is particularly important, and many promising paintings are spoiled by a too-large head or feet that could not possibly be used for their proper function because they are much too small for the body. The best way to check proportions is to hold up a pencil to the subject and slide your thumb up and down it to measure the various elements. This will quickly show you the size of a hand in relation to a forearm and the ratio of head-width to shoulder-width.

Another way to improve your drawing is to look not at the forms themselves, but at the spaces between them. If a model is standing with one arm resting on a hip, there will be a space of a particular shape between these forms. Draw this, not the arm itself, and then move on to any other "negative shapes" you can see. This method is surprisingly accurate.

Composition

It is easy to become so bogged down in the intricacies of the human figure and face that composition is forgotten, but it is every bit as important as in any other branch of painting. Even if you are painting just a head-and-shoulders portrait, always give thought to the placing of the head within the square or rectangle of the paper, the background and the balance of tones.

A plain, light-colored wall might be the ideal foil for a dark-haired sitter, allowing you to concentrate the drama on the face itself, but you will often find you need more background or foreground interest to balance a subject. Placing your sitter in front of a window, for example, will give an interesting pattern of vertical and horizontal lines in the background as well as a subtle fall of light, while a chair or sofa not only serves the purpose of supporting the model, but its curved or straight lines also have pictorial potential.

Figures or groups of figures in an outdoor setting need equally careful pre-planning. You will have to think about whether to make them the focal point of the painting, where to place them in relation to the foreground and background and what other elements you should include – or suppress. It is a good idea to make a series of small thumbnail sketches to work out the composition before you begin to paint.

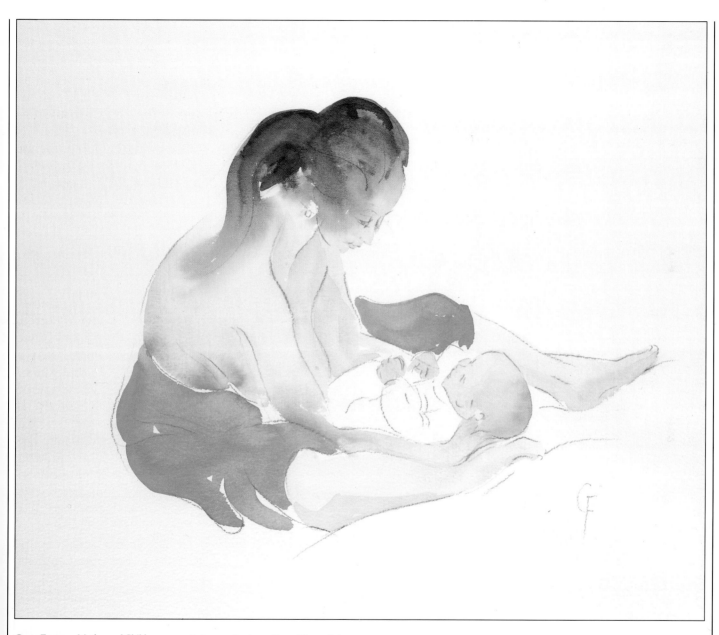

Greta Fenton, *Mother and Child*, 20 × 26
IN (50.8 × 66 CM), WATERCOLOR AND
CONTÉ CRAYON

This lovely, tender group should
quickly disabuse us of the notion
that the figure cannot be painted
in watercolor. In the right hands, it
is the perfect medium. The artist
has painted directly from life,
working mainly WET-IN-WET with a
large Chinese brush and adding
definition with delicate red-crayon
lines.

FIGURE STUDIES

Watercolor may not be the best medium for the highly polished, anatomically correct studies of nudes beloved of the nineteenth-century academic painters, but it is eminently suitable for quick figure studies, whether indoors or out. Making such studies is the best possible way of learning the figure – this is why they are called studies. They are a kind of visual note-taking, and they print impressions on the mind much more effectively than simply looking.

Anyone interested in painting their fellow humans should carry a sketchbook at all times and perhaps a small watercolor box or a few watercolor crayons.

There are countless opportunities to draw and paint unobserved – on buses, in parks and gardens, beside swimming pools and at sports centers. Never attempt a detailed treatment, but try to grasp the essentials as quickly as you can using any method you find you are happy with. LINE AND WASH is much used for this kind of work, as is a combination of pencil and watercolor. You may find it easier to work in monochrome only, drawing with a brush and ink – an expressive and speedy way of conveying movement or blocking in areas of tone. If you do use color, restrict yourself to the minimum and don't bother about mixing the perfect subtle hue. If you want to use your sketches as reference for a later painting, for instance a group of people in a café or a family picnic, write notes about colors on each sketch.

▶ Jake Sutton, *Circus Cyclist*, 30 × 22¼ IN (76 × 56 CM), WATERCOLOR AND CHARCOAL

Sutton draws with his brush (see BRUSH DRAWING) to convey a marvelous sense of excitement and urgency. The variation in the brushstrokes, some like fine pencil scribbles and others swelling and tapering, seem to increase the momentum of the figure, propelling it forward.

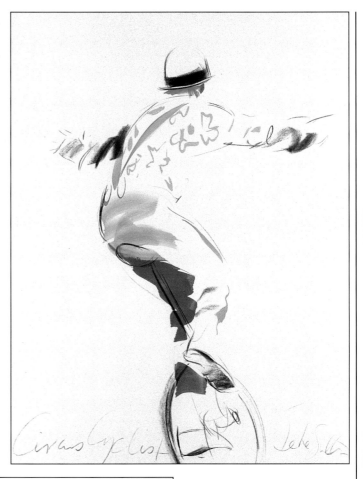

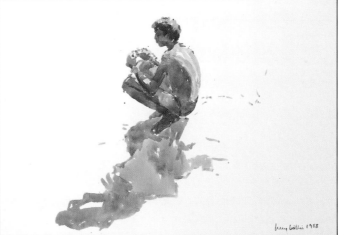

◀ Lucy Willis, *Boy on a Rock*, 10 × 13½ IN (25.4 × 34.3 CM), WATERCOLOR

This lively and spontaneous study conveys a great deal of information in the most economical way possible. The tension of the boy's pose is described extremely accurately by means of broad washes of no more than two or three colors, and a strong sense of a particular light and place is conveyed by the shadow and the little touches of paint at the right suggesting the rock.

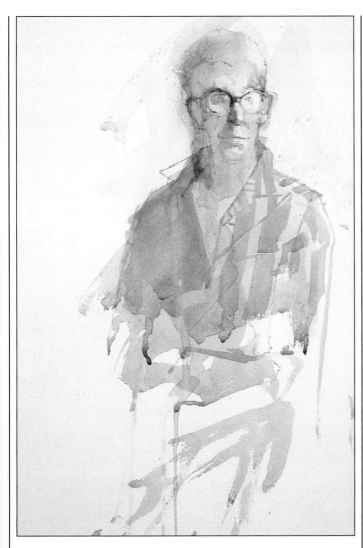

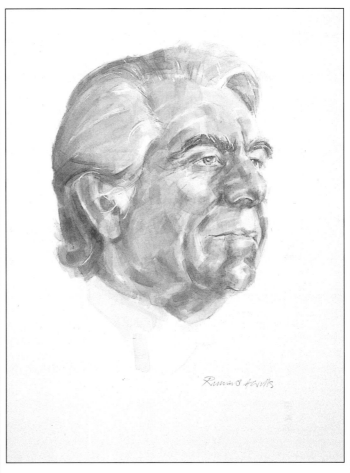

Richard Wills, *Sir Geraint Evans*,
14 × 11 IN (35.6 × 27.9 CM), WATERCOLOR

In this carefully observed and strongly drawn study, a preliminary sketch for an oil portrait, the artist has explored the structure of the head through directional brushstrokes.

Michael McGuinness ARWS, *Sally*,
17¾ × 13⅜ IN (45 × 34 CM), WATERCOLOR AND PENCIL

The lightness and delicacy of the artist's technique, and the way he has applied the paint so that it has dripped down the paper, combine to give a powerful impression of immediacy. Nevertheless, this is a careful and meticulous study, with the shape of the head, the features and the direction and quality of the light 'described with precision.

PORTRAITS

There is no doubt that portraiture is a tricky subject – there are some people who have the knack of capturing faces and expressions without thinking about it, and they are fortunate, but they are not necessarily good artists. However, the idea that painting portraits is particularly difficult in watercolor should be resisted – it is simply not true, and an increasing number of artists are using its subtle qualities to produce fine and sensitive paintings that are also good likenesses.

No good painting, least of all a portrait, can be built on a shaky foundation, so before you begin to paint a face you must understand its structure and be able to draw it convincingly. A good way of getting to know the basics is to use yourself as a model and start with a self-portrait (there are few artists who have not painted themselves at one time or another). You can also practice by drawing from photographs, but, unless they are very good ones, they are not always helpful, as shapes and forms are often obscured by dark shadows and bleached-out highlights. Photographs are more useful in the later stages of a portrait. Most professional portrait painters take them to use as reference for details of clothing and background, but not for the face itself.

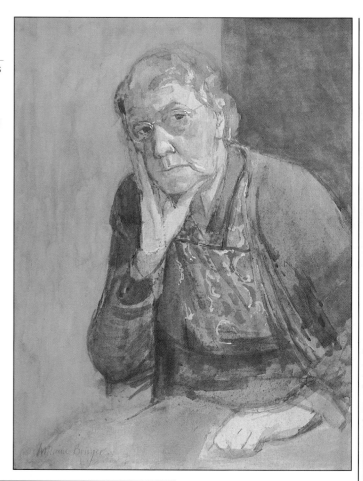

▶ William Bowyer RA, *The Artist's Mother*, 12 × 10 IN (30.5 × 25.4 CM), WATERCOLOR AND GOUACHE

This expressive portrait highlights the importance of composition in figure work. By allowing part of the arm and shoulder to go out of the frame on the right and placing the sitter at a three-quarter angle, the artist has avoided a static, over-symmetrical arrangement and has both balanced and stressed the slant of the figure by the dark vertical of the wall behind. It is a surprisingly small picture, and the paint has been used fairly thinly, with delicate, linear drawing on the face and hand. The lower part of the body and the other hand have been treated more sketchily so that they do not steal attention from the face, always the focal point in a portrait.

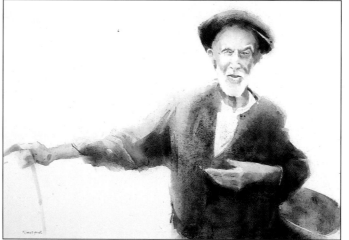

◀ Richard Wills, *Old Man with Bucket*, 30 × 40 IN (76.2 × 101.6 CM), WATERCOLOR AND ACRYLIC

A portrait does not have to be deliberately posed; it can be an informal study of a face seen by chance, as in this studio painting done from location studies. Wills has deliberately created a spontaneous, sketch-like impression by avoiding any background and blurring edges in places to give an impression of movement.

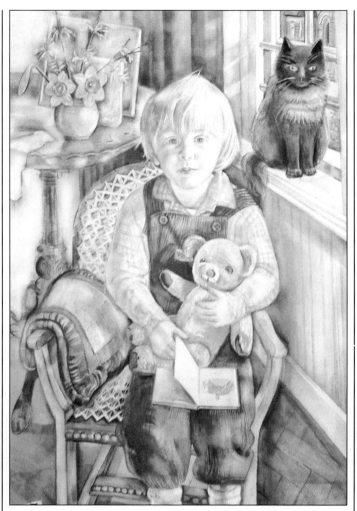

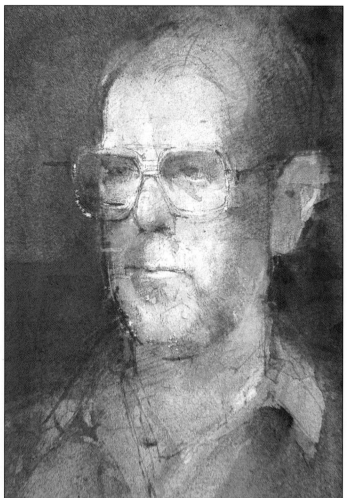

Audrey Macleod, *Portrait of Stephen Ebbett*, 30 × 22 IN (76.2 × 55.9 CM), WATERCOLOR WITH A LITTLE GOUACHE

For commissioned portraits, of which this is one, Macleod paints on Hot Pressed watercolor board, which is smooth enough for detailed work, but tough enough to be scraped if corrections are necessary. She begins establishing the overall design rather than worrying about the likeness and then makes small sketches and transfers them to the board by SQUARING UP. She likes to use surrounding objects to create a sense of identity and here expresses the idea of a very young child through scale – the high table and windowsill with its teddy-bear-sized cat dwarfing the boy's miniature cane-backed chair. The bowl of daffodils, the first spring flowers, adds its own unequivocal message.

Michael McGuinness ARWS, *Bruce*, 9⅞ × 7¾ IN (25 × 19.5 CM), WATERCOLOR AND PENCIL WITH SOME BODY COLOR

McGuinness makes highly effective use of the textures of paint, paper and drawn lines in this taut and finely executed portrait. The brightly lit planes of the face and sharply defined frames of the glasses are thrown into prominence by the soft blurring at the top of the head and around the chin and neck, achieved by a combination of washing out and applying thin white paint to damp paper.

THE FIGURE IN CONTEXT

Because the figure is a complex subject in itself, there is a tendency to lavish all the attention on it and dismiss the setting as unimportant, but few people would think of painting a tree without including the ground from which it grows, and it is just as important to place a person in a specific environment, indoors or out.

Indoor figure paintings have many of the advantages of still life – you can control the lighting, the pose, the background and any other objects, such as furniture, that you may want to include in the composition. Another interesting facet of the subject is that the kind of setting you choose can tell a story about the person. Some of the most successful paintings of figures show people in their place of work or recreation; the marvelous series of ballet dancers by Edgar Degas (1834-1917) are among the best-known examples. So, if you want to paint someone who is fond of reading, think about including books or placing the figure near bookshelves. Degas did this in his portrait of the French writer, Emile Zola.

If you plan a picture of someone who enjoys gardening or some sport, it makes sense to choose an outdoor setting. This is, of course, less controllable, as the light source will change, so you may have to work indoors from sketches made on the spot, but it is a rewarding form of figure painting and well worth experimenting with.

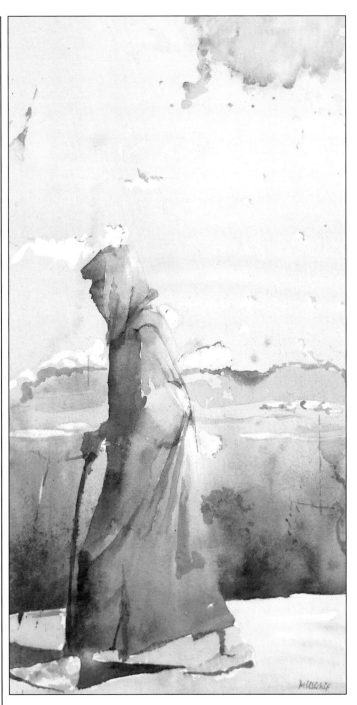

◀ Paul Millichip, *Berber*, 28 × 15 IN (71.1 × 38.1 CM), WATERCOLOR

Here the figure is completely at one with its background, and the painting, although simple in structure, is full of atmosphere, suggesting a whole culture, climate and way of life. Millichip uses a limited palette consisting of no more than six colors, with no premixed greens, browns, grays or violets. He paints very wet on Rough stretched paper, but not WET-IN-WET, waiting for each wash to dry before adding others.

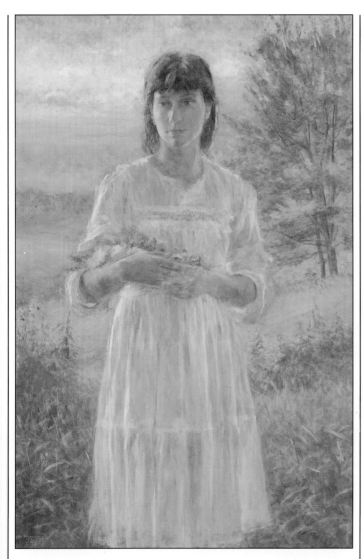

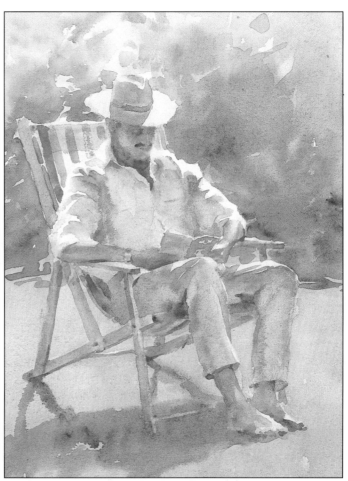

▲ Trevor Chamberlain, *Armchair Gardener*, 12 × 9 IN (30.5 × 22.9 CM), WATERCOLOR

This is a splendid example of a figure painting with an extra dimension. It is a "slice of life" rather than simply a portrayal of a particular person. Everything about it, from the pose of the sitter to the free, spontaneous paint application, conveys the mood of luxurious and contented relaxation on a sunny afternoon.

▲ Jacqueline Rizvi, *Sarah as Perdita*, 35 × 24 IN (88.9 × 61 CM), WATERCOLOR AND BODY COLOR

The choice of an outdoor setting at sunset enhances the period flavor of this delightful portrait, as does Rizvi's delicate and unusual technique. She uses watercolor (not gouache) and opaque white, building up very gradually layer by layer. This picture, on dark brown paper, was worked on over a period of two to three months, with the paint applied very lightly at first with varying admixtures of white. Although it is quite a large painting, she used small brushes throughout. In many areas, transparent touches overlay BODY COLOR so that the underlying colors modify the later ones, as in the GLAZING technique.

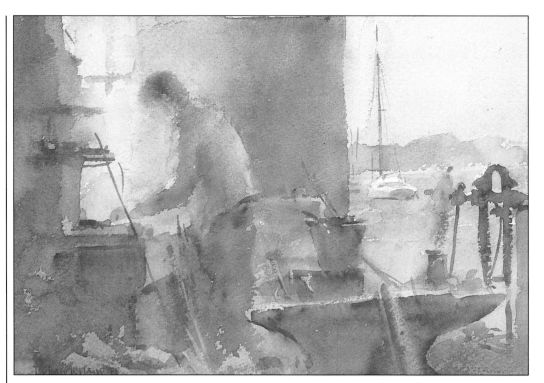

◄ Trevor Chamberlain, *Marine Blacksmith*, 7 × 10 IN (17.8 × 25.4 CM), WATERCOLOR

Chamberlain has concentrated on the light in this scene, creating his soft, diffused effects by working almost entirely WET-IN-WET, with a few small details added at the dry stage. The figure, although the main center of interest, has been treated as broadly as all the other elements, so that the composition has a perfect unity of technique.

► George Large RI, *Hedgecutters*, 12 × 12 IN (30.5 × 30.5 CM), WATERCOLOR AND GOUACHE

This small painting, while stressing abstract and pattern qualities, gives a powerful impression of context. The common activity of the men and the taut shapes of the twisted stems they are working on pull them together as a group, as does the pictorial device of uncovered paper in the outer areas. This is not in fact a toned paper: the flat tint was achieved by laying an overall watercolor wash. Certain areas were then masked (see MASKING) before the gouache was applied.

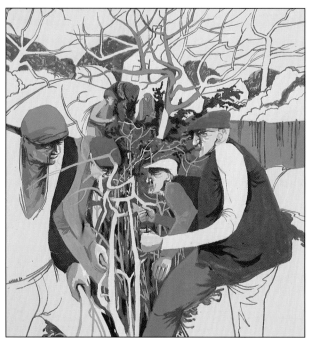

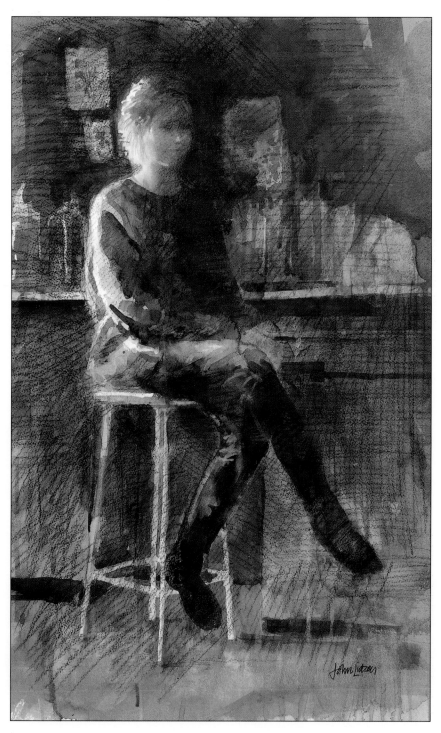

John Lidzey FRSA, *Girl on Stool*, 19 × 13 IN (48.3 × 33 CM), WATERCOLOR, BODY COLOR AND CONTÉ CRAYON

Lidzey, like Chamberlain, has been preoccupied with light, but his tonal contrasts are much stronger than in the painting opposite and his range of colors is considerable. He says that the technique he has used here was inspired by that used by Georges Seurat in his magnificent tonal drawings. The underlayer is pure watercolor, used wet, as in most of his paintings. The highlights were reinforced with white gouache, and the picture was built up with successive layers of cross-hatching with black conté crayon. The carefully varied crayon lines have been broken up by the grain of the paper to create the effect of a soft veil, which enhances the brilliance and depth of the colors below, as in the SCUMBLING technique. This is an inspiring and completely successful use of MIXED MEDIA, with a satisfying harmony between paint and line.

GROUPS

Although people are seen more often in groups than singly, particularly outdoors, multiple figure compositions tend to be avoided by all but the most experienced painters. This is hardly surprising – one figure surely provides enough problems. However, groups are not only an exciting and challenging subject, they are in some ways easier than single figures. If you are painting a family picnic or people sunbathing on a beach, for example, you can treat them more broadly than you would a portrait, concentrating on an overall impression of colors and forms. Such paintings, though, usually have to be done from sketches rather than completed on the spot, as people have a way of packing up and going home just as you have got out your paints.

When you come to compose a group painting from sketches of individual figures, you may find that it is not easy to relate them either to each other or to your chosen setting (they may all be drawn to different scales), so try to regard your sketches as the first steps in a planned painting and make them as informative as possible. Avoid drawing figures in isolation, always indicating the foreground and background as well, if only in broad terms. This will provide a frame of reference and help you to avoid the pitfall of inconsistent scale. You could easily find that you have placed a group in front of a building or tree that is disproportionately small or large. Pay attention also to the lighting and the way the shadows fall, and make notes about the colors.

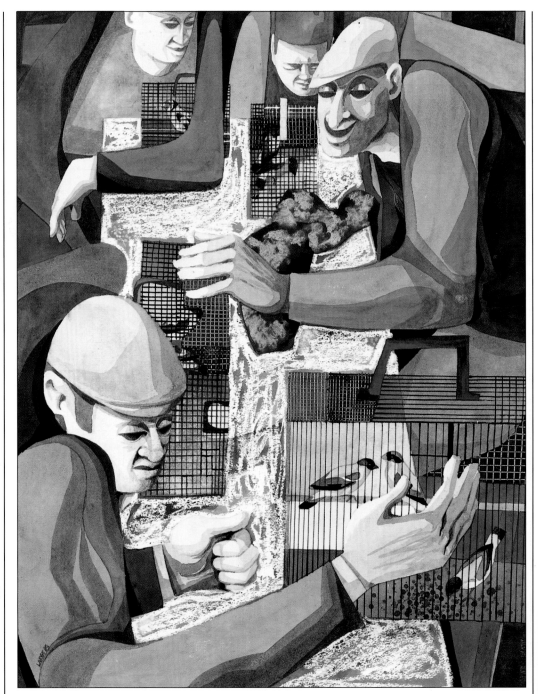

◀ George Large RI, *Finches*, 26 × 20 IN (66 × 50.8 CM), WATERCOLOR

As in his painting on page 112, Large has stylized his group of figures to form a powerful, semi-abstract composition, using a combination of different shapes and textures to give additional movement and interest. The sinuous, flowing lines on the arms of the two main figures on the left and right are counterpointed by the rectangular grids of the bird cages, while the broken color in the center, achieved by the WAX RESIST method, contrasts with the flat areas of solid color. Some areas were blotted with kitchen paper, and the thin lines were cut with a knife blade or scratched with the point of a pair of compasses.

▶ Francis Bowyer, *Changing for a Swim*, 15 × 15 IN (38.1 × 38.1 CM), WATERCOLOR AND BODY COLOR (GOUACHE WHITE)

This charming painting makes the task of painting a group seem less daunting. However, although the treatment of the children is no more detailed than that of the beach, the poses are very carefully observed, and this, together with the suggestion of features on the face of the foreground boy, holds our interest. Bowyer has given a marvelous unity to the composition by repeating versions of the same colors – violet-blues, yellows and warm pinks – throughout the painting.

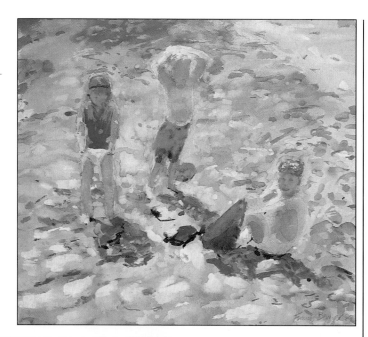

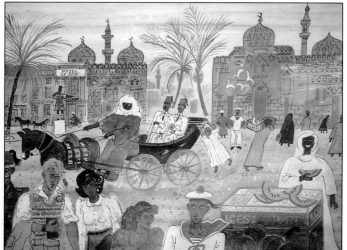

◀ Doreen Osborne, *Durrell's Alexandria*, 22¼ × 15¾ IN (56.5 × 40 CM), GOUACHE AND PEN AND INK

Like Large (opposite), Osborne has stressed the pattern quality of her subject, but in a completely different way. Although she has deliberately flattened the perspective to give a one-dimensional rather than recessive effect, she has treated each figure in some detail, with delightful touches of humor. Her painting is a good example of the LINE AND WASH technique used with great assurance. The line drawing adds to the lively effect but is never allowed to dominate the color.

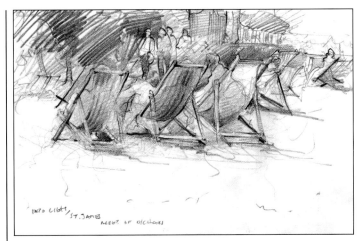

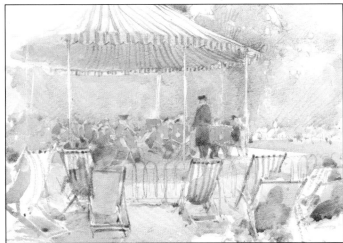

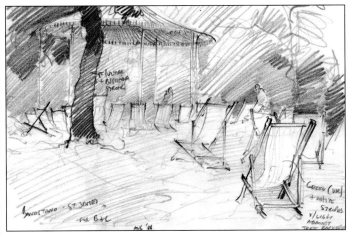

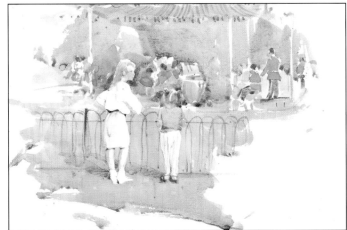

David Curtis works directly from his subject whenever possible, and for a complex subject like this one he makes a series of location sketches and completes the painting in the studio. The secret of working successfully from sketches is to know in advance the kind of visual reference you will need and make sure that your sketches provide it. By using a combination of quick watercolors made in a small sketchbook and pencil drawings with notes about color, Curtis has provided himself with an ample storehouse of information. Notice that he never draws or paints figures in isolation; all the sketches are complete notes about the scene he intends to paint.

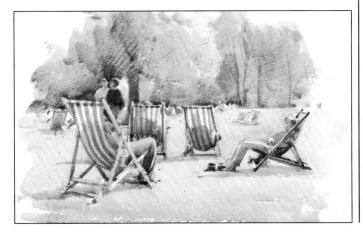

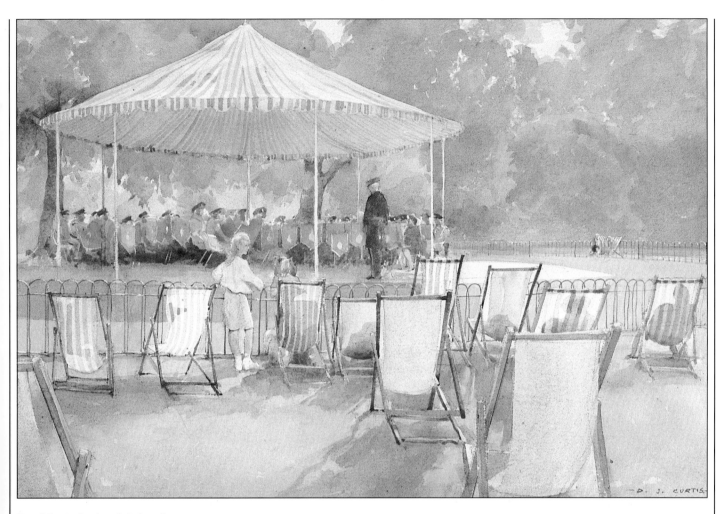

David Curtis, *Bandstand, St. James's Park*, 15 × 22 IN (38.1 × 55.9 CM), WATERCOLOR WITH A LITTLE ACRYLIC

Using the sketches shown opposite as the basis, Curtis made a careful preparatory drawing on stretched paper, after which he applied LIQUID MASK to areas such as the awning and poles. He likes to work freely, maintaining the fresh, translucent quality of the paint, and masking prevents laboring the paint when taking it around small, intricate shapes. Some of the highlight areas in the grass were achieved by mixing a small amount of titanium white acrylic with lemon yellow and phthalocyanine green watercolor, which he finds increases the intensity of color.

Flowers, with their rich and varied array of glowing colors, their intricate forms and delicate structures, are an irresistible subject for painters. What is more, unlike the human and animal world, they do remain still for long enough to be painted. There are many different pictorial approaches to this branch of painting, all eminently suited to the medium of watercolor. Flowers can be painted in their natural habitats or indoors as still life arrangements, they can be treated singly or in mixed groups, they can be painted in fine detail or broadly and impressionistically.

Flower painting in history

Today flower paintings are hugely popular and avidly collected, and good flower painters can command high prices for their work. This is a relatively recent trend in terms of art history, however. In the Medieval and Renaissance periods, when scientists were busily cataloguing herbs and plants, the main reason for drawing and painting them was to convey information, and a host of illustrated books, called herbals, began to appear, explaining the medicinal properties of various plants and flowers. Many of the drawings were crude and inaccurate, but there were notable exceptions where the illustrators seemed to have worked from life, and these were the forerunners in a continuing and still flourishing tradition of botanical illustration.

The concept of painting flowers for their own sake owes more to the Flemish and Dutch still-life schools than any other. The Netherlandish artists had always been more interested in realism and the accurate rendering of everyday subjects than their Italian and French counterparts and, throughout the sixteenth, seventeenth and eighteenth centuries, they vied with one another to produce ever more elaborate flower pieces, with every petal described in minute detail. Artists have been painting flowers ever since, and, although critics in France regarded flower pieces and still life as inferior art forms, even there they had become respectable by the mid-nineteenth century.

Working methods

Because flowers are so intricate and complex, there is always a temptation, whether you are painting them indoors or in the garden, to describe every single petal, bud and leaf in minute detail. In some cases there is nothing wrong with this (for anyone intending to make botanical studies, it is the only possible approach), but too much detail in an arranged flower piece or an outdoor painting can look unnatural and static, and there is also the ever-present danger of overworking the paint and losing the clarity of the colors.

Before you start a painting, make some hard decisions about which particular qualities you are most interested in. If you are inspired by the glowing mixture of colors in a summer flowerbed, treat the subject broadly, perhaps starting by working WET-IN-WET, adding crisper definition in places so that you have a combination of HARD AND SOFT EDGES.

Always remember that flowers are living things, fragile and delicate, so don't kill them off in your painting – try to suit the medium to the subject. You can make a fairly detailed study, while still retaining a sense of freedom and movement, by using the LINE AND WASH technique, combining drawn lines (pen or pencil) with fluid washes. Never allow the line to dominate the color, however, because if you get carried away and start to outline every petal you will destroy the effect. MASKING fluid can be helpful if you want to be able to work freely around small highlights, and attractive effects can be created by the WAX RESIST method.

Finally, even a badly overworked watercolor can often be saved by turning it into a MIXED-MEDIA painting, so before committing hours of work to the wastebasket, consider whether you might be able to redeem it by using pastel, acrylic or opaque gouache on top of the watercolor.

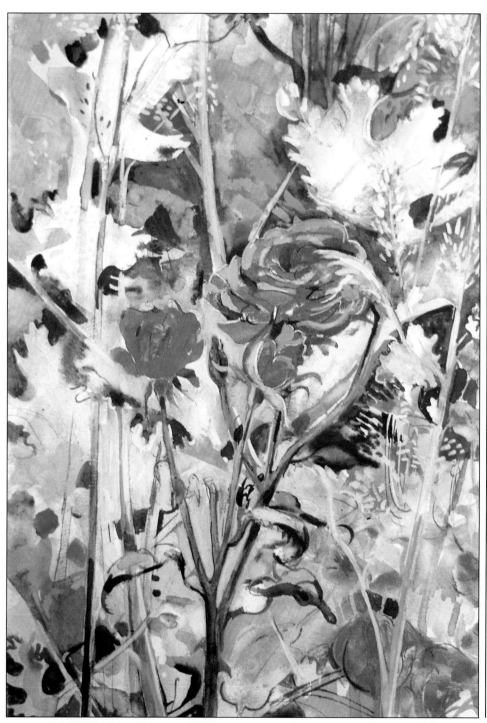

Audrey Macleod, *Red Roses in a Flowerbed*, APPROX. 15 × 11 IN (38.1 × 27.9 CM), WATERCOLOR WITH ADDED GOUACHE

One of Macleod's primary concerns, whether she is painting flowers or portraits, is the overall design of her paintings. Here she has used the different characteristics of the plants to create a strong pattern in which soft, round shapes are contrasted with spikier, more angular ones. Parts of the paper have been left bare to stand as highlights, but the tiny clusters of leaves on the right have been lightly touched in with opaque paint.

SINGLE SPECIMENS

The most obvious example of flowers and plants treated singly rather than as part of a group are botanical paintings. Botanical studies have been made since pre-Renaissance times and are still an important branch of specialized illustration. Many of the best of these drawings and paintings are fine works of art, but their primary aim is to record precise information about a particular species. For the botanical illustrator, pictorial charms are secondary bonuses, but artists, who are more concerned with these than with scientific accuracy, can exploit them in a freer, more painterly way.

However, this is an area where careful drawing and observation is needed. You may be able to get away with imprecise drawing for a broad impression of a flower group, but a subject that is to stand on its own must be convincingly rendered. Looking at illustrated books and photographs can help you to acquire background knowledge of flower and leaf shapes, but it goes without saying that you will also need to draw from life – constantly.

Most flowers can be simplified into basic shapes, such as circles or bells. These, like everything else, are affected by perspective, so that a circle turned away from you becomes an ellipse. It is much easier to draw flowers if you establish these main shapes before you begin to describe each petal or stamen.

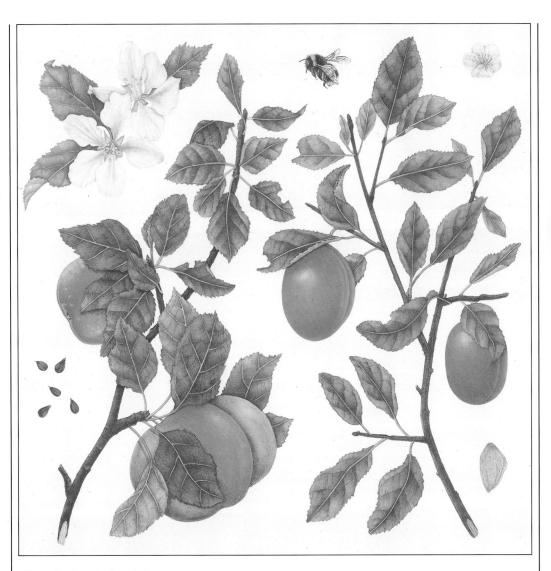

Sharon Beeden, *Apples and Plums*, 10 × 10 IN (25.8 × 25 CM), WATERCOLOR

This artist is a professional botanical illustrator and the painting was one of a series for a book. Its subject was the introduction of fruit, vegetables and herbs to Britain through the centuries, and before she could begin her work, Beeden had to carry out time-consuming research to find old varieties from various periods of history. Each of these specimens was drawn from life, with the blossoms redrawn from sketchbook studies done earlier in the year. The composition was worked out on tracing paper and then transferred to the working paper.

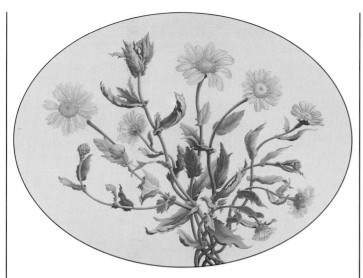

Jean Canter SGFA, *Corn Marigolds*,
9½ × 13 IN (24.1 × 33 CM), OVAL,
WATERCOLOR WITH A LITTLE WHITE
GOUACHE

The oval format chosen for this
delightful study gives it a rather
Victorian flavor. The artist has
created a strong feeling of life and
movement, with the sinuously
curving stems and leaves
seeming to grow outward
toward the boundary of the frame.

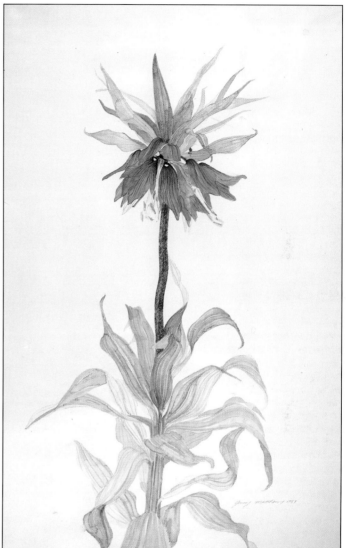

Jenny Matthews, *Crown Imperial*,
WATERCOLOR

The shapes, structures and
colors of some flowers are so
fascinating that they seem to
demand the right to shine out
proud and alone, without the
need for background, foreground
or other diversions. This is
certainly the case here, and the
artist has made the most of her
chosen specimen by her
sensitive but tough use of linear
brushmarks over delicate
washes.

INDOOR ARRANGEMENTS

The great advantage of painting cut flowers indoors is that you can control the set-up and work more or less at your leisure – at any rate until the blooms fade and die. The main problem is that flowers can look over-arranged, destroying the natural, living quality that is the subject's greatest charm. Always try to make them look as natural as possible, allowing some to overlap others, and placing them at different heights, with some of the heads turned away from and others toward you, as they would appear when growing in a flowerbed.

Give equally careful thought to the overall color scheme – of the flowers themselves, the vase you put them in and the background. Too great a mixture of colors can lead to a muddled painting that has no sense of unity because each hue is fighting for attention with its neighbor. The best flower paintings are often those with one predominant color, such as white, blue or yellow, with those in the background and foreground orchestrated to provide just the right element of contrast.

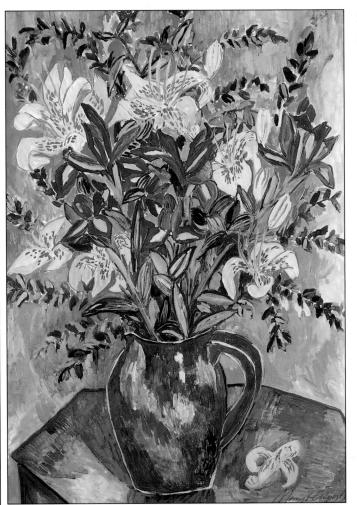

Mary Tempest, *Tiger Lilies*, 20 × 16 IN (50.8 × 40.6 CM), GOUACHE

The marvelously vivid color scheme of this painting has been planned with great care, with the bright yellows and violets repeated throughout. These two colors are complementaries, colors which enhance one another when used together. Tempest has also brought in the other two main complementaries, red and green, so that the whole painting positively vibrates. Although she has placed the vase of flowers centrally, she has avoided a static look by first arranging the flowers so that they reach up on the left, following the curve of the jug, and second by choosing an irregular shape in the foreground.

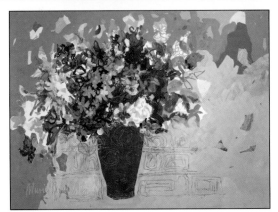

Muriel Pemberton, *Bright Garden Bouquet*, 18 × 24¾ IN (45.7 × 62.9 CM), WATERCOLOR, BODY COLOR, INK AND PASTEL

Here the off-center placing of the vase and the way the flowers lean to the left give a rhythm to the composition, leading the viewer's eye around it from one area to another. Pemberton's technique is equally lively and varied. She makes no preliminary drawing, but begins painting at once, working on the background and flowers at the same time, and building up texture and depth of color with successive layers of paint, pastel and ink. In some places, she applies thin washes over thick, while in others, transparent watercolor is allowed to show through opaque paint, creating a fragile, translucent effect.

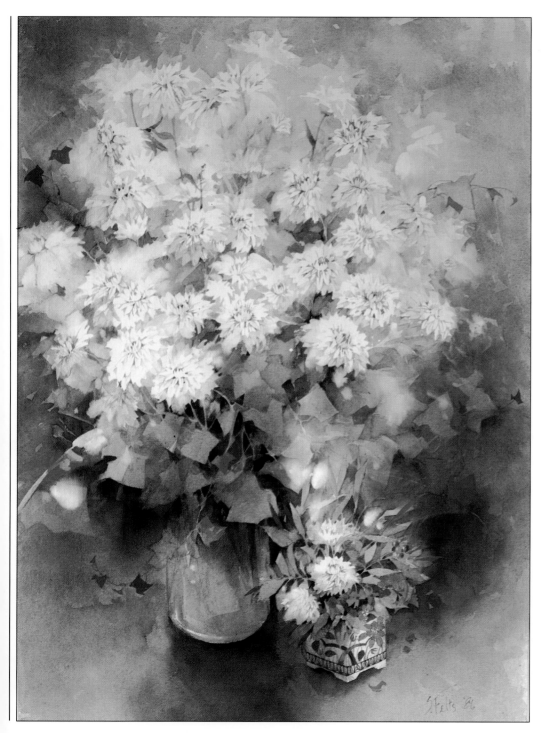

Shirley Felts, *Chrysanthemums with Chinese Vase*, 29 × 21 IN (73.7 × 53.3 CM), WATERCOLOR

One of the considerations in arranging a flower group must be the characteristics of the flowers themselves. A bloom with strong and dramatic shapes, such as a lily, could look exciting by itself or in a small group, but multi-flowered chrysanthemums are best treated as a mass, as here, because that is how they grow. The group is nevertheless very carefully arranged, with a slight asymmetry, and the leaves trailed over the vase on the left to add foreground interest. The little touches of red in the smaller group provide the perfect touch of contrast to the delicate white and green color scheme.

COMPOSITION

A group of flowers tastefully arranged in an attractive vase always looks enticing – that, after all, is the point of putting them there – but it may not make a painting in itself. Placing a vase of flowers in the center of the picture, with no background or foreground interest, is not usually the best way to make the most of the subject – though there are some notable exceptions to this rule. So you will have to think about what other elements you might include to make the composition more interesting without detracting from the main subject.

One of the most-used compositional devices is that of placing the vase asymmetrically and painting from an angle so that the back of the tabletop forms a diagonal instead of horizontal line. Diagonals are a powerful weapon in the artist's armory, as they help to lead the eye in to the center of the picture, while horizontal lines do the opposite.

One of the difficulties with flower groups is that the vase leaves a blank space at the bottom of the picture area. This can sometimes be dealt with by using a cast shadow as part of the composition, or you can scatter one or two blooms or petals beneath or to one side of the vase, thus creating a relationship between foreground and focal point.

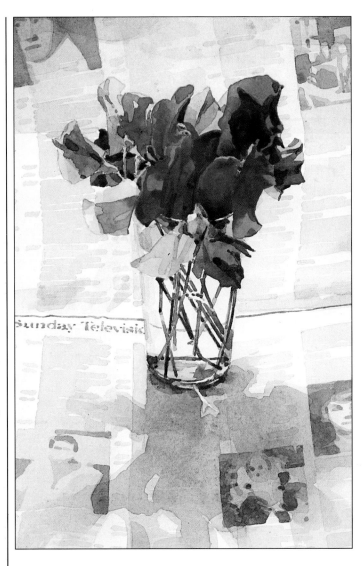

Ronald Jesty, *Sweet Peas in a Tumbler,* 12 × 8 IN (30.5 × 20.3 CM), WATERCOLOR

Jesty's compositions are always bold, and often surprising, as this one is. We are so conditioned by the idea of "correct" settings for flower pieces and still lifes that the idea of placing a vase of flowers on a newspaper seems almost heretical. But it works perfectly, with the newspaper images providing just the right combination of geometric shapes and dark tones to balance the forms and colors of the sweet peas.

▶ Geraldine Girvan, *Studio Mantelpiece*, 22³⁄₈ × 26 IN (57 × 66 CM), GOUACHE

Girvan has used a combination of diagonals and verticals to lead the eye into and around the picture. Our eye follows the line of the mantelpiece, but instead of going out of the frame on the left, it is led upward by the side of the picture frame and then downward through the tall flowers to the glowing heart of the picture – the daffodils. She has avoided isolating this area of bright yellow by using a slightly muted version of it in the reflection behind and has further unified the composition by repeating the reds from one area to another.

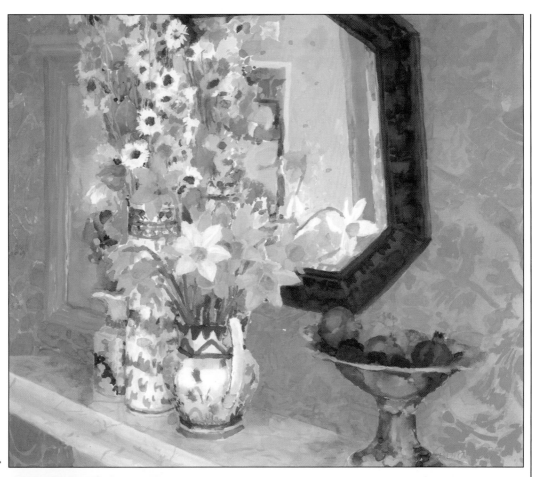

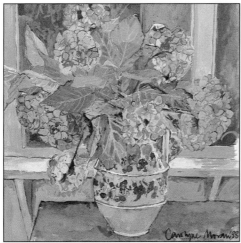

◀ Carolyne Moran, *Hydrangeas in a Blue and White Jug*, 10¹⁄₂ × 10¹⁄₂ IN (26.7 × 26.7 CM), GOUACHE

Here the flowers occupy an uncompromisingly central position, with the rounded shapes of the blooms and vase dominating the picture, but counterpointed by the rectangles formed by the background window frame. Interestingly, we do not immediately perceive this painting as square because the verticals give it an upward thrust. The artist has made cunning use of intersecting diagonals in the foreground to break up the predominantly geometric grid, and has linked the flowers to the background by using the same blue under the windowsill. There is considerable overpainting on the flower heads, as they kept changing color while the artist worked – one of the flower painter's occupational hazards.

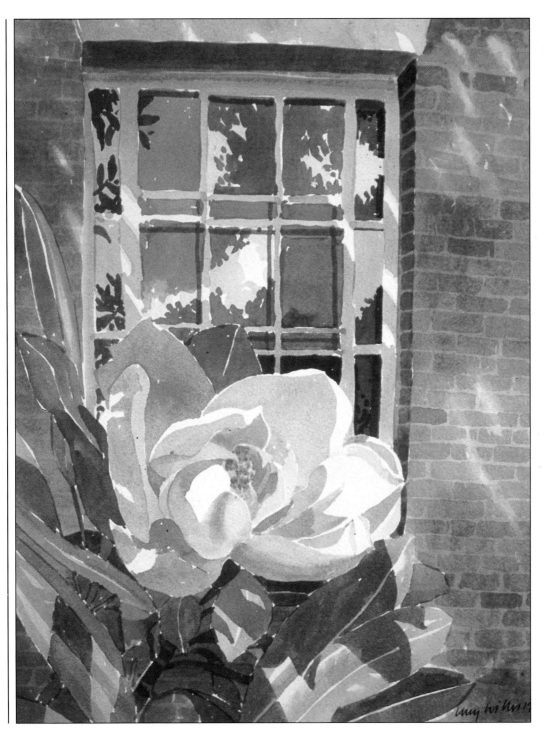

Lucy Willis *Magnolia and Window,*
15 × 11 IN (38.1 × 27.9 CM), WATERCOLOR

This lovely painting, quiet but strong, shows how a simple composition can be as effective, or even more so, as a complex one. Willis, who works directly from life whenever she can and claims to paint no more than what she sees, nevertheless has a highly selective eye and has chosen the perfect background for the sensuous forms of the magnolia. She likes a fairly limited palette and here has used only a small range of colors to produce a perfectly balanced and unified composition.

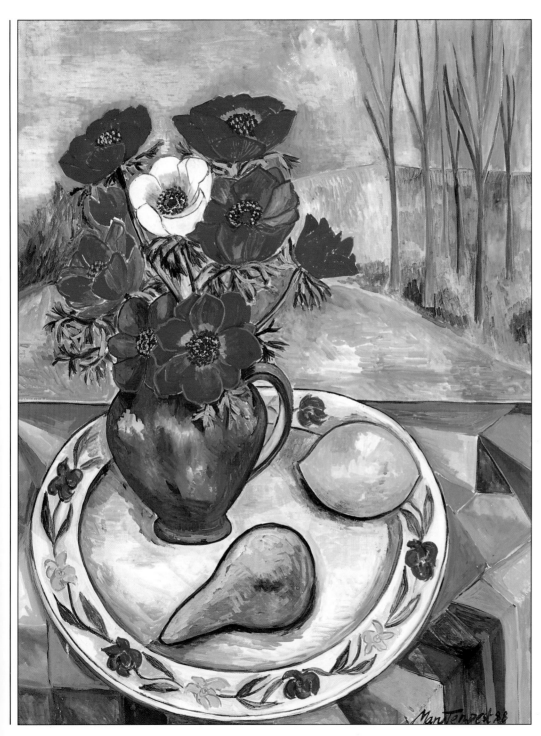

Mary Tempest, *Anemones,* 30 × 22 IN (76.2 × 55.9 CM), GOUACHE

This bold, highly patterned composition, with the emphasis on carefully distributed areas of bright color, is somewhat reminiscent of Henri Matisse. Although the painting is predominantly two-dimensional, there is a considerable degree of modeling in the fruit, jug and flowers, which guarantees their place as the focal point of the painting. Tempest uses gouache almost like oil paint, and for this painting she has mixed it with an impasto medium (Aquapasto) in order to build it up thickly.

NATURAL HABITAT

Oddly, the terms "flower painting" makes us think of cut flowers rather than growing ones, perhaps because most of the paintings of this genre that we see in art galleries are of arranged rather than outdoor subjects. Flowers, however, are at their best in their natural surroundings, and painting them outdoors, whether they are wild specimens in woods, fields or city wastelands or cultivated blooms in the backyard, is both rewarding and enjoyable.

It can, however, present more problems than painting arranged groups indoors, because you cannot control the background or the lighting, and you may have to adopt a ruthlessly selective approach to achieve a satisfactory composition.

You will also have a changing light source to contend with. As the sun moves across the sky, the colors and tones can change dramatically, and a leaf or flower head that was previously obscured by shadow will suddenly be spot-lit so that you can no longer ignore its presence. The best way to deal with this problem, if you think a painting may take more than a few hours to complete, is to work in two or three separate sessions at the same time of day or to make several quick studies that you can then combine into a painting in the studio.

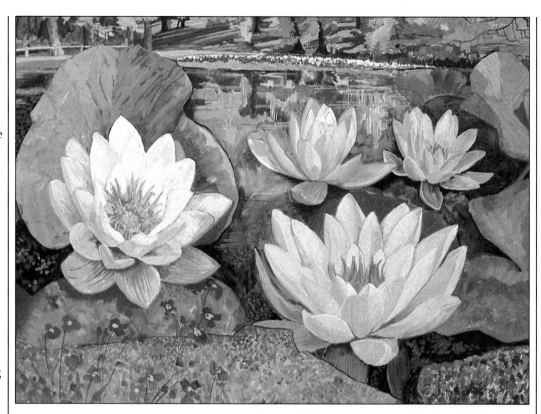

▲ Norma Jameson RBA, ROI, *Waterlilies*, 12 × 16 IN (30.5 × 40.6 CM), GOUACHE AND WATERCOLOR ON CARTRIDGE PAPER

Jameson works partly from life and partly from slides and says that the former gives the necessary element of spontaneity to her work while the photographic studies provide the equally necessary time for consideration. For specific flower forms, she takes numerous slides, from different angles and positions and in close-up, using the camera like a sketchbook and then distilling what interests her most when she begins to paint.

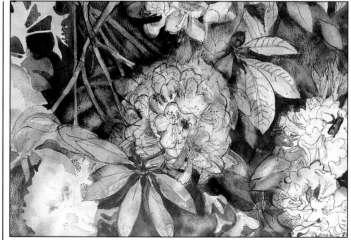

▶ Juliette Palmer, *Pink Roses, White Phlox*, 15 × 11 IN (38.1 × 27.9 CM), WATERCOLOR

This is the artist's own backyard and a spell of good weather gave her the unusual luxury of painting on the spot for as long as she liked. Like Macleod, whose painting is shown opposite, Palmer has a strong sense of design and composition and says that as she observes a subject, various elements will fall into place to form a satisfactory whole. She is not interested in dramatic effects but, as she herself puts it, "elegance of line and the delight of the particular bound in gentle relationships of color and tone."

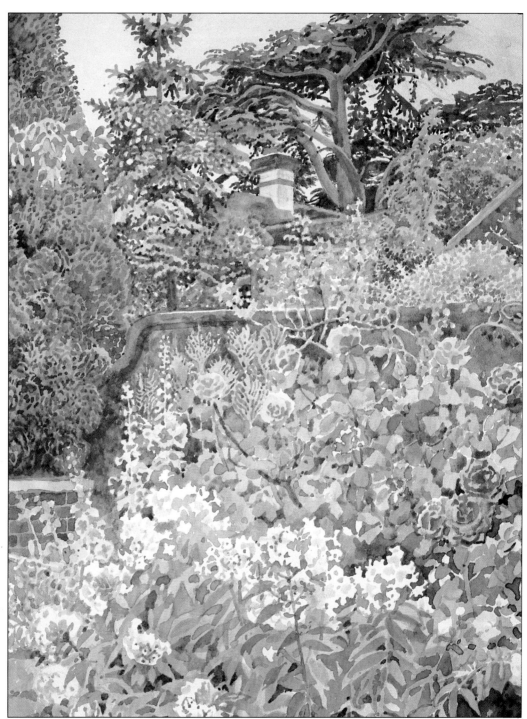

◀ Audrey Macleod, *Rhododendrons in Dulwich Park*, APPROX, 11 × 16 IN (27.9 × 40.6 CM), WATERCOLOR AND PEN DRAWING

Macleod has used the shapes and forms of the plants to create a composition with a strong two-dimensional pattern quality. To express the delicacy of the subject, she has given careful consideration to the medium, exploiting the LINE AND WASH technique to set up an effective hard/soft contrast and retaining the transparency of the paint by touching in the color lightly to the edges of the forms. She has also washed down some areas to soften the color, an effect which can be seen behind and below the central bloom. In contrast, the delicate pen lines, made with watered-down mauve and gray inks, stand out with crisp clarity.

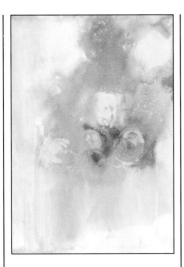

1 John Blockley is not concerned with botanical exactitude but with the massed shape of the group – shimmering with color, translucent and transient. He thinks in terms of the light coming through the flowers and finds he can best express this by working spontaneously, wet-in-wet, in a continual juggling process of adding and removing color. Here he begins by washing over the paper with a 2in (5cm) housepainter's brush and water slightly tinted with pink and blue. This overall wash is then strengthened with varied color and then strengthened again in certain areas. As the sheen begins to disappear, indicating that the paint is beginning to dry, he flicks droplets of water into it, after which he immerses the paper in water and leaves it to dry.

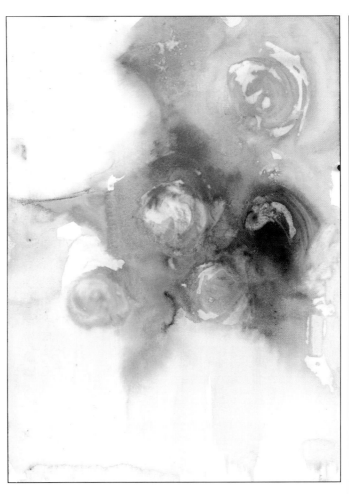

2 The paper is once again dampened with clean water, and fairly stiff paint is brushed into it in roughly circular shapes, but with no attempt to define details. Droplets of water are again flicked into the wash as it begins to dry and the immersion process is repeated, so that the wet parts diffuse to become soft-edged highlights. Blockley does not stretch his paper – he says he would find the effort inhibiting – but uses one tough enough to withstand the amount of water he subjects it to.

3 In the final stages (far right), the color is again strengthened, and dark shades washed in, especially in the top and bottom left corners. A flat-ended brush is used to flick in the leaves, and a few lines are drawn with a brush handle dipped in undiluted paint. Most of the painting was done with the large housepainter's brush, but for smaller details Blockley uses a worn bristle brush. The bristles create lines and striations in the paint surface, which make an interesting contrast to the large, more fluid areas.

He likes the wet-in-wet method because of its immediacy and enjoys the fluidity of the paint dripping down the paper, but accepts the fact that his failure rate is high because of its unpredictability.

▶ The first washes establish the middle tones. Color is then added for the darks and lifted out for the highlights, giving the soft, diffused effect seen in the detail opposite.

▶ This detail from the finished painting shows the interesting textures and hard/soft contrasts achieved by the combination of washing down and drawing with the edge of the brush and a brush handle.

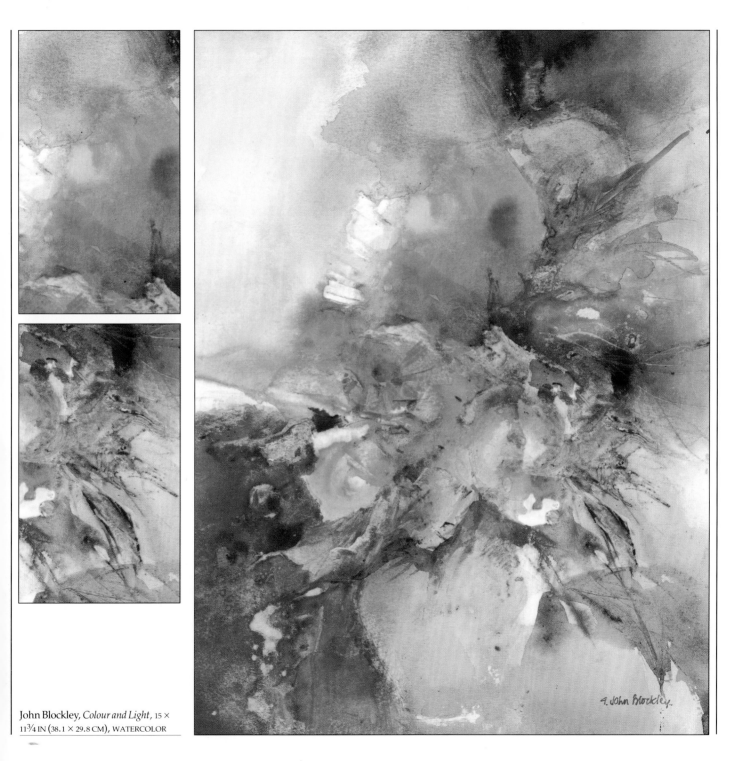

John Blockley, *Colour and Light*, 15 ×
11¾ IN (38.1 × 29.8 CM), WATERCOLOR

Whatever the medium used, landscape is among the most popular of all painting subjects, and among watercolorists, particularly amateurs, it ranks as the undisputed number one. One of the reasons for this is the common belief that it is easier than other subjects. Many who would never attempt a figure painting or flower study turn with relief to country scenes, feeling them to be less exacting and thus more enjoyable. This is perfectly understandable, and even quite a reasonable assumption, after all, it often does not matter too much if the shape of a mountain or tree is not a precise translation of reality. However, a painting will certainly be marred by poor composition or mishandled colors – these things always matter, whatever the subject.

The best landscapes are painted by artists who have chosen to paint the land because they love it, and use the full range of their skills to express their responses to it, not by those who choose it as an easy option.

Direct observation

Another factor that separates the really good from the just-adequate is knowledge, not of painting methods – though this is necessary, too – but of the subject itself. This is why most landscape painters work outdoors whenever they can. Sometimes they only make preliminary sketches, but often they will complete whole paintings on the spot. This, of course, is not always easy, but even if you only jot down some rapid color impressions, it is still the best way to get the feel of a landscape.

If you use photographs as a starting point – and many professional artists do take photos as a back-up to sketches – restrict yourself to a part of the countryside you know well and have perhaps walked through at different times of the year so that you have absorbed its atmosphere. Nature's effects are transient and cannot be captured adequately by the camera, so if you try to copy a photograph of a scene you are not familiar with, your painting is likely to have the same frozen-in-time look as the photograph.

Composition

Nor should you attempt to copy nature itself: painting is about finding pictorial equivalents for the real world, not reproducing it in precise detail. This means that you have to make choices and decide how much to put in or leave out and think about whether you might usefully exaggerate a certain feature in the interests of art. For instance you might emphasize the feeling of space in a wide expanse of countryside by putting in some small figures in the middle distance, or convey the impression of misty light by suppressing detail and treating the whole scene in broad washes.

The medium

Watercolor seems to be almost tailor-made for landscape painting, as its fluidity and translucency are perfectly suited to creating impressions of light and atmosphere. Light and portable, it has always been popular for outdoor work, but until you have gained some practice, it can be tricky to handle as a sketching medium. There is always the temptation to make changes in order to keep up with the changing light, and if there is too much overworking, the colors lose their freshness, defeating the aim of the exercise. There are ways of dealing with this, however. One is to work on a small scale, using the paint with a minimum of water so that you cut down the time spent waiting for each layer to dry, and another is to work rapidly WET-IN-WET, concentrating on putting down impressions rather than literal descriptions. If watercolor proves too frustrating, you may find gouache a good substitute. It can be used thinly, just like watercolor, but dries much more quickly and can be built up in opaque layers for the later stages.

If you intend to complete a whole painting on location rather than just making sketches, it is a good idea, if the subject is at all complex, to make the preparatory drawing the day before. Once the foundation is laid, you can approach the painting with confidence the following day.

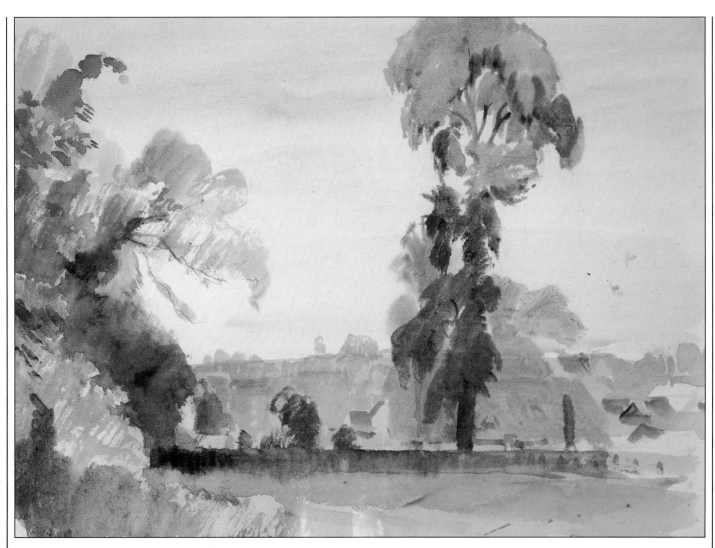

Charles Knight RWS, ROI, *Tall Tree and Buildings*, 11 × 15 IN (27.9 × 38.1 CM), WATERCOLOR

Knight's atmospheric landscapes are marked by the economy with which he describes his shapes, forms and textures. He never uses two brushstrokes when one will suffice. Here he has painted freely but decisively in a combination of WET-IN-WET, WET-ON-DRY and DRY BRUSH, leaving little specks of the paper showing through the paint in places to hint at texture.

TREES AND FOLIAGE

Trees, whether covered in a luxurious blanket of green in summer, glowing with warm reds and yellows in the fall or stark and bare in winter, are among the most enticing of all landscape features.

Unfortunately, they are not the easiest of subjects to paint, particularly when foliage obscures their basic structure and makes its own complex patterns of light and shade.

To paint a leafy tree successfully, it is usually necessary to simplify it to some extent. Start by establishing the broad shape of the tree, noting its dominant characteristics, such as the width of the trunk in relation to the height and spread of the branches. Avoid becoming bogged down in detail, defining individual shapes in a manner that does not detract from the main mass. If you try to give equal weight and importance to every separate clump of foliage, you will create a jumpy, fragmented effect. Look at the subject with your eyes half closed and you will see that some parts of the tree, those in shadow or further away from you, will read as one broad color area, while the sunlit parts and those nearer to you will show sharp contrasts of tone and color.

A useful technique for highlighting areas where you want to avoid hard lines is that of LIFTING OUT, while SPONGE PAINTING is a good way of suggesting the lively broken-color effect of foliage. DRY BRUSH is another favored technique, particularly well suited to winter trees with their delicate, hazy patterns created by clusters of tiny twigs.

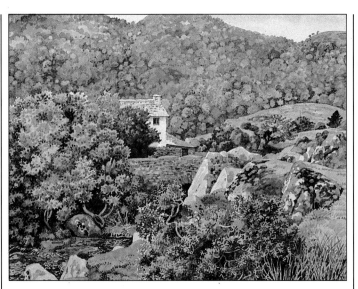

Juliette Palmer, *Fell and River*, APPROX. 14 × 14 IN (35.6 × 35.6 CM), WATERCOLOR

It is interesting to compare this painting with the other on this page, as both artists work WET-ON-DRY, but with very different results. Palmer uses countless tiny brushstrokes to build up a variety of textures, giving her paintings an almost embroidered quality. She reserves HIGHLIGHTS with great skill and care, for example, the blades of grass and light-against-dark leaves in the right foreground were achieved by painstakingly painting around each shape. The painting was done in the studio from an on-the-spot sketch, as the fading evening light did not allow enough time to complete it there and then.

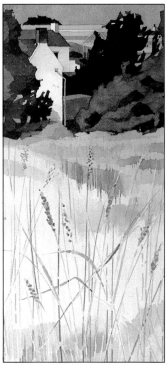

Ronald Jesty RBA, *Torteval, Guernsey*, 13 × 6 IN (33 × 15.2 CM), WATERCOLOR

Jesty also paints WET-ON-DRY, but individual brushstrokes are only visible in the foreground. He has set up an exciting contrast by using very flat paint for the large, strong shapes in the background and delicate BRUSH DRAWING for the slender, spiky grasses. The unusual tall, thin format stresses the vertical emphasis of the composition.

▶ Charles Knight RWS, ROI
Rickmansworth Canal, 11 × 15 IN
(27.9 × 38.1 CM), WATERCOLOR AND PENCIL
ON TINTED PAPER

Knight's expressive landscapes are reminiscent of English eighteenth-century watercolorists, and, like them, he owes his deceptively simple-looking effects to a thorough knowledge of the medium and a willingness to experiment with it. He has used a variety of techniques, including DRY BRUSH, BRUSH DRAWING and WAX RESIST on the trees, but these technical "tricks" are never allowed to dominate the painting. The overall color key is influenced by the use of the TONED GROUND, which is left uncovered in large parts of the composition.

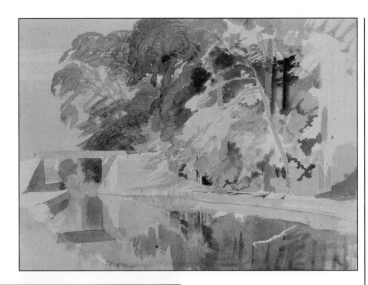

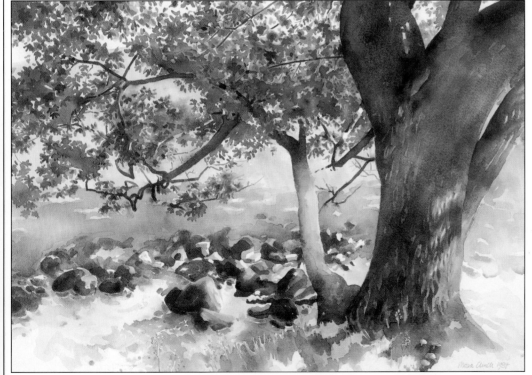

◀ Moira Clinch, *Lakeland Tree*,
13 × 18 IN (33 × 45.7 CM), WATERCOLOR

In this painting, Clinch has used a combination of WET-IN-WET and WET-ON-DRY, which gives excitement and variety to her paint surface. She has also suggested texture on the large tree trunk by exploiting the granular effect caused by overlaying washes (see WASH TEXTURE). She has cleverly prevented the eye from being taken out of the picture with the swing of the large branch on the right by blurring the paint, so that we focus on the crisply delineated area in the center.

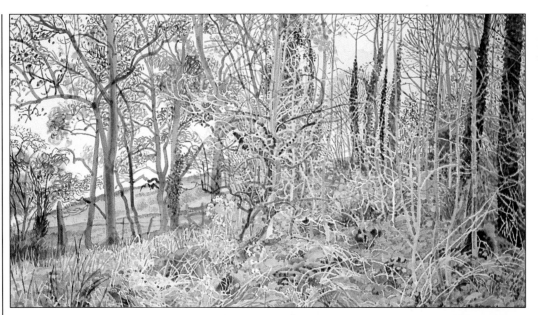

◀ Juliette Palmer, *Wood Edge,*
APPROX. 10 × 20 IN (25.4 × 50.8 CM),
WATERCOLOR

This atmospheric but highly
detailed painting was done
directly from nature. The artist
painted from her car, a practical
alternative to wet feet and
useless, frozen fingers on a winter
day. Many artists would have
used LIQUID MASK fluid for the
pattern of pale, bare twigs, one of
the most attractive features of
winter woodlands, but Palmer,
who is particularly fond of such
effects, creates them entirely by
reserving (painting around the
lights).

▶ Carolyne Moran, *The Apple Tree
Seen Through My Bedroom Window,*
10 × 9 IN (25.4 × 22.9 CM), WATERCOLOR
WITH ZINC WHITE GOUACHE

Both the paintings on this page
have bare branches as their
theme, and both artists were
interested in the patterns they
make, but where Palmer's
painting is delicate and gentle,
Moran's is tough and strong, with
an energetic, linear quality.
Notice how she has paid
particular attention to the
perspective of the branches, with
some crossing others and
coming toward the viewer – one
of the most common mistakes in
painting trees is to make them all
go in the same direction, so that
the tree lacks solidity. Both
sponging and SPATTERING have
been used to give texture and
softness to the trees in the
background.

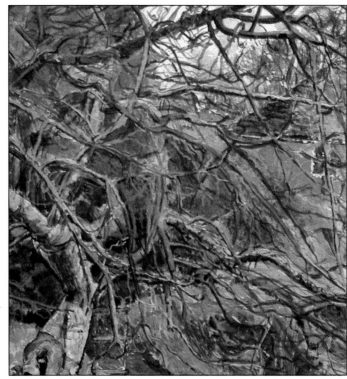

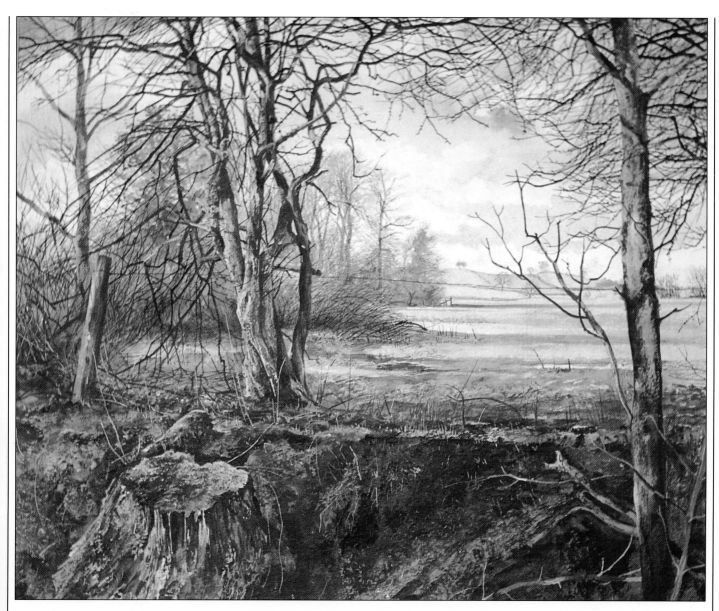

Martin Taylor, *Woodland Bank*
14 × 16 IN (35 × 41.5 CM) WATERCOLOR
AND ACRYLIC

Taylor's method of working is unusual among watercolorists. Having fully absorbed the atmosphere of his chosen scene, he begins to paint from top to bottom, starting with the sky and then working from left to right across the distance. He finishes a complete section before moving to the next and continues in the same way until he reaches the bottom right corner. He says that people often express surprise when watching him paint, but points out that both Stanley Spencer and the Pre-Raphaelites worked in this way. He achieves both his fine detail and his remarkable depth of color by painting over darks with acrylic lights, and then sometimes repeating the process in a version of the GLAZING technique. To attain the right effect of aerial perspective in distances, he will occasionally lay a thin white wash over the whole area.

FIELDS AND HILLS

Hills always make dramatic subjects; their powerful presence needs only the minimum of help from the painter, but quieter country – flat or with gentle contours – can easily become dull and featureless in a painting. It is seldom enough just to paint what you see, so you may have to think of ways of enhancing a subject by exaggerating certain features, stepping up the colors or tonal contrasts, introducing textural interest or using your brushwork more inventively. Interestingly, there have been artists throughout the course of history who have believed that they have been painting exactly what they have seen, but they never really were – consciously or unconsciously improving on nature is part of the process of picture-making.

Part of the problem with this kind of landscape is that, although it is often beautiful and atmospheric, much of its appeal comes from the way it surrounds and envelops you. Once you begin to home in on the one small part of it you can fit onto a piece of paper, you often wonder what you found so exciting – a feeling well known to anyone who takes photographs. So take a leaf from the photographer's book and use a viewfinder – a rectangle cut in a piece of cardboard is all you need. With this, you can isolate various parts of the scene and choose the best. If it is still less interesting than you hoped, add some elements from another area, such as a clump of trees or a plowed field, and consider emphasizing something in the foreground.

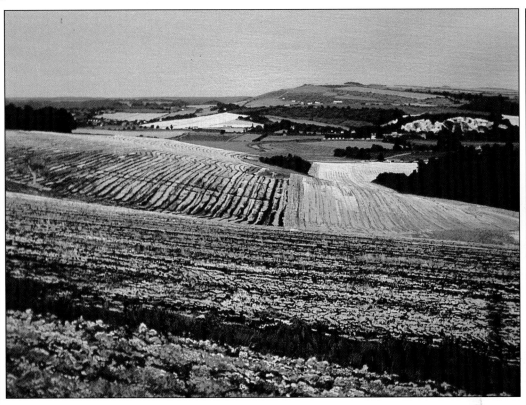

Robert Dodd, *Amberley and Kithurst Hill, Sussex*, 20½ × 28 IN (52 × 71.1CM), GOUACHE

Dodd has given drama to his quiet subject by the use of bold tonal contrasts and inventive exploitation of TEXTURE. He has used his gouache quite thickly, building up areas such as the plowed field in the foreground by MASKING and sponging (see SPONGE PAINTING). The more flatly applied paint used for the background and sky allows the textures to stand out strongly by contrast.

► Martin Taylor, *Castello-in-Chianti*, 10¼ × 13¾ IN (26 × 35 CM), WATERCOLOR AND ACRYLIC

Like many painters before him, Taylor has been excited by the strong Italian light, and this makes itself felt in every area of the painting, from the pale sky and hazy distance to the deep shadows and bright colors of the foreground. Using acrylic white to give body to his watercolor, he builds up his colors and textures gradually, using tiny brushstrokes which create a lovely shimmering quality, and working on one part of a painting at a time.

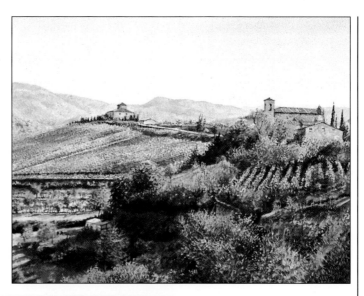

◄ Donald Pass, *Frosty Morning, Autumn*, 26½ × 33½ IN (67.3 × 85 CM), WATERCOLOR

Pass has an unusual watercolor style, using his paints almost like a drawing medium. He makes no preparatory drawing, and begins by laying broad washes of light color. He then builds up each area with a succession of separate, directional or linear brushmarks. It is easy to imagine how this subject might have become dull, but the brushwork, as well as being effective in terms of pure description, creates a marvelous sense of movement: we can almost feel the light wind bending the grass and sending the clouds scudding across the sky.

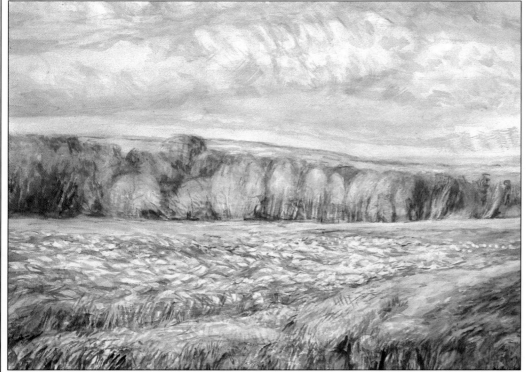

ROCKS AND MOUNTAINS

Mountains are a gift to the painter – they form marvelously exciting shapes, their colors are constantly changing and, best of all, unless you happen to be sitting on one, they are far enough away to be seen as broad shapes without too much worrying detail.

Distant mountains can be depicted using flat or semi-flat washes with details such as individual outcrops lightly indicated on those nearer to hand. For atmospheric effects, such as mist lying between one mountain and another or light cloud blending sky and mountain tops together, try working WET-IN-WET or mixing watercolor with opaque white.

Nearby rocks and cliffs call for a rather different approach, since their most exciting qualities are their hard, sharp edges and their textures – even the rounded, sea-weathered boulders seen on some seashores are pitted and uneven in surface and are far from soft to the touch. One of the best techniques for creating edge qualities is the WET-ON-DRY method, where successive small washes are laid over one another (if you become tired of waiting for them to dry, use a hairdryer to speed up the process). Texture can be built up in a number of ways. The WAX RESIST, SCUMBLING or salt spatter methods (see TEXTURE) are all excellent.

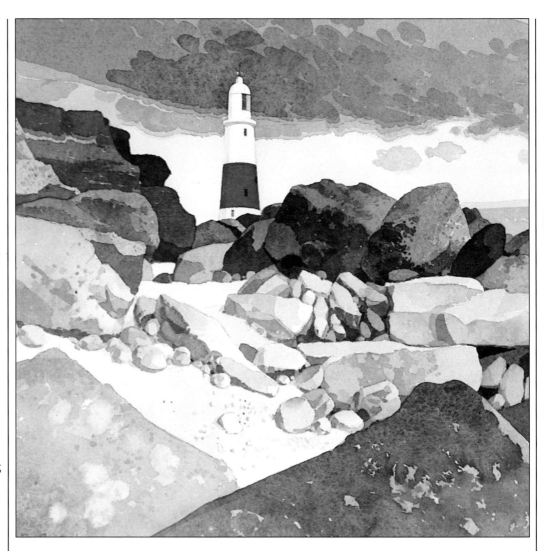

Ronald Jesty RBA, *Portland Lighthouse*, 10 × 10 IN (25.4 × 25.4 CM), WATERCOLOR

Jesty has worked WET-ON-DRY, using flat washes of varying sizes to describe the crisp, hard-edged quality of the rocks. He has created TEXTURE on some of the foreground surfaces by "drawing" with an upright brush to produce dots and other small marks, and has cleverly unified the painting by echoing the small cloud shapes in the light patches on the foreground rock. This was painted in the studio from a pen sketch. Advance planning is a prerequisite for Jesty's very deliberate way of painting, and he works out his compositions and the distribution of lights and darks carefully beforehand.

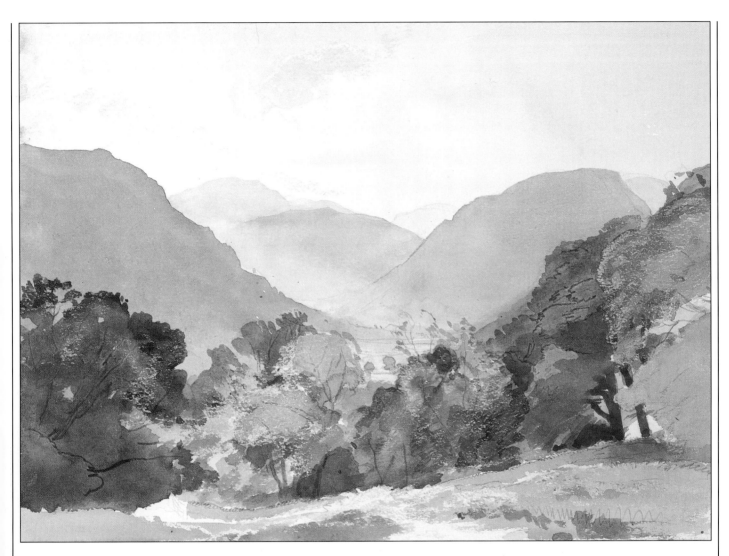

Charles Knight RWS, ROI, *Across the Valley*, 11 × 15 IN (27.9 × 38.1 CM), WATERCOLOR WITH PENCIL AND WAX

Knight has used the shapes and colors of the distant mountains as a dramatic backdrop to the trees and has avoided any details that might bring them forward into competition with the foreground. Nevertheless, they are not painted completely flat: darker and lighter tones have been blended WET-IN-WET within the crisp, clear outlines, and the lighter gray in the center suggests a touch of mist in the valley. The effect of the sunlight on the trees has been achieved by the WAX RESIST technique, and a few branches and tree trunks have been drawn with pencil and fine brushmarks over loose washes.

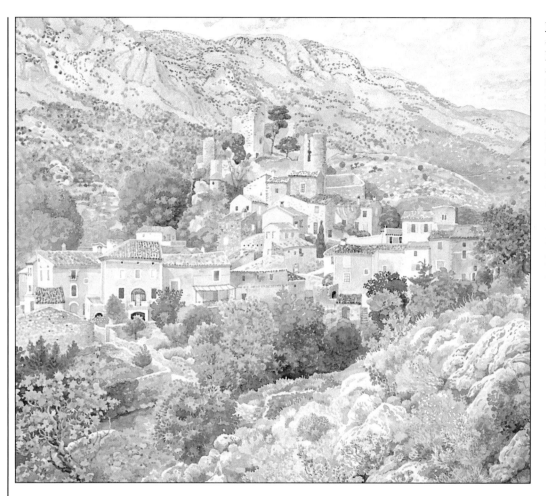

Juliette Palmer, *St. Jean de Buège,* APPROX. 16 × 16 IN (40.6 × 40.6 CM), WATERCOLOR

As is often the case in southern climates, the light was clear and bright, picking out the contours of the mountains and the small trees with pin-sharp clarity. The artist has made the most of this, building up the forms and textures of both mountains and foreground rocks with small, delicate brushstrokes to give a highly patterned but realistic effect. The painting, although begun with a detailed drawing made on the spot, was completed in the studio. As time on location was limited, the drawing was backed up by written notes.

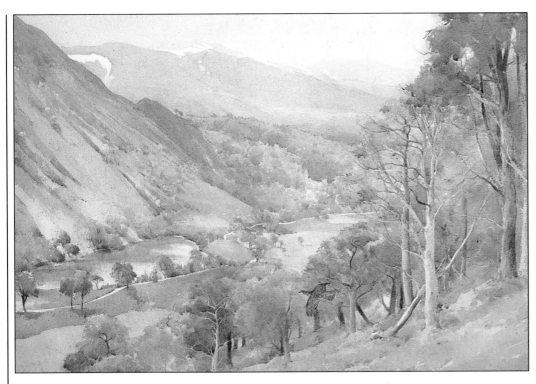

◄ David Curtis ROI, RSMA, *The Pass of Ryvoan*, 23 × 30 IN (58.4 × 76.2 CM), WATERCOLOR

Although this is an unusually large watercolor, it is only partially a studio painting; the first stages were done on location (in Scotland). Contending with sharply sloping ground and squalls of cold rain, the artist made his preliminary drawing, applied liquid mask (see MASKING) to certain small areas such as the path on the left, the dead tree and the patches of snow, and laid the first washes. Having established the general design and the distribution of the whites, he was then able to complete the painting in more comfort. Curtis works outside whenever possible, and believes that such adverse conditions key him up to produce more vigorous and energetic work.

► Michael Chaplin RE, *Welsh Cliffs*, 18 × 21 IN (45.7 × 53.3 CM), WATERCOLOR WITH SOME BODY COLOR

Very light pen lines accentuate the directional brushstrokes used for the sharp verticals of the cliff face, and texture has been suggested in places by sandpapering washes, a technique that works particularly well on the rough paper the artist has used. The addition of BODY COLOR (opaque white) to the paint has produced subtle colors and given a suitably chalky appearance to the cliffs.

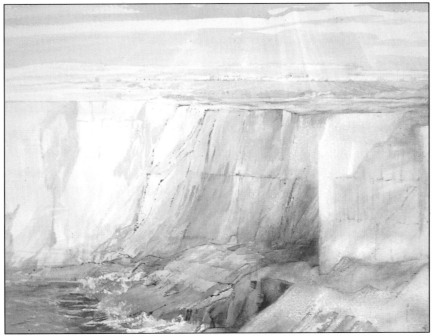

RECESSION

All painting can be seen as a series of optical tricks. The perceived world is three-dimensional, but the painter must translate space and form in a way that makes sense on the flat surface of a piece of paper. The landscape artist does well to realize this, as one of the most attractive qualities of a good landscape painting is the feeling of space it conveys.

Linear perspective makes objects appear smaller the further away they are, while parallel lines, such as furrows in a plowed field, will appear to converge in the distance. Using linear perspective is one way of suggesting recession, but many landscapes have no parallel lines and few objects, and this is where aerial perspective comes in.

The tiny particles of dust and moisture in the air affect the way we see colors, so that they become paler and paler toward the horizon, with the tonal contrasts minimal or imperceptible. Colors also become cooler, with a higher proportion of blue in them. Sometimes a shaft of sunlight catching the side of a faraway mountain can look quite bright, but in fact, it will be infinitely less vivid than a similarly sunlit area directly in front of you, and it will also be very close in tone to the blues or grays surrounding it.

The easiest way to work is from the back to the front of the picture, beginning with flat washes of pale blues and grays and gradually progressing to brighter, warmer colors and stronger light and dark contrasts in the foreground.

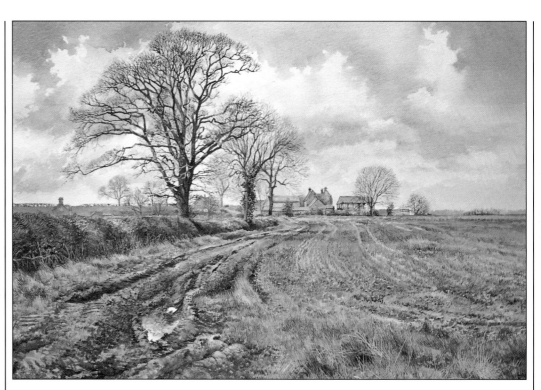

Martin Taylor, *Spring*, 13 × 19 IN (32 × 48 CM), WATERCOLOR

Recession is created in this painting by a combination of linear and aerial perspective, but mainly the former. The curving lines of path and field converge as they recede, while the line of trees slope sharply down to the horizon, diminishing in size and depth of tone. Taylor has heightened the effect of space by the detailed treatment of the foreground, which effectively "pulls" it toward the viewer.

► Robert Dodd, *Tillingbourne Valley, Winter*, 20½ × 28½ IN (52 × 72.4 CM), GOUACHE

Dodd has observed the effects of aerial perspective carefully, controlling his tones and colors with great skill so that the middle ground merges gently into the far distance. The tonal contrasts in the foreground are quite strong, while the far-off hills are only just darker than the sky. His painting creates a strong feeling of place and atmosphere as well as of space and recession.

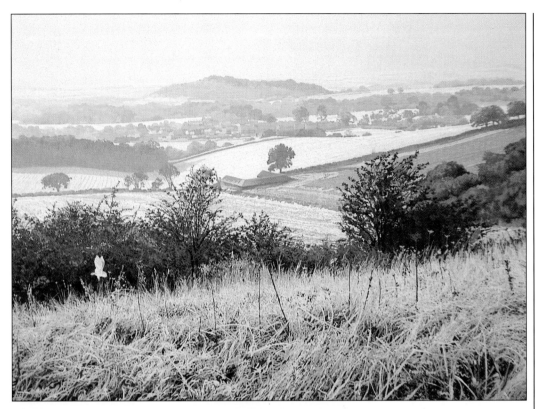

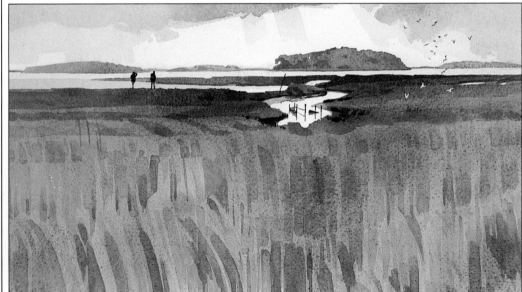

◄ Ronald Jesty RBA, *Poole Harbour from Arne*, 9¾ × 17 IN (24.8 × 43.2 CM), WATERCOLOR

Like the other two paintings shown here, this one makes use of a strong foreground to create depth, but Jesty has also defined the middle distance and created a link between it and the background by the inclusion of the two figures, the flock of birds and the posts in the river. The side of the brush was used to indicate the clumps of bending reeds, with the paint used fairly dry, and the light-against-dark birds on the right were achieved by SCRAPING BACK.

WEATHER AND THE SEASONS

The British landscape painter John Constable (1776-1837) once said that "...the sky is the source of light and governs everything." Sky is, of course, the mirror of the weather, and it is part and parcel of all landscape, transforming it – sometimes in a matter of minutes – from a peaceful, sunny scene to a dark and brooding one. This kind of rapid transition is an obvious example of the landscape/weather interaction, but it is one that takes place all the time, often far more subtly. Even sunlight varies widely: the colors of both sky and land on a hot summer's day are quite unlike those seen in winter, while the light cast by a gray sky can be strong or very weak depending on the amount of cloud cover and the strength and position of the sun above the clouds.

A landscape painting – even one with no visible sky – should always give the viewer a feeling of the weather conditions under which it is seen, and the best way to experience these is at first hand. Another great British painter, J.M.W. Turner (1775-1851), who was fascinated by the subject, made endless outdoor studies of landscapes under different skies and at different times of the year. This was in spite of the fact that he had a near-perfect visual memory and was able to re-create the effects of a thunderstorm in the Alps years after seeing it.

▶ Ronald Jesty RBA, *Winter, Sedge Moor*, 16 × 9 IN (40.6 × 22.9 CM), WATERCOLOR

In this bold composition, the dark tree and low, red sun counterpoint the brilliance of the white snow – the paper left uncovered. The brooding purple-gray sky often seen on a late winter afternoon has been exaggerated, both to make a more powerful statement and to provide warm/cool contrast. The fluid use of the paint and simplification of the tree into broad shapes accentuates the drama of the scene.

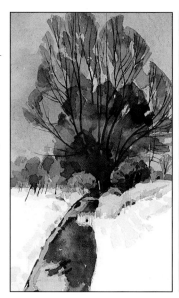

▼ Charles Knight RWS, ROI, *Evening*, 9¾ × 13¼ IN (25 × 33.6 CM), WATERCOLOR WITH WAX AND PENCIL

The evening mist has been beautifully described by means of wet washes of pale, pearly colors. In places, notably in the central tree area, the overlaying of washes has created lines (see HARD AND SOFT EDGES), which provide subtle touches of definition. The effect of the setting sun behind the trees has been achieved by lightly sponging the area and flooding some warmer color into it, while lightly scribbled lines of wax crayon (see WAX RESIST) and pencil suggest ripples and highlights on the water.

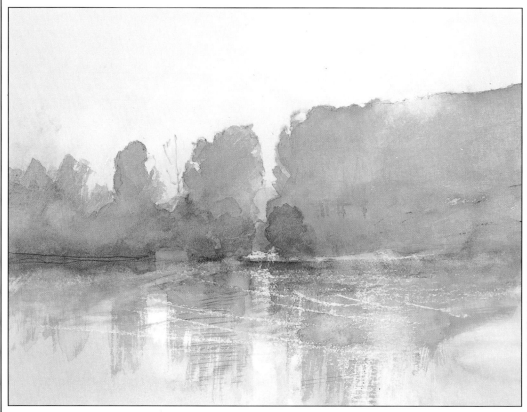

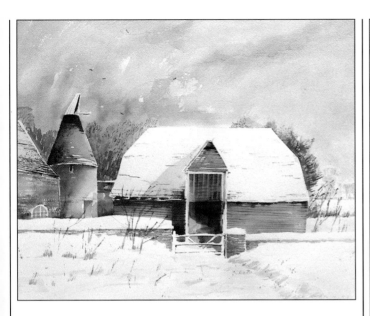

Michael Chaplin RE, *Grove Green Farm*, 13 × 18 IN (33 × 45.7 CM), WATERCOLOR

We tend to think of snow as always being white, whatever the weather conditions, but the land always reflects color from the sky, and since white surfaces are more reflective than dark ones, snow is a direct mirror of the prevailing light. In this well-observed painting (done on the spot, wearing three pairs of socks) there are no whites, only pale and darker grays, emphasized by the warm red-browns of the buildings and trees. The impression of cold is palpable.

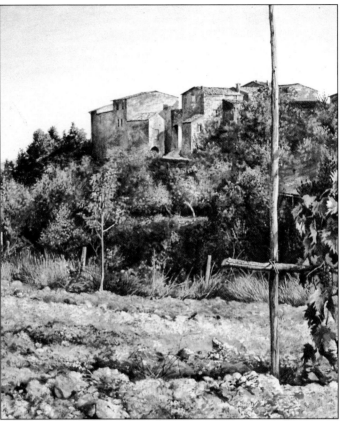

Martin Taylor, *Castello di Tocchi, Tuscany*, 14½ × 11¾ IN (37 × 30 CM), WATERCOLOR AND ACRYLIC

If you were to take only one small section of the foreground of this painting and mask out the rest, you would recognize the clear, bright light of a Mediterranean country. As in all his paintings, Taylor has built up strong contrasts of tone and depth of color by means of considerable overpainting with small, careful brushstrokes. Because he mixes watercolor and acrylic, he is able to lay light colors over dark and vice versa, working for long periods on one area of a painting until he achieves the right effect.

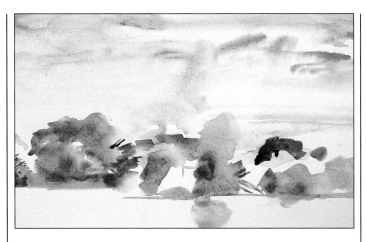

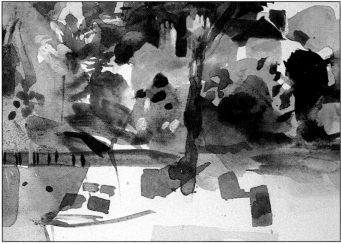

1 To use Kate Gwynn's own words, she uses "anything that comes to hand" when painting, and here she builds up a variety of shapes and textures by combining different media and techniques. She begins in pure watercolor with the addition of a little GUM ARABIC, using the side of the brush to define the sharp areas of foliage on the left.

3 Opaque white is added to the paint for the buildings, echoed in the small dots on the tree below, which effectively link the two areas. Notice the variety of BRUSHMARKS and the lively effect created by the overlapping washes. In the foreground, pure watercolor is taken carefully around the boat to leave a crisp, sharp outline, which will be reinforced with line at a later stage.

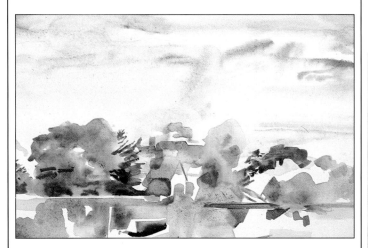

2 She continues to cover the paper with broad, loose washes, adding interest to the central tree and reflection by SPATTERING thick, slightly darker paint.

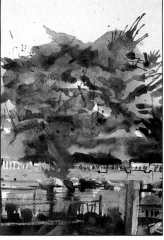

4 The reflections are mainly pure watercolor, but BODY COLOR is used for the posts, with a line or two of pastel on the left suggesting ripples on the water surface. The spiky shapes of the evergreen tree are achieved by blown blots (see BLOTS).

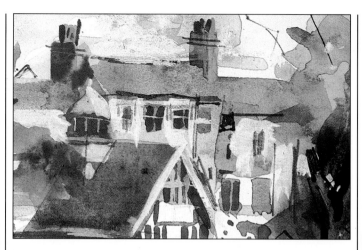

6 The group of boats on the right of the painting is left to stand more or less as a white area in order to avoid competing with the center of interest, but some decisive felt-tip pen lines and patches of blue pastel provide just the right touch of detail.

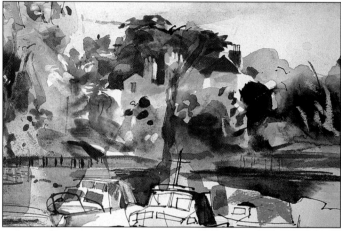

5 The central group of houses, the focal point of the painting, is given more definition than those on the right, which are deliberately left as little more than hints (see 3). This detail shows how exciting textural contrasts can be obtained by juxtaposing translucent washes and opaque paint. Dark crayon lines roughly scribbled onto the house front add to the lively effect. The lines at the extreme bottom right have been made by drawing with a brush handle dipped into undiluted paint.

7 The finished painting has a sparkling, busy appearance, with a strong sense of movement created by the wide variety of brushmarks, linear elements and textures.

Kate Gwynn, *The River in Summer,* 16 × 20 IN (40.6 × 50.8 CM), WATERCOLOR WITH GOUACHE AND LINE ON STRETCHED BOCKINGFORD PAPER

SKIES

It may seem odd to devote a whole section to skies – they are, after all, an integral part of landscape – but, from the painter's point of view, they are a major subject in themselves. They demand close observation and a degree of technical knowhow, partly because of their infinite variety and partly because they are not subject to the same rules that govern the solid earth below. A mountain, cliff or tree will change in appearance under different lighting conditions, but its structure will remain stable, while clouds, seemingly solid but in fact composed of nothing but air and moisture, are constantly on the move, forming and re-forming in ways that can only partially be predicted and are never the same twice. Most important of all, the sky is the light source without which the landscape could not exist, and weather conditions above relate directly to the colors, tones and prevailing mood of the land below. Thus the surest way to spoil a landscape is by failing to analyze or express this interdependent relationship.

Clear skies

We tend to think of cloudless skies as simply blue, but in fact they vary widely according to the season and climate. A midsummer's sky in a hot country will be a warm blue, sometimes tending to violet and often surprisingly dark in tone, while a winter sky in a temperate zone is a paler and cooler blue. Nor is a clear sky the same color all over. A frequent mistake is to paint blue skies in one uniform wash, but there are always variations – sometimes slight, but often quite marked. As a general rule, skies are darker and warmer in color at the top and paler and cooler on the horizon, following the same rules of aerial perspective as the land (see LANDSCAPE, RECESSION on page 144). There is, however, an important exception to this. Sky directly over the sea will absorb particles of moisture, giving a darker band of color at the horizon, and a similar effect can often be seen in cities, where the dark band is caused by smoke, dust or other pollution.

"Learning" clouds

There are few people, whether they paint or not, who can fail to be enthralled by cloud effects – great dark thunderheads, delicate "mackerel" skies or the magical effects created by a low evening sun breaking through after a day's rain. Sadly, these effects are fleeting, so the landscape painter needs to be in constant readiness to watch, memorize and sketch.

The British painter John Constable (1776-1837) was fascinated by skies and well understood their leading role in landscape painting. He made endless oil sketches of nothing but skies. Often these were done in a few minutes, but provided him with a storehouse of information that he drew on for his finished paintings. Such quick studies provide the ideal means of recording these transient effects: even a rapid pencil sketch of cloud shapes with written notes of the colors will act as an *aide-mémoire* and help you to observe constructively. Photographs are also useful in this context, as long as you use them as part of a learning process and not as models to copy for a painting.

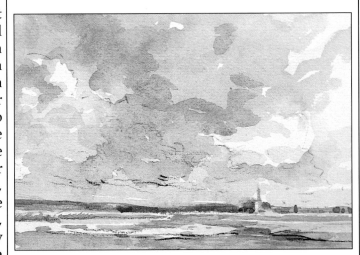

Christopher Baker, *Bosham Estuary*, 6 × 9 IN (45 × 22.5 CM), WATERCOLOR AND CONTÉ CRAYON

The scudding clouds are painted lightly and deftly, with definition restricted to the few lines of crayon that formed the preliminary drawing.

Methods

For novice watercolor painters, skies, particularly those with complex cloud formations, are a daunting subject. You aim at a soft impression and find you have unwanted hard edges, or you try to build up some really dramatic tonal contrast for a stormy sky and overwork the paint, completely ruining the effect. But really, clouds are not so very difficult. The trick is to understand the medium well enough to develop your own tricks of the trade. Always be ready to use the element of happy accident. Unintentional BACKRUNS and spreading paint may suggest the perfect way of painting rain clouds, while some experiments with the LIFTING OUT technique will quickly show you how to paint wind clouds or achieve soft, fluffy white edges without having to go through the more laborious process of reserving highlights.

Robert Tilling RI, *Winter Sky,*
16 × 23 IN (40.6 × 58.4 CM), WATERCOLOR

Working on a light stretched paper with a Not surface, and with his board well tilted, the artist uses large brushes to lay very wet washes, later adding further ones WET-ON-DRY.

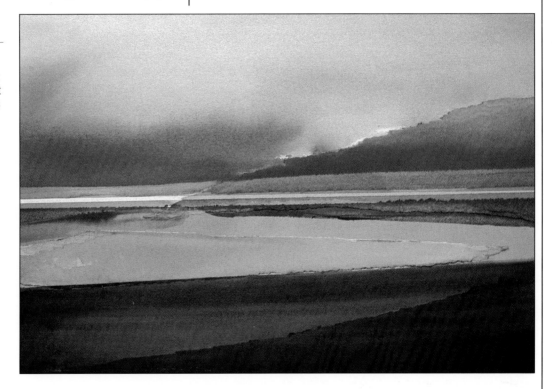

CLOUDS IN COMPOSITION

The possibilities of using clouds as an integral part of a composition are often ignored, which seems strange in view of the fact that skies are often the dominant element in a landscape. Perhaps it is simply that so many people are afraid of painting skies. But the landscape painter must tackle this problem: clouds form exciting shapes in themselves, and these can be manipulated or exaggerated to add extra movement and drama to a subject. Shapes in the sky can also be planned to provide a balance for those in the foreground or middle distance, such as clumps of trees or rounded hills, and if colors as well as shapes are repeated from sky to land, the two parts of the painting will come together to form a satisfying whole. Since the sky is reflected to some extent in the land below, you will often see touches of blue or violet from the undersides of clouds occurring again in shadows or distant hills.

Not all paintings, of course, need this kind of sky interest. A mountain scene, for instance, or winter trees in stark silhouette, will be more successful if the sky is allowed to take second place, but a flat landscape can often be saved from dullness by an eventful sky, so keep a special sketchbook for recording cloud effects so that you can use them in landscapes painted indoors. Skies are very difficult to re-create from memory alone, so in addition to sketches, you could also use photographs of skies, but do so with caution – they can badly misrepresent colors and tones.

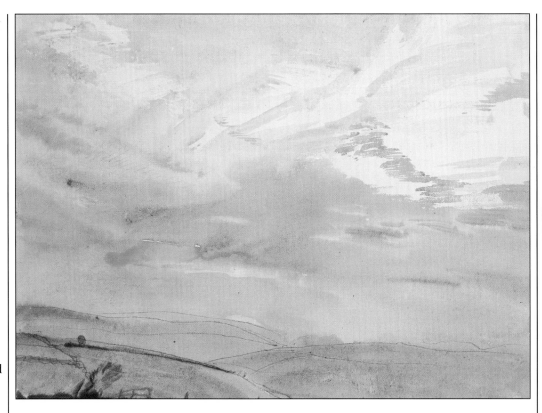

Charles Knight RWS, ROI, *Sunset, South Downs*, 11 × 15 IN (27.9 × 38.1 CM), WATERCOLOR AND PENCIL

In this painting, the sky is virtually the whole composition, with the hills and fields serving as an anchor to the movement above. Much of the sky and foreground has been painted WET-IN-WET, and in the central area the orange and gray washes have been allowed to flood together, giving a realistically soft effect. But the artist has not overdone the technique: below the orange patch there are clearer, harder edges, which are echoed by the crisp pencil lines defining the hills below, and the small clouds toward the top have been worked WET-ON-DRY.

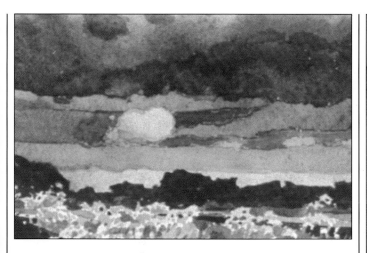

Ronald Jesty RBA, *Cloud Study,*
7 × 9 IN (17.8 × 22.9 CM), WATERCOLOR

This dramatic painting, although giving the appearance of a planned and studio-composed piece, was in fact a study sketch made on the spot after a storm. Which just goes to show that nature will do at least some of the composing if you are receptive enough to her suggestions. The painting is quite small and was done quickly, of necessity, with superimposed washes and the dark clouds at the top painted WET-IN-WET. Wet paint was lifted out in places (see LIFTING OUT), and the white cow parsley was suggested by stippling around the shapes with the point of a brush.

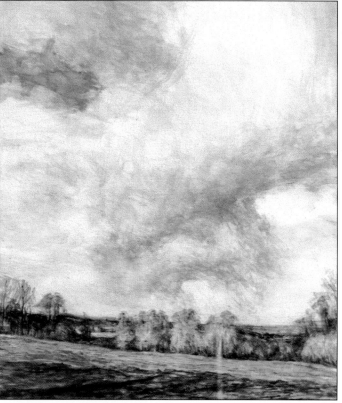

Donald Pass, *Spring Shower,*
21 × 18 IN (53.3 × 45.7 CM), WATERCOLOR

This is the perfect example of clouds used as an integral part of a compositon. The painting is full of movement, and our eye is encouraged to travel around it as we follow the direction of the dramatic, curving cloud – up to the right, around to the left and then downward through the bright patches of blue to the sunlit trees. The artist has tied the sky to the land both by using the same kind of brushwork throughout the picture and by echoing shapes: the vertical cloud seems a logical extension of the central group of tall trees.

CLOUD FORMATIONS

Clouds are always on the move – gathering, dispersing, forming and re-forming – but they do not behave in a random way. There are different types of cloud, each with its own individual structure and characteristics.

In children's geography books, you will sometimes see "prototype" pictures of the basic formations. It is not necessary to know the name of each type, but to paint clouds convincingly you need to recognize the differences. It is also helpful to realize that they form on different levels, because this affects their tones and colors.

Cirrus clouds, high in the sky, are fine and vaporous, forming delicate, feathery plumes where they are blown by the wind. The two types of cloud that form on the lowest level are cumulus clouds, with horizontal bases and cauliflower-like tops, and storm clouds (or thunderclouds) – great, heavy masses that rise up vertically, often resembling mountains or towers. Both these low-level clouds show strong contrasts of light and dark. A storm cloud will sometimes look almost black against a blue sky, and cumulus clouds are extremely bright where the sun strikes them and surprisingly dark on their shadowed undersides. Between these two extremes of high and low, there is often an intermediate level of cloud with gentler contrasts than the low layer, so a single sky with a mixture of all these types of clouds can present a fascinating ready-made composition of varied shapes and colors.

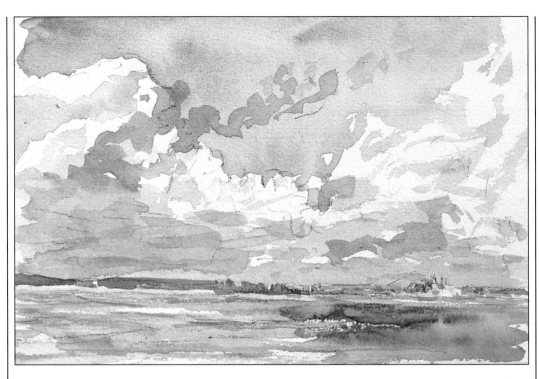

Christopher Baker, *Bosham Clouds*, 7 × 10 IN (47.8 × 25.4 CM), WATERCOLOR AND CONTÉ CRAYON

The light conté-crayon drawing made to establish the main shapes has been deliberately used as part of the painting. Working on rag paper, which gives a pleasing texture to the picture surface, Baker has worked swiftly, with almost no overpainting. The subtle warm grays of the clouds were achieved by mixtures of ultramarine and light red, with some viridian and raw sienna in places.

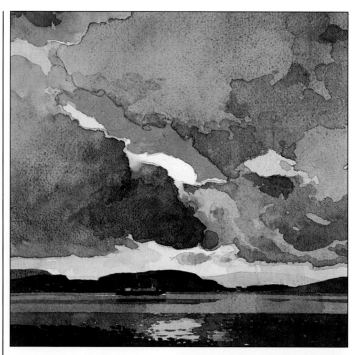

◄ Ronald Jesty RBA, *Out of Oban*,
13 × 13 IN (33 × 33 CM), WATERCOLOR

This dramatic cloud study was painted in the studio from a pen sketch. Built up entirely by means of superimposed washes painted WET-ON-DRY, the colors are nevertheless fresh and clear. Although many watercolorists avoid overlaying washes for subjects such as these, which are easily spoiled by too great a build-up of paint, Jesty succeeds because he takes care to make his first washes as positive as possible. Notice the granulated paint in the clouds caused by laying a wet wash over a previous dry one (see WASH: TEXTURES), an effect often used to add extra surface interest.

Moira Clinch, *Mountain Retreat*, 15½
× 19 IN (39.4 × 48.3 CM), WATERCOLOR

There is often quite sharp definition as well as strong contrasts of tone in the low level of cloud (that nearest to us). Clinch has given form to the clouds by using a combination of WET-IN-WET, which creates soft, diffused shapes, and WET-ON-DRY, which forms crisp edges where one wash overlaps another. The effect of the squall of rain has been achieved by careful LIFTING OUT.

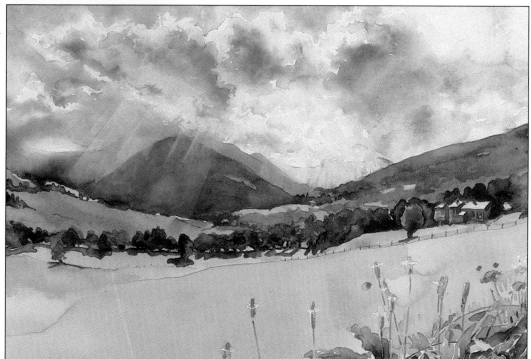

CLOUD COLORS

Clouds present a marvelous kaleidoscope of colors, but these are far from being accidental. They are caused by the position of the sun and by the reflections of surrounding colors.

At noon, when the sun is high, clouds are largely robbed of color – this is when you see the "fleece balls" that amateur painters often depict – but the low sun of early morning or evening presents a very different picture. At such times, there is a panorama of hues – yellows, warm pinks, browns and violets, with the edges of clouds being a wonderful, glowing gold where they reflect the sun. A cloud high in the sky will be blue-gray or violet on the underside because it takes on some of the blue from the sky, while a similar cloud lower on the horizon will be browner because it reflects less of the blue.

It is useful to know these general rules, particularly when you are painting indoors from notes and sketches. An ever-changing sky can be a headache, however, if you are working on the spot. Each new effect and set of colors will seem to be better than the last, and you will find it difficult not to make changes. This could lead to disaster, as pushing the paint around too much is the surest way to destroy the airy evanescence of a sky. The best way to work is fast, keeping your color mixtures simple and your brushwork free and unfussy. The same applies to a studio painting, so to avoid overworking the paint, plan which colors you will use and put them on with assurance.

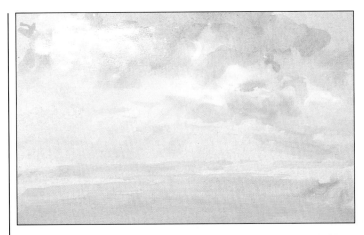

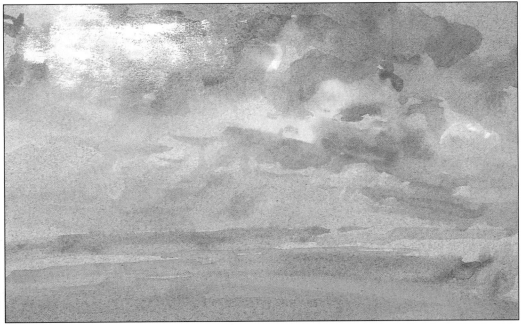

1 John Martin's cloud study, painted in gouache on a TONED GROUND, shows careful observation of the colors seen in an early evening sky. If gouache is used too thickly from the outset, later layers will stir up and muddy the earlier ones, so he begins by using it as watercolor, blocking in the main shapes lightly.

2 He continues to build up the forms and colors of the clouds, thickening the paint only marginally in most areas, but introducing some opaque white at top left.

3 The final touch (below) is to overpaint a touch of bright, deep blue at the top of the sky, separating the main cloud masses, and to add a few touches of light-toned, thick paint to the foreground. These link it to the sky by suggesting patches of sunlight, but no attempt is made at precise definition of the fields and hills, as this would steal attention from the real subject of the painting.

▶ This detail shows the dry, cream-colored paint scrubbed over a darker mauve-gray. This SCUMBLING technique is well suited to skies, as it allows one color to shine through another to give a shimmering, vaporous effect.

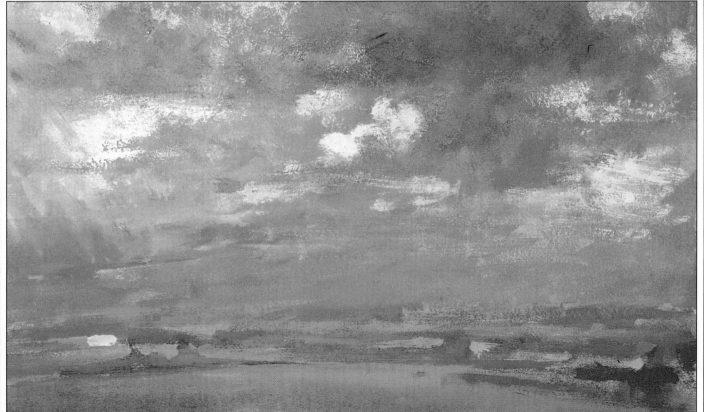

John Martin, *Cloud Study*, APPROX. 9 × 14 IN (22.9 × 35.6 CM), GOUACHE ON TONED PAPER

RAIN AND MIST

Watercolor is particularly well suited to capturing soft, pale, misty skies, wet-looking rainclouds and delicate shafts of light, but such effects can easily look drab in a painting unless you introduce variety in subtle ways.

An overcast sky is seldom a completely flat gray – if it is, there is little point in painting it. The most fascinating wet-weather effects are created by blue sky or a weak sun reflecting back through the fine gauzy layers of clouds to give suggestions of other colors in places such as blues. In misty conditions, these colors are always gentle and subdued, so control your palette very carefully, using the minimum of tonal contrast. This applies equally to the landscape (or seascape) beneath the sky, as a bright color accent or over-dark tone introduced into an otherwise muted color scheme will destroy the whole atmosphere.

A painting like this can be almost monochromatic, but it will not be dull if you provide some extra interest, such as varied brushwork or the surface texture provided by working on rough paper. Directional brushwork creates an impression of movement, while squalls of rain can be described quickly and economically by dragging wet paint down the paper with a stiff bristle brush. BACKRUNS can be exploited to give both interest and verisimilitude to soft, wet clouds, while techniques such as SPATTERING and SPONGE PAINTING can be used to enliven a too-flat area of color.

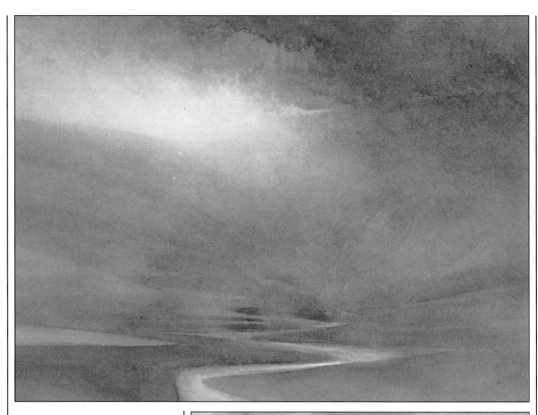

▲ Colin Paynton, *Welsh Elements 1*, 19½ × 26½ IN (49.5 × 67.3 CM), WATERCOLOR

At first glance, this wonderfully atmospheric painting looks almost monochromatic, but there are subtle touches of green-gray toward the horizon, which are echoed in the sky. The control of tones is extremely skillful, as is the use of paint: notice the long, sweeping brushstrokes radiating upward from the center of the horizon and the deliberate BACKRUN at the top of the sky. The artist has used a certain amount of washing out (see LIFTING OUT) to achieve his soft effects and has worked on unstretched but heavy paper with a Not surface.

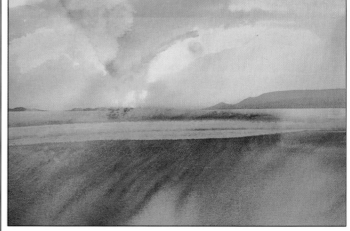

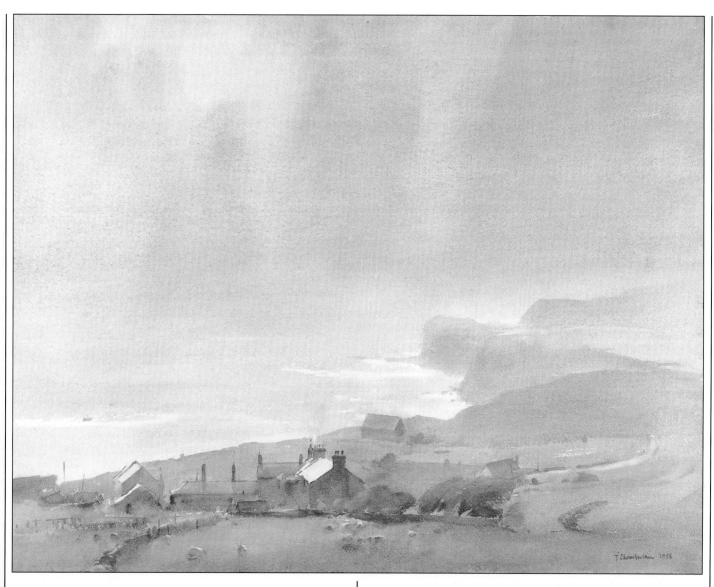

◄ Robert Tilling RI, *Winter Headland,*
WATERCOLOR

Tilling is fascinated by dramatic light effects, and most of his watercolors are devoted to exploring the interaction of sky, sea and land. He works very wet, using large brushes, but controls his paint carefully. Here, for instance, he has held the dark gray-purple wash away from the headland to create an eloquent line of light above it.

▲ Trevor Chamberlain, *Hazy Sun and Damp Mist, Boulby Down,* 20¼ × 28¾ IN (51.4 × 73 CM), WATERCOLOR

This lovely evocation almost makes us feel the damp but warm atmosphere with the sun about to break through. The artist has worked WET-IN-WET, controlling the tones and colors with the precision demanded by such a subject.

There was a time when drawing objects such as plaster casts, bottles and bowls of fruit was regarded as the first step in the training of art students. Only after a year or two spent perfecting their drawing technique would they be allowed to move on to using actual paint, while the really "difficult" subjects such as the human figure were reserved for the final year. This now seems an arid approach, almost designed to stifle any personal ideas and talent, but like many of the teaching methods of the past, it contained a grain or two of sense – drawing and painting "captive" subjects is undeniably a valuable exercise in learning to understand form and manipulate paint. But still-life painting can be very much more than this. It is enormously enjoyable, and presents almost unlimited possibilities for experimenting with shapes, colors and composition as well as technique.

The great beauty of still life lies in its controllability. You, as artist, are entirely in charge: you decide which objects you want to paint, arrange a set-up that shows them off to advantage and orchestrate the color scheme, lighting and background. Best of all, particularly for those who dislike being rushed, you can take more or less as long as you like over the painting. If you choose fruit and vegetables, they will, of course, shrivel or rot in time, but at least they will not move. This degree of choice allows you to express your own ideas in an individual manner, whereas in a portrait or landscape painting, you are more tied to a specific subject.

The still-life tradition
Almost all artists have at some time turned their hands to still life, and long before it became an art form in its own right, lovely little still lifes often appeared among the incidental detail in portraits and religious paintings. The first pure still-life paintings were those with an allegorical significance that became popular in the sixteenth century. Typical of these paintings, known as *vanitas*, were subjects such as flowers set beside a skull, signifying the inevitable triumph of death. It was the Flemish and Dutch painters of the seventeenth and eighteenth centuries, though, who really put still-life and flower painting on the map, with their marvelously lavish arrangements of exotic fruit and flowers, rich fabrics and fine china and glass. The *vanitas* still lifes reminded their religious patrons of the transience of life, but these exuberant and unashamedly materialistic works, painted for the wealthy merchant classes, were celebrations of its pleasures.

Still-life painting has remained popular with artists ever since, and, although it was regarded as an inferior art form by the French Academy, who favored paintings with grand historical or mythological themes, it gained respectability when the Impressionists altered the course of painting forever. The still-life paintings of Edouard Manet (1832-83), Paul Cézanne (1839-1906) and Vincent Van Gogh (1853-90) rank among the finest works of any kind ever produced, the everyday subject matter being transcended in such a way that paintings became personal and passionate artistic statements.

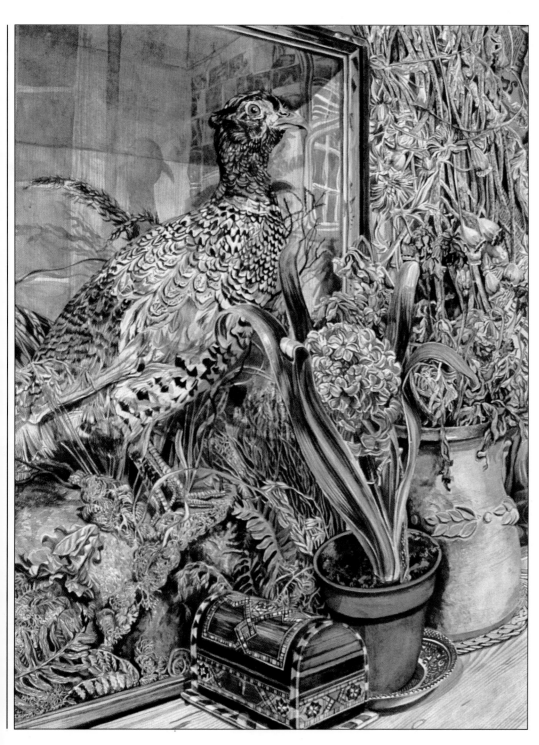

Cherryl Fountain, *Still Life with Pheasant and Hyacinth,* 20 × 13 IN (50.8 × 33 CM), WATERCOLOR

This artist also paints landscapes, in the same highly detailed style, but she likes still life particularly because she can control her set-up in a way that allows her to express her love of pattern and texture.

"FOUND" GROUPS

A still-life painting can be of more or less anything – the only thing common to all paintings in this genre, naturally, is that the subjects do not move.

Many still-life paintings are the result of carefully planned arrangements. Paul Cézanne (1839-1905) reputedly spent days setting up his groups of fruit and vegetables before so much as lifting his brush. Sometimes, though, you may just happen to see a subject, such as plates and cups on a table or a few vegetables lying on a piece of newspaper, that seems perfect in itself, or needs only small adjustments to make it so. These "found" groups have a particular charm of their own, hinting at impermanence and the routines of everyday life – the vegetables will shortly be made into soup, and the dishes will be washed and put back into the cupboard.

Found groups obviously have to be painted more quickly than arranged ones, but this is in some ways an advantage, since you want to achieve a spontaneous, unposed effect. So make your technique express this also and paint freely, putting down broad impressions of shapes, color and light.

Alternatively, you can use the idea of the found group as the basis for a more deliberate set-up, placing the objects in a more convenient place for painting or one where they have better light. Be careful, however, not to destroy the essence of the subject by over-planning and including too many extra elements.

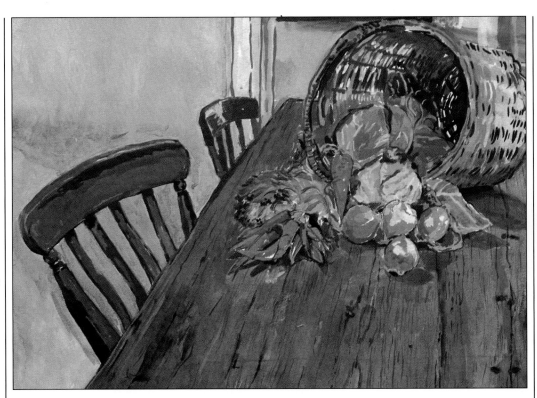

Carolyne Moran, *Kitchen Table with Basket and Vegetables*, 14½ × 21½ IN (36.8 × 54.6 CM), GOUACHE

This painting gives a powerful impression of spontaneity and immediacy, partly through the sense of movement created by the spilling vegetables, but equally through the manner of painting. Although the drawing is accurate – chairs, basket and vegetables all make sense in terms of structure and proportion – there is no unnecessary detail.

The light coming through the cane of the basket is described deftly but with no niggling, and the brushwork throughout the painting is vigorous and expressive. On the left-hand wall, the artist has allowed her brush to follow the sweeping lines of the upright chair struts, and on the table she has smeared still-wet paint with her fingers to simulate the grain of the wood.

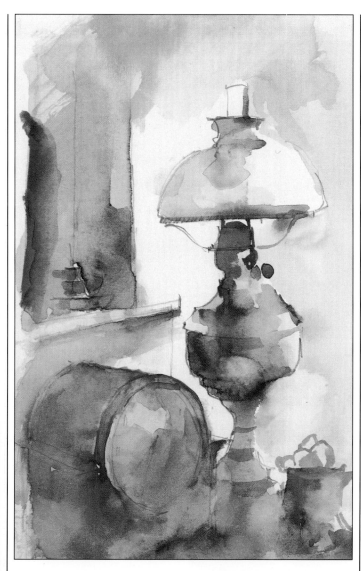

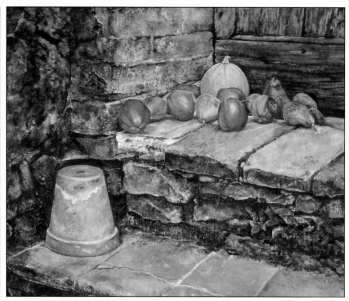

▲ Martin Taylor, *Still Life with Pumpkin*, 9 × 13 IN (23 × 33 CM), WATERCOLOR

We are not all fortunate enough to have such a perfect still life setting as this old stone building. But neither does Martin Taylor – he happened on this arrangement of fruit and vegetables quite by chance during a trip to Italy, and promptly settled down to paint it. The picture's most striking feature is the way he has built up the rough textures of the stone and contrasted them with the smooth ones of the fruit and vegetables, which glow out like beacons from their neutral-colored surroundings.

▲ John Lidzey FRSA, *Oil Lamp*, 9½ × 6 IN (15.2 × 24.1 CM), WATERCOLOR

This, a page from the artist's sketchbook, is the quintessential "found" still life, painted rapidly and freely with no overworking. Heavily sized paper, such as the cartridge paper used for sketchbooks, has a non-absorbent surface which causes the paint to mix freely but unevenly. Lidzey has exploited this effect to the full. Using plenty of water, he allowed the paint to flood onto the paper, controlling it with damp absorbent cotton. He used only three colors, ultramarine, yellow ocher and burnt sienna, but encouraged them to run into one another and mix, treating the paper almost like a palette.

THEMES

A successful still life is seldom if ever a random collection of objects – there should always be some kind of theme. One of the most popular types of still life is the culinary one, where fruit, vegetables and kitchen equipment are grouped together. Attractive in themselves, they also are related in subject, so that the viewer is not worried by the discordant notes of objects that seem not to belong. Another kind of theme is the "literary" one. Some still lifes tell a story about the personal interests of the artist. The best-known examples of such still lifes are those of Vincent Van Gogh (1853-90), whose paintings of his room at Arles and his moving portrayals of his own work-soiled boots are almost a form of pictorial biography, telling us as much about the artist and his way of life as about the objects themselves. This approach to painting makes a lot of sense – most people possess some objects that have particular value because they evoke memories, so what better than to make them the starting point for a personal still life.

You can also take colors and shapes as the theme, choosing objects that seem to be linked visually or set up exciting contrasts. Visual themes need very careful handling at the painting stage – if the objects are widely dissimilar in kind you may have to treat them in a semi-abstract way, allowing them to hide their identity behind their general forms or outlines.

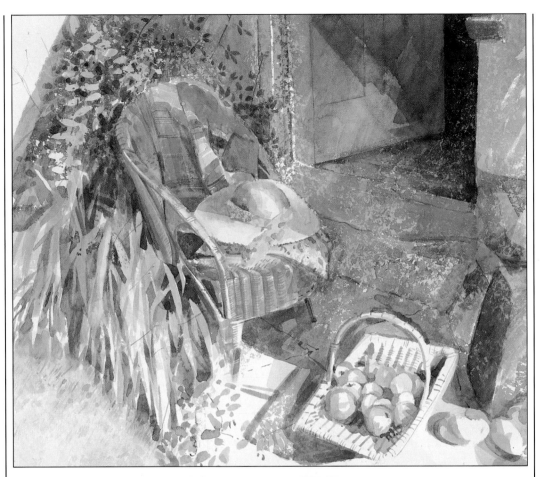

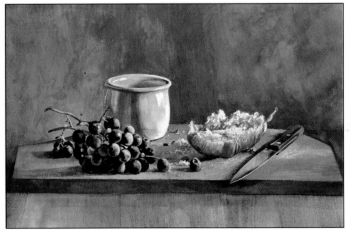

◀ Martin Taylor, *Grapes and Bread*, 9 × 13 IN (23 × 33 CM), WATERCOLOR AND ACRYLIC

Foodstuffs have always been a popular still life theme, and this lovely, simple little group is very much in the Dutch tradition of minute observation and truth to the realities of everyday life. Painted in Italy at the end of a vacation, it had an extra significance for the artist, the grapes (wine) and bread symbolizing the Italian way of life as well as suggesting a "last supper."

◄ Michael Emmett, *By the Cottage Door*, 14½ × 16½ IN (36.8 × 41.9 CM), WATERCOLOR

This delightful outdoor group is an example of a still life with a narrative content: we can see that someone, perhaps the painter's wife, has been sitting in the sun preparing fruit and vegetables, but has now abandoned her task. This adds an extra dimension to the picture, inviting us to participate in the domestic scene, but the implied story plays only a secondary role; once drawn in, we can admire the carefully planned composition and the artist's technical skill. He has painted mainly WET-ON-DRY, building up subtle but varied colors by means of successive overlapping washes, and the effect of dappled sunlight by the door has been cleverly suggested by the SPATTERING technique.

► Moira Huntly RI, RSMA, *Still Life with African Artefact*, 19½ × 14 IN (49.5 × 35.5 CM), WATERCOLOR AND GOUACHE

Here the main theme is color and shape; if you look at the painting through half-closed eyes, you can see an abstract pattern, perfectly balanced and carefully controlled. One of the surest ways to tie all the elements in a still life together is to repeat colors and shapes from one area to another, and there could be few better examples than this painting. Every color in the foreground has its echo in the background or foreground, while the zigzag patterns on the tablecloth are picked up again in the top left-hand corner.

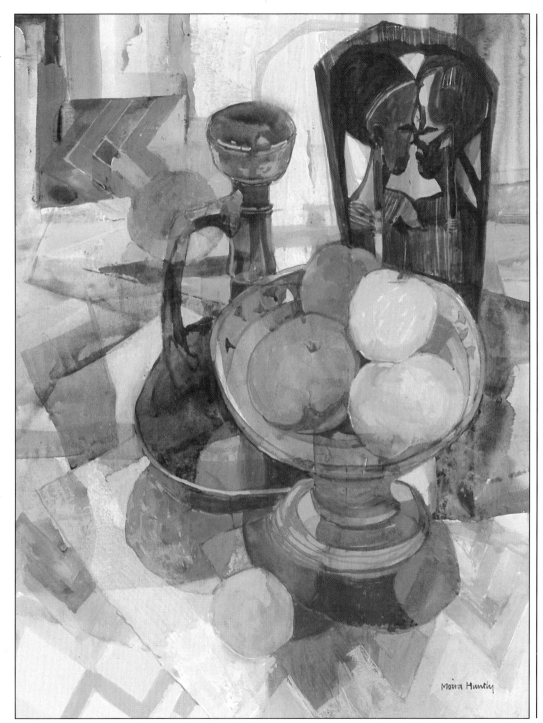

ARRANGING THE GROUP

Planning the disposition of objects in a still-life group so that they provide a satisfactory balance of shapes and colors is as important as painting it, so never rush at this stage, and think carefully about the composition.

A good still life, like any other painting, should have movement and dynamism, so that your eye is drawn into the picture and led around it from one object to another. It is wise to avoid the parallel horizontals formed by the back and front of a tabletop: the eye naturally travels along straight lines and these will lead out of the painting instead of into it. A device often used to break up such horizontals is to arrange a piece of drapery so that it hangs over the front of the table and forms a rhythmic curve around the objects. An alternative is to place the table at an angle so that it provides diagonal lines that will lead in toward the center of the picture.

Never arrange all the objects in a regimented row with equal spaces between them, as this will look static and uninteresting. Try to relate them to one another in pictorial terms by letting some overlap others, and give a sense of depth to the painting by placing them on different spatial planes, with some near the front of the table and others toward the back. Finally, make sure that the spaces between objects form pleasing shapes – these "negative shapes" are often overlooked, but they play an important part in composition.

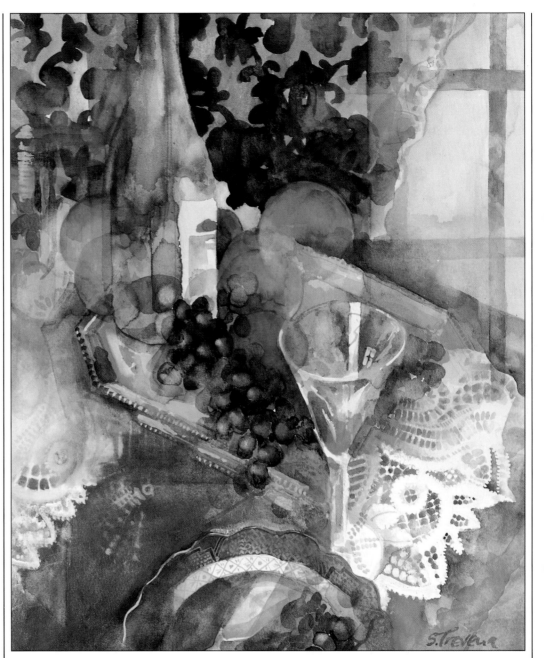

◀ Shirley Trevena, *Black Grapes and Wine*, 20 × 16 IN (50.8 × 40.6 CM), WATERCOLOR AND GOUACHE

Trevena works straight from her arranged group, with no sketching or preliminary pencil drawing, and composes as she paints, constantly improving on her group to create balance, harmony and contrast. She likes to vary the texture of her paint, using thin watercolor washes in places and thickly built up layers of gouache in others. The lace is the original white paper left untouched. Her work has a lyrical, semi-abstract quality: the objects are all recognizable, but we are drawn to the painting by the shapes and colors.

▶ Geraldine Girvan, *Winter Oranges*, 12³⁄₄ × 13¹⁄₂ IN (32.4 × 36.8 CM), GOUACHE

This arrangement relies for its effect on simplicity, but it is carefully planned, as are all good paintings. Notice how the artist has made use of strong tonal contrasts and diagonal lines to lead the eye into the center of the picture, and how she has used blues – small, dark accents on the bowl and paler, less assertive, gray-blues in the background – to counterpoint the marvelous, glowing oranges. Girvan's main interest is color, and she favors gouache because it allows her to build up the strong, vibrant harmonies she loves.

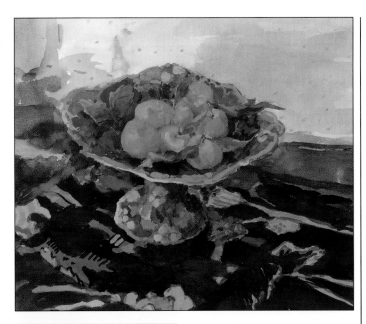

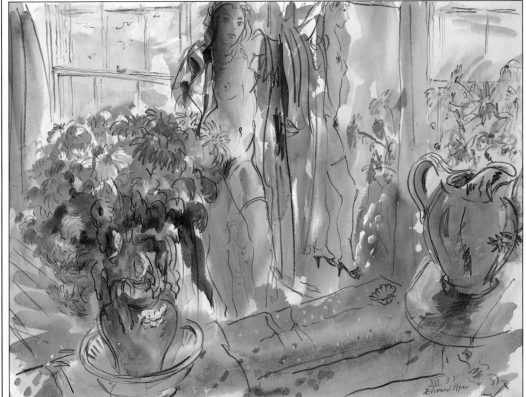

◀ Edward Piper, *Nude in a Mauve Negligée*, 18 × 24 IN (45.7 × 61 CM), WATERCOLOR AND LINE

In a way, this painting breaks the rules of still life because it includes a human figure. But because the treatment is not naturalistic, it blends perfectly with the other components of the group, looking at first glance rather like one of the plaster casts that appear frequently in Cézanne's still life paintings. Piper, like Girvan, is interested in color, but he uses it in a completely different way, establishing broad areas that relate to, but do not describe, the forms, and adding crisp but free definition by means of drawn lines – a bold use of the LINE AND WASH technique. Notice how the group of flowers on the left, with its strong contrast of tone, draws the eye into the bright area of red, pink and purple at the center.

BACKGROUNDS

One of the most common mistakes in still-life painting is to treat the background as unimportant. It is easy to feel that only the objects really matter and that the spaces behind and between them are areas that just need to be filled in somehow. All the elements in a painting should work together, however, and backgrounds, although they may play a secondary role, require as much consideration as the placing of the objects.

The kind of background you choose for an arranged group will depend entirely on the kind of picture you plan. A plain white or off-white wall could provide a good foil for a group of elegantly shaped objects, such as glass bottles or tall vases, because the dominant theme in this case would be shape rather than color, but a group you have chosen because it allows you to exploit color and pattern would be better served by a bright background, perhaps with some pattern itself.

The most important thing to remember is that the background color or colors must be in tune with the overall color key of the painting. You can stress the relationship of foreground to background when you begin to paint, tying the two areas of the picture together by repeating colors from one to another. For example, if your group has a predominance of browns and blues, try to introduce one of these colors into the background also. It is usually better in any case not to paint it completely flat.

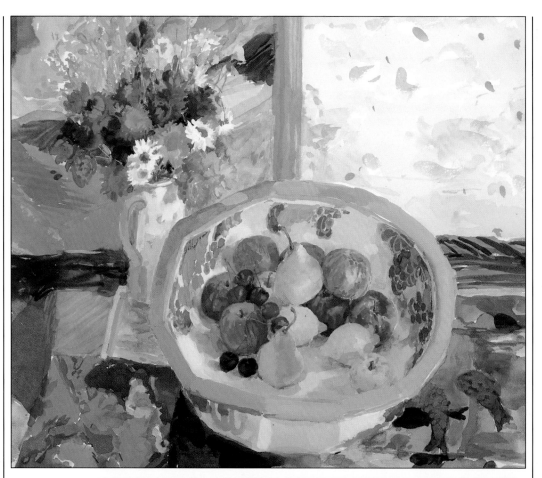

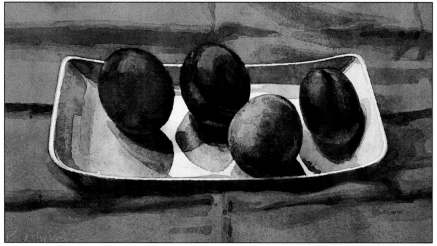

◀ Geraldine Girvan, *Victoria Day,* 19 × 20⅞ IN (48.3 × 53 CM), GOUACHE

Here the background is as busy and eventful as the foreground, as befits a painting in which color and pattern are the dominant themes. Notice how the artist has echoed the shapes of the blue fish (bottom right) in the patterned wallpaper above.

▶ Shirley Felts, *Still Life with Apples,* 16 × 12 IN (40.6 × 30.5 CM), WATERCOLOR

For this lovely painting, delicate but strong, the artist has chosen a plain brown background that picks up the color of the tabletop. But she has not painted it flat: there are several different colors and tones in the "brown," including a deep blue, and she has given movement and drama to it by the use of brushstrokes that follow the direction of the spiky leaves. Her technique is interesting. She builds up her rich colors and softly modeled forms gradually by laying wash over wash, but avoids tired and muddy paint by repeated soaking of the paper. Highlights are lifted out (see LIFTING OUT) while the paper is wet, and the shadows are deepened later.

◀ Ronald Jesty RBA, *Plums in a Dish,* 11 × 9 IN (28 × 29.9 CM), WATERCOLOR

This artist likes to exploit unusual viewpoints in his still life paintings, and in this example he has chosen to paint his subject from above. This not only neatly solves the problem of a separate background and foreground, it also allows him to make the most of the elegant shape of the metal platter.

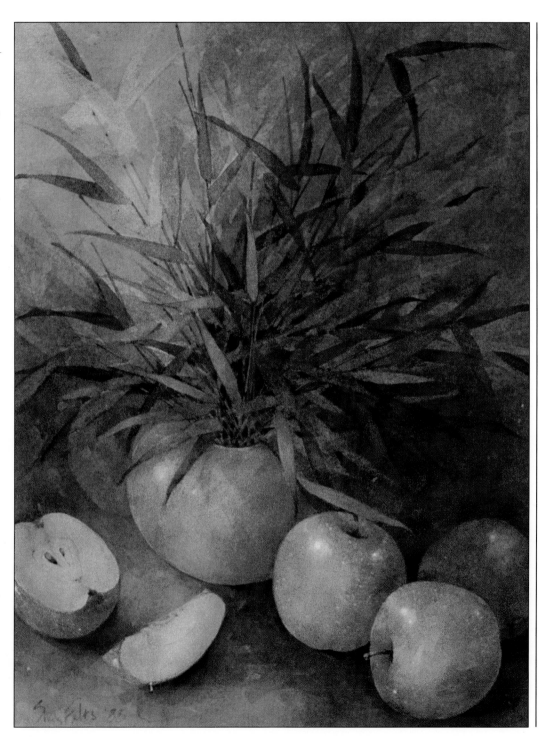
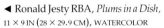

SETTINGS

The majority of still lifes are done indoors for the very simple reason that it is more convenient from the painting point of view, as well as giving you greater control over the set-up and lighting. There is, however, a wide range of indoor settings: you can paint in the corner of a room with your group lit by artificial light, you can arrange your objects on a windowsill with natural light behind them, you can even paint in a shed or glasshouse.

There is no reason why you should not paint outside – a picture of a group of garden tools and a wheelbarrow is just as valid a still-life subject as a collection of bottles on a table.

Always consider the possibilities of more unusual settings, but never choose them randomly – the objects should look as though they belong, not as though they have been unwillingly transplanted.

Whether you decide on an outdoor subject or one lit by daylight coming through a window, you will, of course, have to cope with the problem of a changing light source.

Daylight indoors can create exciting shadow patterns that you can use as an element in the composition, but they will not remain the same for long, so you will either have to work fast or in two or more separate sessions at the same time of day.

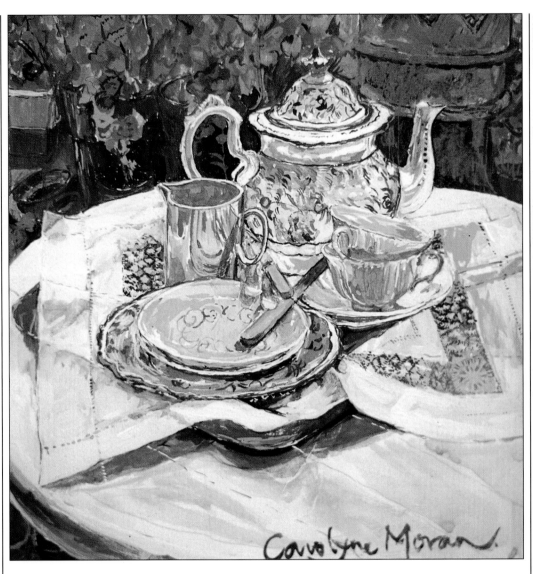

Carolyne Moran, *Time for Tea*,
10½ × 12¾ IN (26.7 × 27.3 CM), GOUACHE ON BOCKINGFORD PAPER

It is surprising how few still lifes are painted out of doors, but it seems like the obvious setting for a group like this, as well as providing an interesting and natural-looking background. A changing light source can be a problem, but here the artist has avoided any dramatic light and shade effects to concentrate on the shapes and colors of the objects set against the dark background of pots and foliage.

Cherryl Fountain, *January Windowsill*,
21¾ × 30 IN (55.2 × 76.3 CM),
WATERCOLOR

Here the artist has chosen to
group her objects so that they are
lit by the cold winter light coming
in from outside, which partially
silhouettes the cactus and the tail
of the bird, as well as dictating the
color key for the painting. An
additional advantage of this
setting is that the window frame
provides a stabilizing set of
verticals and horizontals which
act as a counterpoint to the
curving shapes of leaves and
pots.

Paul Dawson, *The Pink Umbrella*,
13 × 18 IN (33 × 45.7 CM), WATERCOLOR,
GOUACHE AND ACRYLIC

We tend to think of still life as a
group of objects arranged
against a background, but here
the whole painting is the still life —
the chair and parasol, the hat on
the table, the floor with its pattern
of shadows, and the wooden wall
and shuttered window.
Everything is treated with the
same loving attention to detail.
Dawson uses a variety of
techniques to obtain his
meticulously realistic effects. The
floorboards, table and walls were
painted by DRY BRUSH over a
preliminary wash, with the leaves
added in thick gouache on top.
The procedure for the chair was
more complex. First an overall
wash was laid, then the cane was
defined with waterproof white ink
and a fine brush, and finally thin
glazes of acrylic were used to
give the chair its color and form.
Altogether, an exercise in
technical ingenuity.

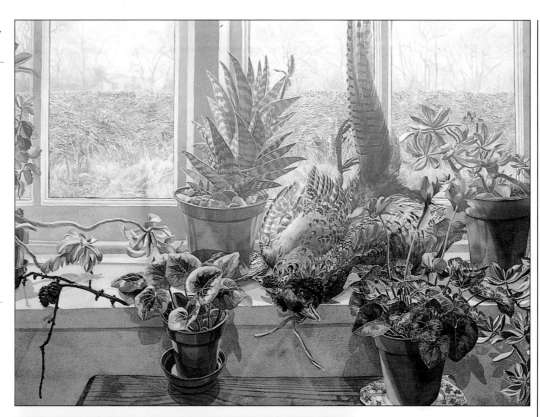

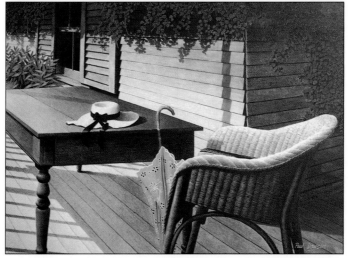

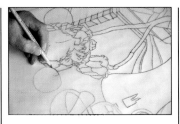

1 Ronald Jesty is an artist who likes to exercise full control over his medium, and he works almost exclusively WET-ON-DRY. This painting has been planned very carefully and is built up in a series of separate stages. Here he is transferring a full-scale drawing to the watercolor paper by drawing over a tracing.

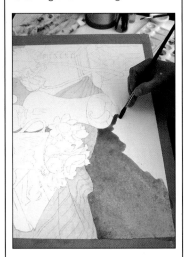

2 He begins with several small, neutral-colored washes and then paints the golden-brown background. Notice that he has turned the board sideways to make it easier to take the paint around the edges of the bottle.

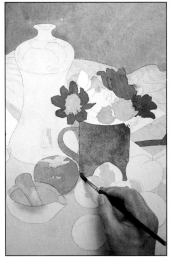

3 It is important to establish the color key early, so once the background is complete, he puts down a pale pinkish gray for the tabletop and areas of vivid red for the petals of the anemones. Without the background, it would have been difficult to assess the strength of color needed for these. The next stages are the persimmon and the mug that holds the flowers, close in tone and color, but with clearly perceptible differences. None of these areas of color is completely flat: the modeling on the persimmon and the jug begins immediately, with darker, cooler colors in the shadow areas, linked to the blue-gray of the pestle and mortar.

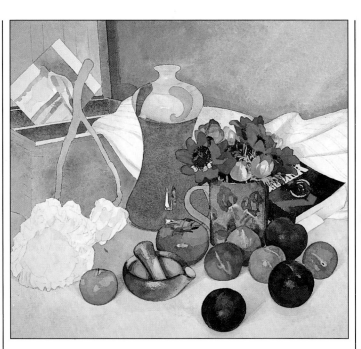

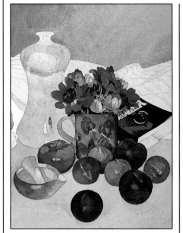

4 The flowers and fruit are now virtually complete, with the dark, rich colors built up in a series of small, overlapping washes to leave HIGHLIGHTS of varying intensity. The light blue-gray of the vase on the left represents the color and tone to be reserved for highlights.

5 The box on the left is painted in a color that picks up that of the persimmons and yellow plums. Although the painting is vivid and colorful, the colors are deliberately orchestrated to give an overall strength and unity to the composition. A further wash is laid on the blue vase to provide the mid-toned highlights when the darkest tones have been added.

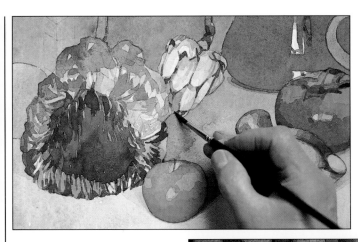

6 The complex forms of the artichoke head are described with delicate but accurate brush-strokes. Again, the colors used are versions of those elsewhere in the painting – there are no blacks or dead browns even in the darkest outlines.

7 With the deep blues and purples of the jug now complete, the painting has a sure and definite focal point. Although the whole picture is eventful and there are some delightful touches, such as the book title we cannot quite read and the sketch on the extreme left (which probably has some significance for the artist), our attention is drawn to the center by the strong, dark tones and glowing colors. It is not easy to achieve this intensity in watercolor without muddying the paint by overworking, and this is why Jesty plans so thoroughly. He overlays washes to a considerable extent, but avoids overworking by using barely diluted paint from the outset where the tones are to be dark.

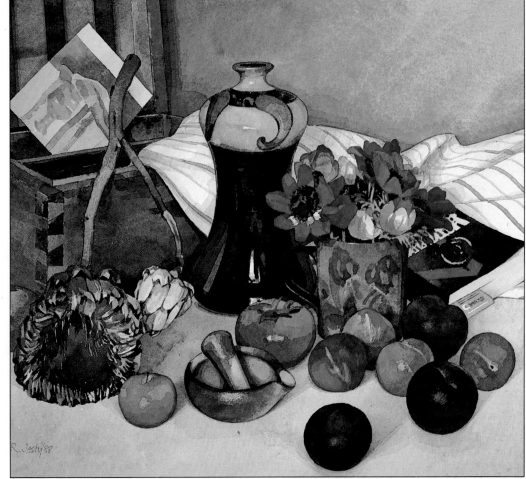

Ronald Jesty, *Persimmon and Plums*, 16 × 20 IN (40.6 × 50.8 CM), WATERCOLOR ON STRETCHED BOCKINGFORD PAPER

Water is one of the most appealing and challenging of all subjects. Like the sky, it presents a multitude of different faces – from wild, wind-tossed waves or turbulent waterfalls to the glassy surface of a still pond. Also, like the sky, it is elusive and insubstantial.

Observe and simplify

Perhaps more than any other subject, water requires very close observation. The shapes and colors of trees or hills can, to some extent, be re-created from memory, but water has no permanent shape or presence of its own. A completely still lake will present a mirror image of the sky and any prominent land features behind it, but one tiny breeze can remove these images in a matter of seconds, transforming the water surface into a steely gray, solid-looking mass. A fast-running stream seen from a certain distance away may provide a reassuringly simple surface and an even color, but as soon as you sit down beside it, the real paradox of water becomes apparent. It is undeniably there, but at the same time it is transparent, an ethereal presence through which you can clearly see the sand and rocks below.

To paint water successfully, it is necessary to simplify what you see, but you cannot hope to distill the essence of a subject until you are familiar with its complexities. All artists know that water is not easily captured in paint. The great Impressionist painter Claude Monet (1840-1926), for whom it amounted almost to an obsession, spent years trying to reconcile its special qualities with those of paint and canvas, while J.M.W. Turner (1775-1851) became a popular subject of contemporary cartoons because of his habit of taking his paints and canvas onto boats in the Thames so that he could study the effects of water more fully.

So be prepared to spend time watching water – it is a pleasing enough pastime in itself. If you sit quietly by a river or on the seashore, you will begin to see that the movements of water, like its changing colors, follow certain patterns, as do the movements of the sky. Understanding, for instance, the way the sea swells to become a wave, which then curls over and under before breaking into foam will enable you to paint it with assurance and freedom.

Painting methods

As soon as you begin to labor the paint, the effect of movement and fluidity will be destroyed. There are several techniques that are particularly suited to the subject, some of which are shown in the examples on the following pages, but, as a general rule, any method that involves much overlaying of paint should be avoided. Broad, flat or broken washes are ideal for still lakes or calm sea, and a DRY BRUSH dragged across rough white paper is a wonderfully economical means of suggesting lines or patches of wind-ruffled water in the distance. Ripples and reflections can be described in a kind of shorthand by calligraphic brush marks and squiggles, while the WET-IN-WET method is marvelous for a soft, diffused impression and beautifully conveys a misty day when all the colors merge together with no hard lines. Everyone has their own way of painting, however, and ultimately the only way to find out the best way of approaching the subject is by trial and error – the latter will at least show you what not to do.

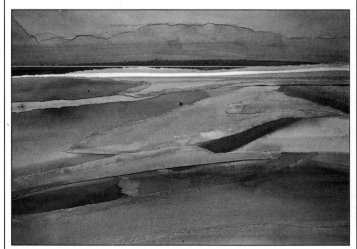

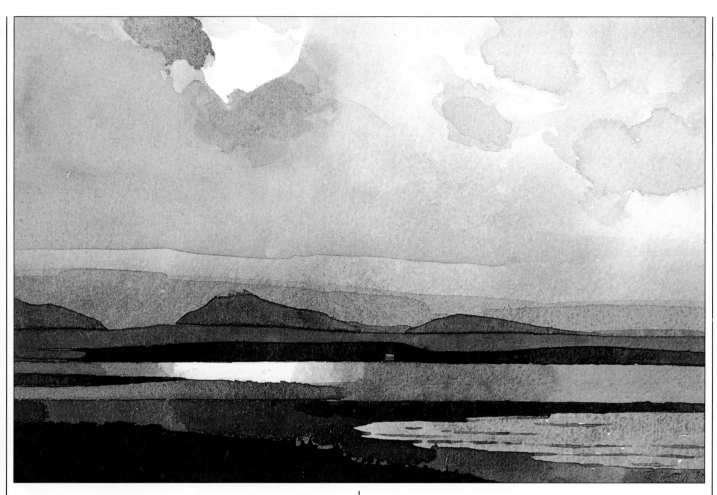

◄ Robert Tilling, *Low Tide Textures*, 20 × 28 IN (50.8 × 71.1 CM), WATERCOLOR, GOUACHE AND COLLAGE

Robert Tilling lives in the Channel Islands, and most of his watercolors are based on what he calls the "edge of the sea." As can be seen in this painting, he is fascinated by the abstract qualities of such seascapes. He usually works in pure watercolor, used in broad, wet washes, but here he has used a collage technique, involving gluing torn (stretched) paper to the working surface and then applying washes on top. Some color was then scraped off with a piece of stiff cardboard, more washes applied, and some gouache lines added as a final stage.

▲ Ronald Jesty, *Loch Etive at Taynuilt*, 7½ × 11 IN (19 × 27.9 CM), WATERCOLOR

Jesty has set up such a strong contrast of darks and lights that the patch of white water reflected from the bright area of sky seems almost to be illuminated from behind. The combination of deep-toned, hard-edged washes and the slightly granular texture of the paper is particularly striking.

LIGHT ON WATER

The effects of light on water are almost irresistible, particularly the more dramatic and fleeting ones caused by a changeable sky. Obviously they can seldom be painted on the spot; a shaft of sunlight suddenly breaking through cloud to spotlight an area of water could disappear before you lay out your colors. But you can recapture such effects in the studio as long as you have observed them closely, committed them to memory and made sketches of the general lie of the land.

When you begin to paint, remember that the effect you want to convey is one of transience, so try to make your technique express this quality. This does not mean splashing on the paint with no forethought – this is unlikely to be successful. One of the paradoxes of watercolor painting is that the most seemingly spontaneous effects are in fact the result of careful planning.

Work out the colors and tones in advance so that you do not have to correct them by overlaying wash over wash. It can be helpful to make a series of small preparatory color sketches to try out various techniques and color combinations. Knowing exactly what you intend to do enables you to paint freely and without hesitation. If you decide to paint WET-IN-WET, first practice controlling the paint by tilting the board. If you prefer to work WET-ON-DRY, establish exactly where your highlights are to be and then leave them strictly alone or, alternatively, put them in last with opaque white used drily.

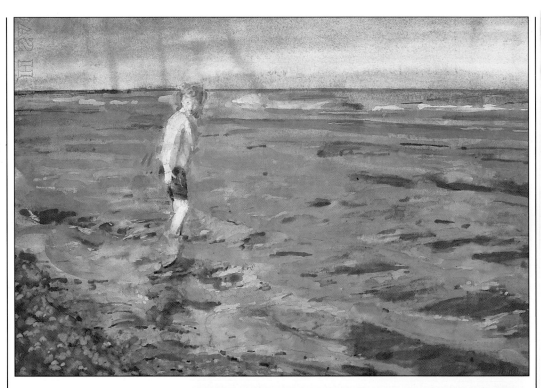

▲ Francis Bowyer, *It's Freezing!*, 15 × 21 IN (38.1 × 53.3 CM), WATERCOLOR AND BODY COLOR (GOUACHE WHITE)

The effect of the low sun on the choppy water has been beautifully observed and painted rapidly and decisively, with each brushstroke of vivid color put down and then left alone. In places, such as the more distant waves, the paint is thin enough for the paper to be visible, while in the foreground the shapes of the brushmarks have been exploited to give a feeling of movement to the wavelets breaking on the beach.

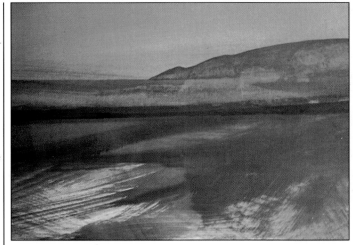

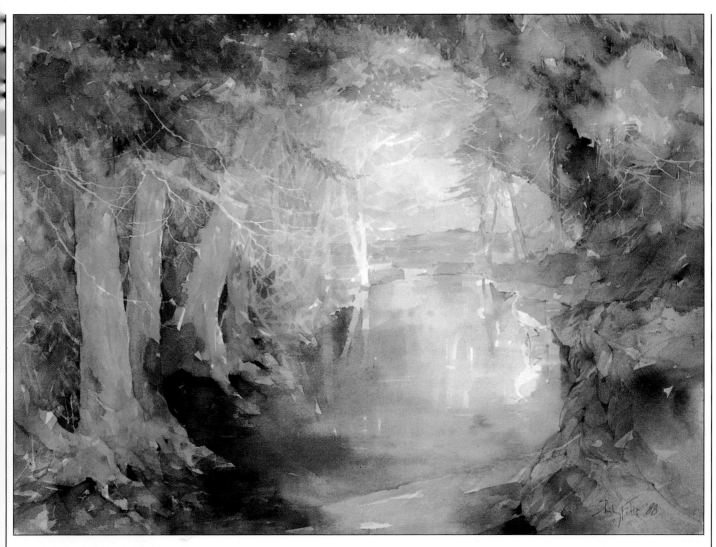

◀ Robert Tilling RI, *Winter Tide*,
16 × 23 IN (40.6 × 58.4 CM), WATERCOLOR

Tilling begins his watercolors by
laying very wet, broad washes
with large brushes (No. 12 up).
Here he has also used stiff-
bristled housepainting brushes to
create the striated effect of the wet
beach, combining brushwork with
SCRAPING BACK (using scraps of
cardboard) to build up a lively and
descriptive paint surface.

▲ Shirley Felts, *The River Guadalupe*,
21 × 29 IN (53.3 × 73.7 CM), WATERCOLOR

This lovely painting shows a
breathtakingly skillful use of
reserved HIGHLIGHTS. Each pale
reflection, tiny sunlit twig and point
of light has been achieved by
painting around the area. This can
result in tired, overworked paint,
but here nothing of the luminosity
of the watercolor has been
sacrificed and it remains fresh
and sparkling.

MOVING WATER

Most people have experienced the disappointment of finding that a photograph of a waterfall or rushing stream has completely failed to capture the movement and excitement of the subject. This is because the camera freezes movement by its insistence on including every tiny detail, and this provides an important lesson for the painter. You can never hope to paint moving water unless you simplify it, so learn to make "less say more" by looking for the main patterns and ruthlessly suppressing the secondary ones.

Rippling water under a strong light shows very distinct contrasts of tone and color, often with hard edges between the sunlit tops and the shadows caused by broken reflections. Working WET-ON-DRY is the best way of describing this edgy, jumpy quality, but avoid too much overlaying of washes, as this can quickly muddy the colors and destroy the crispness and clarity. LIQUID MASK is very helpful here, as you can block out small highlights on the tops of ripples or wavelets while you work freely on the darker tones.

The WAX RESIST method is tailor-made for suggesting the ruffled effect of windblown water or the broken spray on the tops of breakers, while the delicate, lace-like patterns formed when a wave draws back from the beach can be very accurately "painted" by SCRAPING BACK.

Whatever technique or combinations of techniques you decide on, use as few brushstrokes as possible – the more paint you put on, the less wet the water will look.

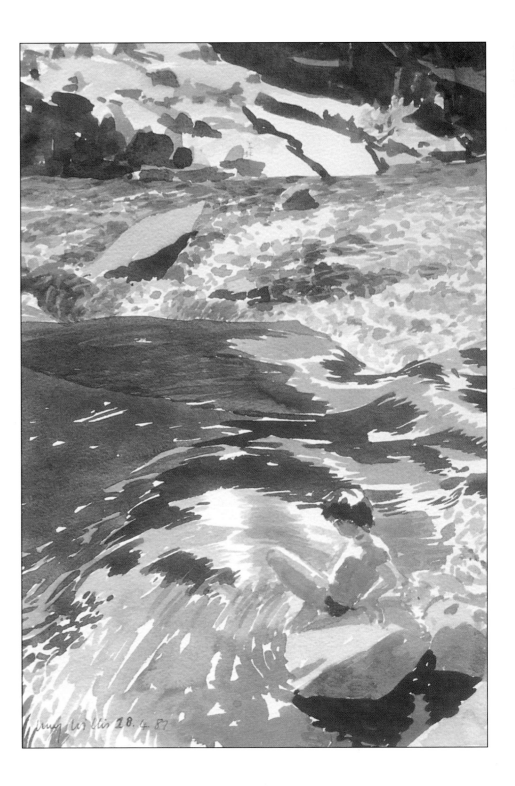

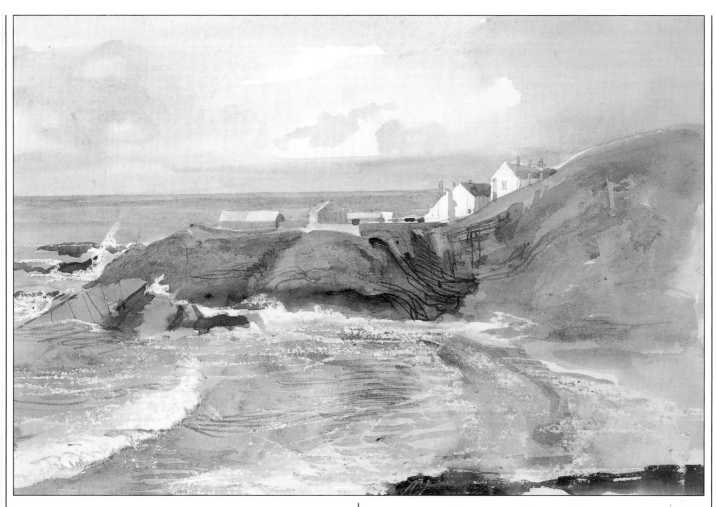

◀ Lucy Willis, *Pinhao Rapids,*
15 × 11 IN (38.1 × 27.9 CM), WATERCOLOR
The artist says that what attracted her about this subject was the contrast between the smooth, glassy water in the foreground, sliding toward the rapids, and the turbulence beyond. She found that the effect of the water's flow could be described entirely through the pattern of dark and light reflections which, as she observed, remained more or less the same even though the water itself was in fast movement. Willis has expressed the hard-edged quality of the water, with its abrupt transitions from light to very dark, by working WET-ON-DRY, with a very precise use of differently shaped brushstrokes.

▲ Charles Knight RWS, ROI, *Headland,* 10¾ × 14¾ IN (27.3 × 37.5 CM), WATERCOLOR, PENCIL AND WAX
Knight is a committed land- and seascape painter, and a master of the watercolor medium. This wonderfully atmospheric painting provides the perfect illustration of the secondary role played by technique in art. He has made excellent use of WAX RESIST for the waves and given a lovely feeling of movement and drama to the headland with crisp, dark pencil lines, but his techniques, although fascinating to analyze, remain "in their place" as no more than the vehicles which allow him to express his ideas.

STILL WATER

There are few sights more tempting to the painter than the tranquil, mirror-like surface of a lake on a still day or a calm, unruffled sea at dawn or dusk. But although it would be reasonable to believe still water to be an easy subject, particularly in a medium that has such an obvious affinity with it, it is surprising how often such paintings go wrong.

The most frequent reason for failure is simply poor observation. A calm expanse of water is seldom exactly the same color and tone all over, because it is a reflective surface. Even if there are no objects such as boats, rocks or cliffs to provide clearly defined reflections, the water is still mirroring the sky and will show similar variations. These shifts in color and tone – often very subtle – are also affected by the angle of viewing. Water usually looks darker in the foreground because it is closer to you and thus reflects less light.

It is also important to remember that a lake or area of sea is a horizontal plane. This sounds obvious, but has powerful implications for painting. A horizontal plane painted in an unvaried tone will instantly assume the properties of a vertical one because no recession is implied. It can sometimes be necessary to stress flatness and recession by exaggerating a darker tone or even inventing a ripple or two to bring the foreground forward.

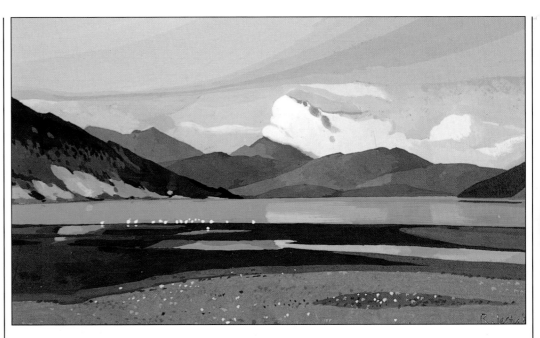

▲ Ronald Jesty RBA, *The White Cloud, Loch Etive*, 6½ × 11 IN (16.5 × 27.9 CM), GOUACHE

It is interesting to compare this painting with the one opposite, by the same artist. The majority of his paintings are in pure watercolor, but here he uses gouache applied in broad areas of very flat color to give an almost print-like effect, in which the juxtaposition of shapes and colors are all-important. He has produced an exciting composition by echoing the sweeping curve of the cloud in the light area of foreground, while the reflections in the water serve to break up the central area of blue-gray.

▶ Robert Tilling RI, *Noirmont Evening, Jersey*, 16 × 23 IN (40.6 × 58.4 CM), WATERCOLOR

The magical effects of still water under a setting sun have been achieved by a skillful use of the WET-IN-WET technique. Tilling works on paper with a Not surface, stretched on large blockboard supports. He mixes paint in considerable quantities in old teacups or small food cans and applies it with large brushes, tilting his board at an angle of 60° or sometimes even more to allow the paint to run. This method, although looking delightfully spontaneous, can easily get out of control, so he watches carefully what happens at every stage, ready to lessen the angle of the board if necessary to halt the flow of the colors. The dark wash for the headland was painted when the first wet-in-wet stage had dried.

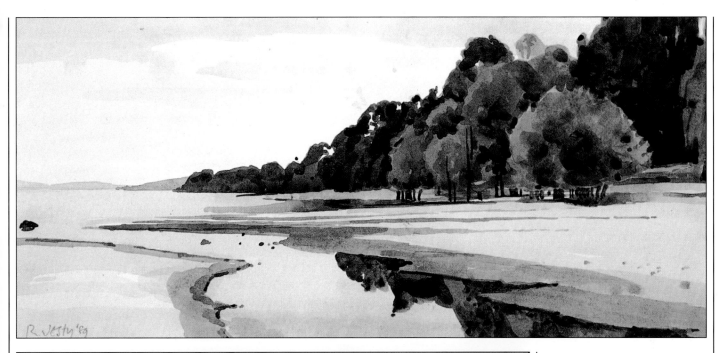

▲ Ronald Jesty RBA, *Loch Rannoch, Low Water*, 6 × 13½ IN (15.2 × 34.3 CM), WATERCOLOR

There is not a single unnecessary brushstroke to disturb the calm tranquillity of this scene. The artist has cleverly enhanced the bright surface of the water and its pale, sandy banks by setting up strong contrasts of tone while keeping the colors muted. The crisply painted reflections of the dark trees on the right and the little lines of shadow on the left define the river with perfect accuracy. The water surface is not painted completely flat: a sense of space and recession is created by the slightly darker patch of color directly in the foreground as well as by the linear perspective that narrows the river banks as it flows toward the lake.

REFLECTIONS

Reflections are one of the many bonuses of water provided free of charge to the painter. Not only do they form lovely patterns in themselves, they can also be used as a powerful element in a composition, allowing you to balance solid shapes with their watery images and to repeat colors in one area of a painting in another.

The most exciting effects are seen when small movements of water cause ripples or swells that break up the reflections into separate shapes, with jagged or wavering outlines.

Water can, of course, be so still that it becomes quite literally a mirror, but this does not necessarily make a good painting subject because it loses much of its identity as water.

As in all water subjects, try to simplify reflections and keep the paint fresh and crisp. Let your brush describe the shapes by drawing with it in a calligraphic way (see BRUSH DRAWING) and never put on more paint than you need. The amount of detail you put into a reflection will depend on how near the front of the picture it is. A distant one will be more generalized because the ripples will decrease in size as they recede from you, so avoid using the same size of brushmark for both near and far reflections or the water will appear to be flowing uphill. You could emphasize foreground reflections by painting WET-ON-DRY, and give a softer, more diffused, quality to those in the background by using the WET-IN-WET or LIFTING OUT methods.

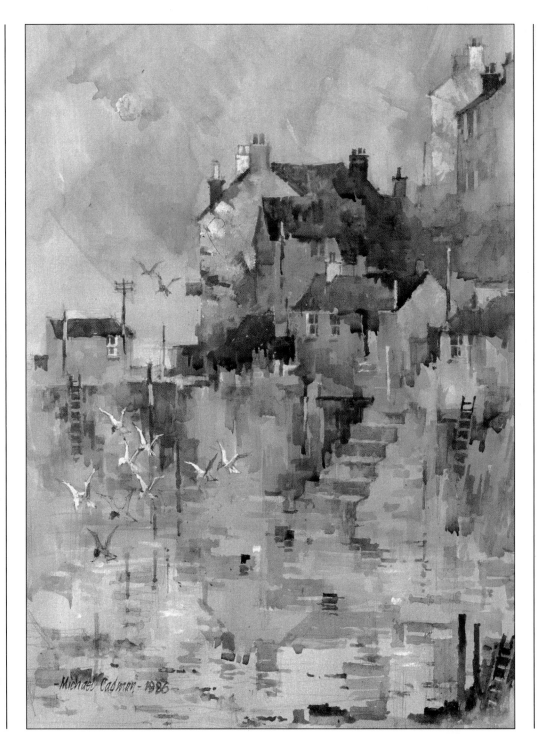

◄ Michael Cadman RI, ARCA, *Cornish Harbour, Low Tide*, 18 × 13 IN (45.7 × 33 CM), ACRYLIC AND WATERCOLOR ON TONED PAPER

Here the artist has exploited the potential of acrylic to the full, using brushmarks as an integral part of the painting, so that water, buildings and sky are all broken up into small areas of color. The reflections are hinted at rather than literally described. Because we cannot be quite sure where the water ends and the steps and harbor wall begin, the two parts of the picture seem to flow into one another to create a sense of complete unity, reinforced by the overall golden color key. To help him achieve this, Cadman has painted on a TONED GROUND (oyster-colored Canson Mi-Teintes paper) and in places has used his paint quite thinly so that the paper stands as a color in its own right. Although in the main, this is a fairly direct painting, in some areas, notably the light on the main building, a dark underpainting of burnt sienna and violet was used and allowed to show through successive coats of overpainted impasto. These were then glazed (see GLAZING) in places.

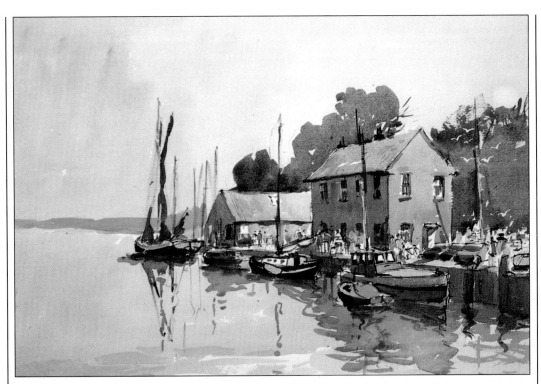

▲ John Tookey, *Snape*, 13¼ × 20¼ IN (33.6 × 52.7 CM), WATERCOLOR AND PEN

This painting aptly illustrates the idea of "making less say more." The main area of water consists of only two washes, with the initial pale one left to show through the subsequent slightly darker one in the foreground. These pale patches hint at soft ripples, which have then been defined more precisely with a few shapes of darker blue-gray. There is no hesitant niggling and the reflections have been painted similarly freely, with calligraphic brushmarks, broken lines and squiggles suggesting the way they are broken up by the gentle movement of the water.

▶ Ronald Jesty RBA, *Old Harry Rocks*, 19 × 12 IN (48.3 × 30.5 CM), WATERCOLOR

In this bold composition, the reflection, rather than being an incidental detail, forms part of the painting's focal point. The treatment is stylized to some extent, but nevertheless extremely accurate. There is no unnecessary detail, but there is enough variation in the reflection to suggest both the structure of the rock above and the slightly broken surface of the water. The artist has painted WET-ON-DRY, his preferred method, and has made clever use of the shape and direction of his brushmarks to lead the eye into the center of the picture.

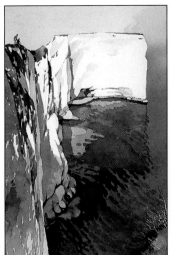

Many of us avoid painting urban scenes because of the clutter of cars and feel outraged when a brash new motor vehicle spoils our view of a pretty village. But the relationship of water and boats is a time-hallowed one and they have always been among the most popular of painting subjects. With their swelling curves and exciting colours and textures, boats (particularly old ones) are exciting in themselves, and they also provide an opportunity to make use of reflections in a composition. Their forms, however, are more complex than one might think and practice is essential if you are to learn to draw them convincingly. Work from life whenever possible and try to learn the basic structure and the way it is affected by perspective.

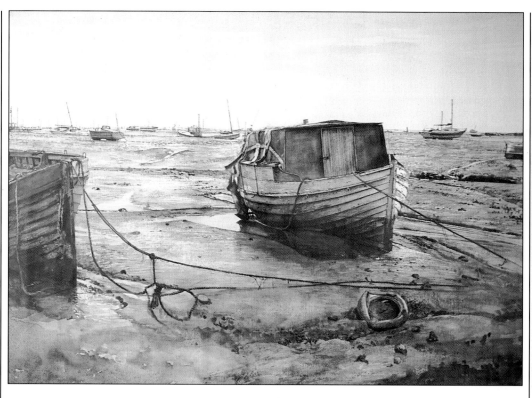

Martin Taylor, *Morning, Leigh-on-Sea,* 21¼ × 28⅜ IN (54 × 72 CM), WATERCOLOR AND BODY COLOR

This quiet, atmospheric painting is a visual essay in light and texture. Taylor always works from top to bottom in his landscapes, establishing the color and shades of the sky and middle distance to set the key for the rest of the painting. He mixes white gouache with watercolor blues for skies, and often works on them for hours, dabbing with a sponge or tissue paper and working into and over preliminary washes.

TEXTURE is obtained in a number of ways, sometimes simply by allowing the grain of the paper to show through and sometimes by working with a DRY BRUSH over earlier washes. On the boats, the blade of an art knife has been used to scuff the paper, a method the artist uses quite frequently, often painting over the scraped area and then repeating the process until he is satisfied with the result.

Once he has covered all the white paper, he goes back over the whole painting, tying it all together to achieve the right quality of light. He finds this final stage the most exciting of all – the final "expression" after the hard work has been done.

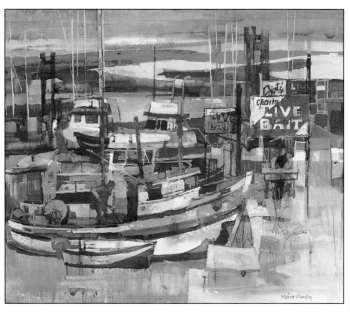

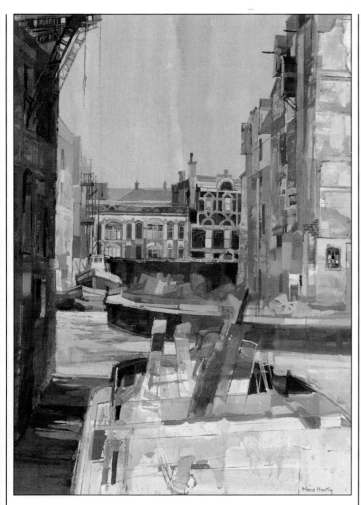

Moira Huntly RI, RSMA, *Charlie's Live Bait Stand. Campbell River*, 11¾ × 14½ IN (30 × 27 CM), WATERCOLOR AND GOUACHE

Huntly's paintings, whether landscape or still life, have a strong abstract quality, and here she has used the shapes of the boats to create a pattern of intersecting curves and verticals. Nevertheless, the boats are carefully drawn and perfectly convincing in terms of actuality, and the color scheme of greens, blue-grays and muted reds gives a strong feeling of place and atmosphere.

Moira Huntly RI, RSMA, *Butler's Wharf. London*, 15½ × 19½ IN (39.5 × 149.5 CM), WATERCOLOR AND GOUACHE

This painting, like that on the left by the same artist, stresses the relationship of shapes and the barges have been simplified into a series of blocks of color. Warm washes of transparent watercolor have been overlaid with gouache in places and textural effects were achieved by a simple printing technique. This, which is demonstrated on page 102, involves brushing watercolor onto a small piece of thick paper and pressing it onto the working surface before the paint dries.

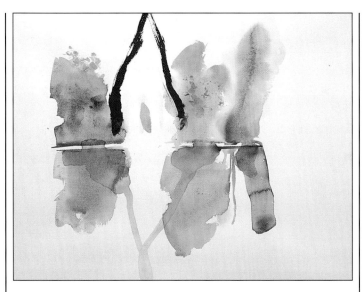

1 Kate Gwynn is an inventive artist who seldom restricts herself to one technique, and here she uses various methods, improvising as she works. First she establishes the main composition, overlaying washes in the water area to create hard edges.

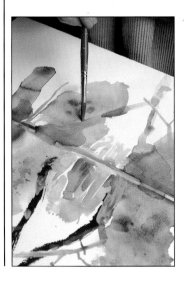

2 Having laid further washes, she now works WET-IN-WET with the point of the brush to suggest the effect of the reflected foliage.

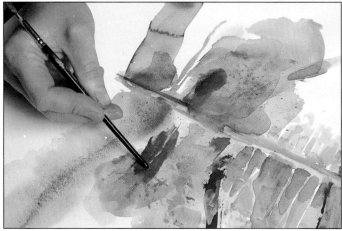

3 The brushmarks made in the last stage have now been overlaid with loose, wet washes to achieve a soft, diffused effect. The pale tree trunks seen on the right in this picture have been reserved in the traditional manner (see HIGHLIGHTS), but here the handle of the brush is used to draw into paint slightly thickened with BODY COLOR, providing an effective contrast to the loose wash on the right.

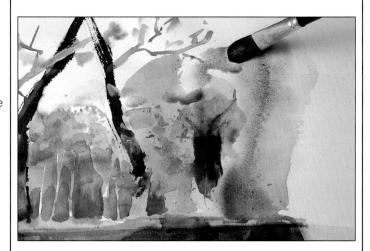

4 Sky is suggested with a wet brushstroke of blue, which is allowed to run into the yellow wash below.

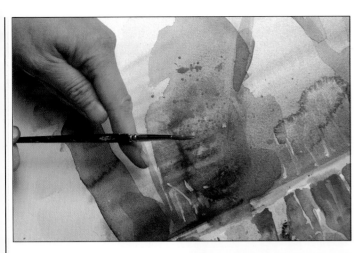

6 The soft, undefined impression has been maintained throughout the painting, with no attempt at precise description. The intersecting diagonals of the central trees provide a focal point, and the crisp, dark strokes of rather dry paint contrast with the paler, more fluid reflections below.

5 The SPATTERING technique is used to build up the impression of texture. Again, the paint has been slightly thickened with opaque white. Notice the deliberate use of the BACKRUN to accentuate the aqueous effect and the horizontal brushmarks suggesting slight ripples.

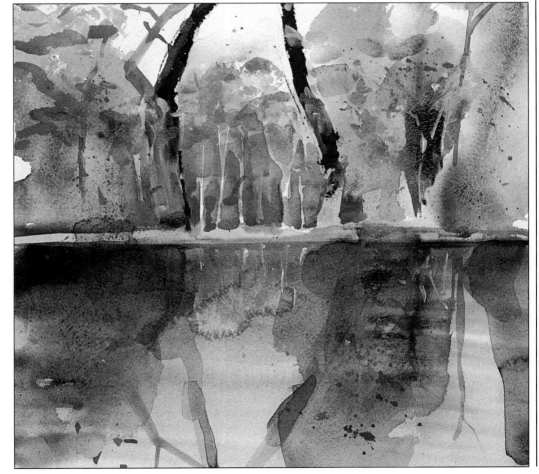

Kate Gwynn, *Trees and Water,*
16 × 20 IN (40.6 × 50.8 CM), WATERCOLOR
WITH SOME BODY COLOR ON STRETCHED
BOCKINGFORD PAPER

190

CREDITS

Frontispiece Samuel Palmer, courtesy of the Fitzwilliam Museum, Cambridge. **p8** John Lidzey. **p11** (b) William Tillyer, courtesy of Bernard Jacobson Galley, London. **p14** Jacqueline Rizvi. **p15** (t) Moira Huntly (b) Robert Dodd. **p16** (t) Michael Cadman (b) John McPake. **p17** Lucy Willis, courtesy of Chris Beetles Ltd, St James's, London. **p18** (t) Jacqueline Rizvi (b) Christopher Baker. **p19** Christopher Baker. **p20** (t) John Tookey (b) Donald Pass. **p21** (t) Juliette Palmer (b) Ronald Jesty. **p23** Ian Sidaway. **p32** William Tillyer, courtesy of Bernard Jacobson Gallery, London. **p33** Paul Riley, courtesy of Chris Beetles Ltd, St James's, London. **p38** Edward Piper, courtesy of Catto Gallery, London. **p39** (l) Doreen Osborne (r) Audrey Macleod. **p42** Michael Cadman. **p44** Ian Simpson. **p45** Ian Sidaway. **p47** Hazel Harrison. **p50** Arthur J Barbour. **p57** (t) Charles Knight, courtesy of Chris Beetles Ltd, St James's, London. (b) John Martin. **p60** Robert Tilling, courtesy of Bernard Jacobson Gallery, London. **p62** Christopher Baker. **p63** (t) Colin Paynton (b) Charles Knight, courtesy of Chris Beetles Ltd, St James's, London. **p67** Moira Huntly. **p70** (t) Ronald Jesty (b) Juliette Palmer. **p71** Jean Canter. **p72** Geraldine Girvan, courtesy of Chris Beetles Ltd, St James's, London. **p75** Laura Wade. **p76** Paul Dawson. **p77** David Boys. **p78** Lucy Willis, courtesy of Chris Beetles Gallery, London. **p79** (l) Jake Sutton, courtesy of Francis Kyle Gallery, London (b) Richard Wills. **p80** (t) Ronald Jesty (b) Lucy Willis, courtesy of Chris Beetles Gallery, St James's, London. **p81** Richard Wills. **p82** John Wilder. **p83** (l) David Boys (b) Sally Michel. **p87** Julia Gurney. **p88** (t & b) Sandra Walker. **p89** (l) Martin Taylor (r) John Lidzey. **p90** Paul Millichip. **p91** Trevor Chamberlain. **p92** (t) Christopher Baker (b) John Tookey. **p93** (l) John Lidzey (collection of Yvonne Joyce) (r) John Martin. **p94** (t) John Tookey (b) Michael Cadman. **p95** (t) Michael Cadman (b) Trevor Chamberlain. **p96** Martin Taylor. **p97** (l) Julia Gurney (r) Jill Mirza. **p98** Juliette Palmer, **p99** (t) Edward Piper, courtesy of Catto Gallery, London (b) David Curtis. **p100** Jill Mirza. **p101** Martin Taylor. **p103** Moira Huntly. **p105** Greta Fenton, courtesy of Duncan Campbell Fine Art, London. **p106** (t) Jake Sutton, courtesy of Francis Kyle Gallery, London. (b) Lucy Willis. **p107** (l) Michael McGuinness (r) Richard Wills. **p108** (t) William Bowyer, courtesy of Metrographic Arts London (b) Richard Wills. **p109** (l) Audrey Macleod (r) Michael McGuinness. **p1100** Paul Millichip. **p111** (l) Jacqueline Rizvi (r) Trevor Chamberlain. **p112** (t) Trevor Chamberlain (b) George Large, courtesy of Duncan Campbell Fine Art, London. **p113** John Lidzey. **p114** George Large, courtesy of Duncan Campbell Fine Art, London. **p115** (t) Francis Bowyer, courtesy of Metrographic Arts, London (b) Doreen Osborne. **p117** David Curtis. **p119** Audrey Macleod. **p120** Sharon Beeden. **p121** (l) Jean Canter (r) Jenny Matthews, courtesy of the Royal Botanic Gardens, Edinburgh. **p122** (t) Mary Tempest, courtesy of Duncan Campbell Fine Art, London (b) Muriel Pemberton, courtesy of the Catto Gallery, London. **p123** Shirley Felts. **p124** Ronald Jesty. **p125** (t) Geraldine Girvan, courtesy of Chris Beetles Ltd, St James's, London (b) Carolyne Moran. **p126** Lucy Willis. **p127** Mary Tempest, courtesy of Duncan Campbell Fine Art, London. **p128** (t) Norma Jameson (b) Audrey Macleod. **p129** Juliette Palmer. **p133** Charles Knight, courtesy of Chris Beetles Ltd, St James's, London. **p134** (l) Julliette Palmer (r) Ronald Jesty. **p135** (t) Charles Knight, courtesy of Chris Beetles Ltd, St James's London (b) Moira Clinch. **p136** (t) Juliette Palmer (b) Carolyne Moran. **p137** Martin Taylor. **p138** Robert Dodd. **p139** (t) Martin Taylor (b) Donald Pass. **p140** Ronald Jesty. **p141** Charles Knight, courtesy of Chris Beetles Ltd, St James's, London. **p142** Juliette Palmer. **p143** (t) David Curtis (b) Michael Chaplin (collection of Ian & Julie Kury) **p144** Martin Taylor. **p145** (t) Robert Dodd (b) Ronald Jesty. **p146** (t) Ronald Jesty (b) Charles Knight, courtesy of Chris Beetles Ltd, St James's, London. **p147** (l) Michael Chaplin (collection of Eric & Gill Mitchell) (r) Martin Taylor. **p149** Kate Gwynn. **p150** Christopher Baker. **p151** Robert Tilling. **p152** Charles Knight, courtesy of Chris Beetles Ltd, St James's, London. **p153** (l) Ronald Jesty (r) Donald Pass. **p154** Christopher Baker. **p155** (t) Ronald Jesty (b) Moira Clinch. **p157** John Martin. **p158** (t) Colin Paynton (b) Robert Tilling. **p159** Trevor Chamberlain. **p161** Cherryl Fountain. **p162** Carolyne Moran. **p163** (l) John Lidzey (r) Martin Taylor. **p164** (t) Michael Emmett, courtesy of the Catto Gallery, London (b) Martin Taylor. **p165** Moira Huntly. **p166** Shirley Trevena (collection of Jo Webb). **p167** (t) Geraldine Girvan, courtesy of Chris Beetles Ltd, St James's, London (b) Edward Piper, courtesy of the Catto Gallery, London. **p168** (t) Geraldine Girvan, courtesy of Chris Beetles Ltd, St James's, London (b) Ronald Jesty. **p169** Shirley Felts. **p170** Carolyne Moran. **p171** (t) Cherryl Fountain (b) Paul Dawson. **p173** Ronald Jesty. **p174** Robert Tilling. **p175** Ronald Jesty. **p176** (t) Francis Bowyer, courtesy of Metrographic Arts, London (b) Robert Tilling. **p177** Shirley Felts. **p178** Lucy Willis. **p179** Charles Knight, courtesy of Chris Beetles Ltd, St James's, London. **p180** Ronald Jesty. **p181** (t) Ronald Jesty (b) Robert Tilling. **p182** Michael Cadman. **p183** (l) John Tookey (b) Ronald Jesty. **p184** Martin Taylor. **p185** (l & r) Moira Huntly. **p187** Kate Gwynn.

Demonstration paintings by: Chloë Alexander (**p13**) John Blockley (**130-131**) Jean Canter (**p46, p55-56, p61**) David Curtis (**p116-117**) Kate Gwynn (**p24-25, p27, p28-31, p34-37, p43, p48-49, p53, p64-65, p68-69, p84-85, p148-149, -186-187**) Hazel Harrison (**p10-11, p12, p26, p42-43, p60, p62, p66**) Moira Huntly (**p102-103**) Ronald Jesty (**p156-157**) Tom Robb (**p46** (t) **P51, p58**) Ian Sidaway (**p22**).